**W9-BVE-934**

GEORGE F. HOFMANN, PhD.
5575 Little Flower Ave.
Cincinnati, Ohio 45239

Force and Statecraft

FORCE AND STATECRAFT

Diplomatic Problems of Our Time

GORDON A. CRAIG
ALEXANDER L. GEORGE

New York   Oxford
OXFORD UNIVERSITY PRESS
1983

Library of Congress Cataloging in Publication Data
Craig, Gordon Alexander, 1913-
Force and statecraft.
Bibliography: p.   Includes index.
1. World politics—20th century.   2. World politics—
19th century.   3. World politics—To 1900.
4. International relations.   5. Diplomacy.
I. George, Alexander L.   II. Title.
D443.C73   327′.09′04   81-22304
ISBN 0-19-503115-6   AACR2
ISBN 0-19-503116-4 (pbk.)

Printing (last digit): 9 8 7 6 5 4 3 2 1

Printed in the United States of America

Acknowledgments

We are grateful to all of the undergraduate and graduate students who during the past three years were members of our course on contemporary problems of foreign policy, and from whom we have learned much. We owe particular thanks to Major Clinton Ancker III, U.S. Army, Captain Alan Carver, U.S. Army, and Captain Richard S. Hoffman, U.S. Army, who prepared in their original form the case studies that appear in the second half of this book.

We are grateful also to Loraine Sinclair of the Department of History and Wilma Fuller and Alyce Adams of the Department of Political Science, Stanford University, for typing the manuscript.

Stanford, California   G. A. C.
December, 1981   A. L. G.

Contents

III   Ethical Imperatives and Foreign Policy

Introduction

Since the emergence of war as a feature of relations between communities, reflective and concerned persons have had apocalyptic visions of its potentiality for destruction and have searched for ways to prevent conflict. In general, they have placed their hopes on five different means: on religious and moral codes forbidding resort to war; on agreements to restrict or abolish the use of certain kinds of weapons; on agreements to limit military operations or to regulate the usages of war; on doctrines designed to make war more efficient, to match the level of violence to the political objective and thus to avoid unnecessary destruction; and, finally, on political systems designed to reduce the friction between groups or nations to the point where wars would be unprofitable or dangerous to the aggressor.

With the first four of these experiments, only modest success has been achieved. Religion has not only failed to discourage war but has often motivated it; attempts at arms control and disarmament have had minor successes that all too often, once achieved, encouraged evasion; the rules of war that alleviated the brutalities of eighteenth-century conflict are clearly ineffective in an age of nuclear weaponry; and recent experience hardly encourages one to believe in the capacity of modern governments to employ war strictly as an instrument of policy, restraining its inherent expansive tendencies. In the history of the West from the Middle Ages to the present, the most effective restraint upon the warlike tendencies of the individual, group, or state has been the pressure exerted by external forces, and the periods least affected by interstate violence have been those in which there existed a viable international community and an accepted body of law and custom to guide and control it.

Such periods were, to be sure, at least before the nineteenth century, brief and far between; the age of the Italian city states before the papacy of Alexander VI and the period sometimes called the age of Walpole in the first half of the eighteenth century are lonely exceptions in a long history of disorder and armed tumult. But after the twenty-five years of warfare caused by the French Revolution and the ambitions of Napoleon Bonaparte, the Congress of Vienna in 1814–1815 created an international system that secured the peace for two generations and then, as modified by Bismarck, for most of the rest of the century. That example has served, if not as a model, at least as an admonition to later statesmen. After World War I, Woodrow Wilson attempted to establish a new system of collective security to replace the one that had finally collapsed so disastrously in 1914, and during World War II Franklin D. Roosevelt tried to set the stage for a postwar system that would extend into peacetime the cooperative working relations that characterized the wartime alliance of the United States with the Soviet Union and Great Britain. More recently, Richard Nixon and Henry Kissinger attempted to develop a relationship with the Soviet Union that would serve as the foundation for an international system that would overcome the strains of the Cold War.

Both the fact that it took until the nineteenth century for the European states to create an effective concert of powers and the failure of recent attempts to achieve the relative success of that earlier experiment can be explained by the requirements of a viable international system. These are threefold: (1) an agreement among the principal states concerning aims and objectives that reflects the dominant values that they are seeking to preserve and enhance in creating and participating in the system; (2) a structure appropriate to the number of states interacting with each other, the geographical boundaries or scope of the system, the distribution of power among member states, and the stratification and status hierarchy among them; and (3) commonly accepted procedures—that is, norms, rules, practices, and institutions for the achievement of the aims and objectives of the system. During the long stretch of time that intervened between the breakdown of the authority of the Holy Roman Empire and the religious wars that followed the Reformation, centuries in which Europe was composed of a welter of political units of indeterminate sovereignty and ill-defined borders, not even the most gifted political leaders could be expected to conceive of, let alone develop, anything so systematic. As will become apparent, it was only in the seventeenth century, when modern states came into existence that possessed efficient institutions, strong armed forces, and a rational theory of statecraft, that any progress toward effective collaboration became possible, and even then it took a century of intermittent conflict and the threat of domination by a single power before the major European states were able to achieve an agreement with respect to basic objectives and the structural and methodological requirements of a viable system.

The eventual collapse of the nineteenth-century experiment and the twentieth-century failure to find a substitute for it can be explained by another characteristic of an effective international system, namely, that it must be able to adapt to environmental developments and to internal changes within its member states that affect its performance and its ability to maintain itself. The modern period has been one of profound and continuing changes in socioeconomic organization, military technology, transportation, and communication, to say nothing of those mutations in the internal political structure of states that have resulted from the rise of public opinion, the emergence of a large variety of organized interest groups, and the increasing scope and complexity of governmental organization. It has also been an age of intense nationalism, which has been reflected in the breakup of the old colonial empires and the multiplication of new sovereign states, and of ideological conflict on a global scale. All of these forces, singly and in combination, have had an impact upon international politics that amounts to a diplomatic revolution; and this has made it increasingly difficult to maintain old structures or to devise new ones. Adaptation to accelerated change has become the major problem of modern statecraft, testing the ingenuity and the fortitude of those charged with responsibility both for devising means of controlling international violence and for maintaining the security of their own countries.

The first part of this book deals with the emergence of the modern states, the conflict in the eighteenth century between their desire for order and their anarchic tendencies, the laborious and painful birth of the nineteenth-century system, its procedures, and the various changes in its structure before its collapse in 1914. But its more particular theme is the impact of the diplomatic revolution just alluded to, and the ways in which this crippled the system-building experiments of Woodrow Wilson, Franklin D. Roosevelt, and Richard Nixon.

Because statesmen have not succeeded in inventing the perfect international system, interstate violence remains a major factor in contemporary world politics, and the period since 1945 has seen three major conflicts in the Far East, three short but destructive wars in the Middle East between Israel and the Arab states and another between Iran and Iraq, numerous civil and interstate conflicts in Africa and Latin America, and a war in the South Atlantic between Great Britain and Argentina that is still unresolved as these words are written. This book will not attempt to deal with the causes or the operational and strategical aspects of these confrontations or of military conflict in general. Nevertheless, international violence is never remote from the heart of its concern, and the focus of its second part is upon the uses of force as an instrument of statecraft. One of the marked characteristics of our time is the frequency with which states employ threats of force to deter or to halt encroachments upon their interests, a practice that requires some analysis in the pages that follow of the techniques of deterrence and coercive diplomacy.

Again, competition and rivalry between states, abetted sometimes by misperceptions and miscalculations, often plunges them into tense diplomatic confrontations and brings them to the brink of war; and the problem of protecting their essential interests in such situations, without warfare and without escalation of low-level military conflict, poses a difficult dilemma for policy makers. In the age of thermonuclear weapons, the successful management of crises is more critical than ever, and an appropriate theme for special attention, the more so because crises not only pose threats but often offer opportunities for constructive change in interstate relations. Indeed, the potentially constructive role of crises in international relations has led some observers to argue that in the present age crises have become a substitute for war. If so, it is hardly necessary to enjoin policy makers to take seriously the requirements and modalities of crisis management, but it is certainly permissible in a book like this to try to analyze them in such a way as to make it possible to distinguish between effective and faulty procedure.

Finally, because, as we have discovered to our cost, nations do get into wars, it is necessary to consider the best ways of getting out of them. Terminating a conflict by means short of surrender is often much more difficult than starting one, and because the process has received so little analytical attention, it seemed advisable to include here an examination of the forces that prolong wars and of the conditions and processes that seem, on the basis of experience, best designed to lead to cease-fires and peace agreements.

Tensions that arise in interstate relations do not, fortunately, always lead to war. A dangerous crisis may have a sobering effect on both sides and create a mutual desire to relax tensions, and this may be followed by diplomatic efforts to reach a mutually acceptable accommodation or a resolution of conflicting interests. One side may recognize the legitimacy of some of its adversary's grievances and seek to appease it; as the two sides resolve their salient disagreements, they may also recognize interests that they have in common and work out the basis for a cooperative relationship. The reorientation of the relationship from one of initial hostility to cooperation is generally, in our day, called détente, although, as we shall see, it is an imprecise and ambiguous term. For that very reason, however, and because the process has become a point of contention between the United States and its European allies, it requires analysis.

Fundamental to all of these diplomatic procedures—to deterrence and coercive diplomacy, to crisis management and war termination, and to détente—is negotiation, as vital to the relations of contemporary great powers, and as worthy a subject for study and reflection, as it was in the days of Machiavelli and Wicquefort and Callières. Because of its central importance, it is the first of the topics considered in the second part of the book.

Finally, at a time when increasing numbers of citizens have religious or conscientious doubts about the tendencies, the methods, and the dangers of contemporary international relations, it seemed appropriate to include in Part III two admittedly tentative chapters on the difficult problem of the role of ethics and morality in world politics.

This book grew out of the authors' long-standing concern over the challenging tasks confronting American foreign policy and their conviction that it would be worthwhile to examine the kind of problems of force and statecraft that confront policy makers from the combined perspectives of the diplomatic historian and the specialist in strategy. Accordingly, we developed a course with these objectives in mind and have taught it together several times at Stanford University. In our course, as in this book, we selected for controlled comparison a wide variety of case studies drawn from the diplomatic history of the nineteenth and twentieth centuries in order to throw some light upon contemporary problems of foreign policy. It was our intention there—and this was the reason for employing the comparative method—to make some tentative generalizations about the diplomatic procedures and techniques that we discussed with our students. In the pages that follow, and particularly in Parts II and III, we have carried our classroom conclusions a bit further and have had the temerity to formulate theories about the requirements of successful employment of the instruments and techniques under discussion, as well as about their appropriate uses and limitations.

It need hardly be added that these formulations are in the nature of working hypotheses that are subject to modification and elaboration. Still, we do not apologize for offering them to our readers. This is a time for serious reflection upon foreign affairs and, if these pages help to provoke it, we shall be satisfied even if our views suffer serious correction.

DISCIPULIS NOSTRIS
QUORUM INDULGENTIA ET SEDULITAS
AUCTORIBUS EXEMPLO
FUERUNT

I

The International System
from the Seventeenth Century
to the Present

1

The Emergence
of the Great Powers

I

Although the term *great power* was used in a treaty for the first time only in 1815, it had been part of the general political vocabulary since the middle of the eighteenth century and was generally understood to mean Great Britain, France, Austria, Prussia, and Russia. This would not have been true in the year 1600, when the term itself would have meant nothing and a ranking of the European states in terms of political weight and influence would not have included three of the countries just mentioned. In 1600, Russia, for instance, was a remote and ineffectual land, separated from Europe by the large territory that was called Poland-Lithuania with whose rulers it waged periodic territorial conflicts, as it did with the Ottoman Turks to the south; Prussia did not exist in its later sense but, as the Electorate of Brandenburg, lived a purely German existence, like Bavaria or Württemberg, with no European significance; and Great Britain, a country of some commercial importance, was not accorded primary political significance, although it had, in 1588, demonstrated its will and its capacity for self-defense in repelling the Spanish Armada. In 1600, it is fair to say that, politically, the strongest center in Europe was the old Holy Roman Empire, with its capital in Vienna and its alliances with Spain (one of the most formidable military powers in Europe) and the Catholic states of southern Germany—an empire inspired by a militant Catholicism that dreamed of restoring Charles V's claims of universal dominion. In comparison with Austria and Spain,

3

France seemed destined to play a minor role in European politics, because of the state of internal anarchy and religious strife that followed the murder of Henri IV in 1610.

Why did this situation not persist? Or, to put it another way, why was the European system transformed so radically that the empire became an insignificant political force and the continent came in the eighteenth century to be dominated by Great Britain, France, Austria, Prussia, and Russia? The answer, of course, is war, or, rather more precisely, wars—a long series of religious and dynastic conflicts which raged intermittently from 1618 until 1721 and changed the rank order of European states by exhausting some and exalting others. As if bent upon supplying materials for the nineteenth-century Darwinians, the states mentioned above proved themselves in the grinding struggle of the seventeenth century to be the fittest, the ones best organized to meet the demands of protracted international competition.

The process of transformation began with the Thirty Years War, which stretched from 1618 to 1648. It is sometimes called the last of the religious wars, a description that is justified by the fact that it was motivated originally by the desire of the House of Habsburg and its Jesuit advisers to restore the Protestant parts of the empire to the true faith and because, in thirty years of fighting, the religious motive gave way to political considerations and, in the spreading of the conflict from its German center to embrace all of Europe, some governments, notably France, waged war against their own coreligionists for material reasons. For the states that initiated this wasting conflict, which before it was over had reduced the population of central Europe by at least a third, the war was an unmitigated disaster. The House of Habsburg was so debilitated by it that it lost the control it had formerly possessed over the German states, which meant that they became sovereign in their own right and that the empire now became a mere adjunct of the Austrian crown lands. Austria was, moreover, so weakened by the exertions and losses of that war that in the period after 1648 it had the greatest difficulty in protecting its eastern possessions from the depredations of the Turks and in 1683 was threatened with capture of Vienna by a Turkish army. Until this threat was contained, Austria ceased to be a potent factor in European affairs. At the same time, its strongest ally, Spain, had thrown away an infantry once judged to be the best in Europe in battles like that at Nördlingen in 1634, one of those victories that bleed a nation white. Spain's decline began not with the failure of the Armada, but with the terrible losses suffered in Germany and the Netherlands during the Thirty Years War.

In contrast, the states that profited from the war were the Netherlands, which completed the winning of its independence from Spain in the course of the war and became a commercial and financial center of major importance; the kingdom of Sweden, which under the leadership of Gustavus Adolphus, the Lion of the North, plunged into the conflict in 1630 and emerged as the strongest power in the Baltic region; and France, which entered the war formally in 1635 and came out of it as the most powerful state in western Europe.

It is perhaps no accident that these particular states were so successful, for they were excellent examples of the process that historians have described as the emergence of the modern state, the three principal characteristics of which were effective armed forces, an able bureaucracy, and a theory of state that restrained dynastic exuberance and defined political interest in practical terms. The seventeenth century saw the emergence of what came to be called *raison d'état* or *ragione di stato*— the idea that the state was more than its ruler and more than the expression of his wishes; that it transcended crown and land, prince and people; that it had its particular set of interests and a particular set of necessities based upon them; and that the art of government lay in recognizing those interests and necessities and acting in accordance with them, even if this might violate ordinary religious or ethical standards. The effective state must have the kind of servants who would interpret *raison d'état* wisely and the kind of material and physical resources necessary to implement it. In the first part of the seventeenth century, the Dutch, under leaders like Maurice of Nassau and Jan de Witt, the Swedes, under Gustavus Adolphus and Oxenstierna, and the French, under the inspired ministry of Richelieu, developed the administration and the forces and theoretical skills that exemplify this ideal of modern statehood. That they survived the rigors of the Thirty Years War was not an accident, but rather the result of the fact that they never lost sight of their objectives and never sought objectives that were in excess of their capabilities. Gustavus Adolphus doubtless brought his country into the Thirty Years War to save the cause of Protestantism when it was at a low ebb, but he never for a moment forgot the imperatives of national interest that impelled him to see the war also as a means of winning Swedish supremacy along the shore of the Baltic Sea. Cardinal Richelieu has been called the greatest public servant France ever had, but that title, as Sir George

Clark has drily remarked, "was not achieved without many acts little fitting the character of a churchman." It was his clear recognition of France's needs and his absolute unconditionality in pursuing them that made him the most respected statesman of his age.

The Thirty Years War, then, brought a sensible change in the balance of forces in Europe, gravely weakening Austria, starting the irreversible decline of Spain, and bringing to the fore the most modern, best organized, and, if you will, most rationally motivated states: the Netherlands, Sweden, and France. This, however, was a somewhat misleading result, and the Netherlands was soon to yield its commercial and naval primacy to Great Britain (which had been paralyzed by civil conflict during the Thirty Years War), while Sweden, under a less rational ruler, was to throw its great gains away.

The gains made by France were more substantial, so much so that in the second half of the century, in the heyday of Louis XIV, they became oppressive. For that ruler was intoxicated by the power that Richelieu and his successor Mazarin had brought to France, and he wished to enhance it. As he wrote in his memoirs:

> The love of glory assuredly takes precedence over all other [passions] in my soul. . . . The hot blood of my youth and the violent desire I had to heighten my reputation instilled in me a strong passion for action. . . . *La Gloire*, when all is said and done, is not a mistress that one can ever neglect; nor can one be ever worthy of her slightest favors if one does not constantly long for fresh ones.

No one can say that Louis XIV was a man of small ambition. He dreamed in universal terms and sought to realize those dreams by a combination of diplomatic and military means. He maintained alliances with the Swedes in the north and the Turks in the south and thus prevented Russian interference while he placed his own candidate, Jan Sobieski, on the throne of Poland. His Turkish connection he used also to harry the eastern frontiers of Austria, and if he did not incite Kara Mustafa's expedition against Vienna in 1683, he knew of it. Austria's distractions enabled him to dabble freely in German politics. Bavaria and the Palatinate were bound to the French court by marriage, and almost all of the other German princes accepted subsidies at one time or another from France. It did not seem unlikely on one occasion that Louis would put himself or his son forward as candidate for Holy Roman emperor. The same method of infiltration was practiced in Italy, Portugal, and

Spain, where the young king married a French princess and French ambassadors exerted so much influence in internal affairs that they succeeded in discrediting the strongest antagonist to French influence, Don Juan of Austria, the victor over the Turks at the battle of Lepanto. In addition to all of this, Louis sought to undermine the independence of the Netherlands and gave the English king Charles II a pension in order to reduce the possibility of British interference as he did so.

French influence was so great in Europe in the second half of the seventeenth century that it threatened the independent development of other nations. This was particularly true, the German historian Leopold von Ranke was to write in the nineteenth century, because it

> was supported by a preeminence in literature. Italian literature had already run its course, English literature had not yet risen to general significance, and German literature did not exist at that time. French literature, light, brilliant and animated, in strictly regulated but charming form, intelligible to everyone and yet of individual, national character was beginning to dominate Europe. . . . [It] completely corresponded to the state and helped the latter to attain its supremacy. Paris was the capital of Europe. She wielded a dominion as did no other city, over language, over custom, and particularly over the world of fashion and the ruling classes. Here was the center of the community of Europe.

The effect upon the cultural independence of other parts of Europe—and one cannot separate cultural independence from political will—was devastating. In Germany, the dependence upon French example was almost abject, and the writer Moscherosch commented bitterly about "our little Germans who trot to the French and have no heart of their own, no speech of their own; but French opinion is their opinion, French speech, food, drink, morals and deportment their speech, food, drink, morals and deportment whether they are good or bad."

But this kind of dominance was bound to invite resistance on the part of others, and out of that resistance combinations and alliances were bound to take place. And this indeed happened. In Ranke's words, "The concept of the European balance of power was developed in order that the union of many other states might resist the pretensions of the 'exorbitant' court, as it was called." This is a statement worth noting. The principle of the balance of power had been practiced in Machiavelli's time in the intermittent warfare between the city states of the Italian peninsula. Now it was being deliberately invoked as a principle of

7

European statecraft, as a safeguard against universal domination. We shall have occasion to note the evolution and elaboration of this term in the eighteenth century and in the nineteenth, when it became one of the basic principles of the European system.

Opposition to France's universal pretensions centered first upon the Dutch, who were threatened most directly in a territorial sense by the French, and their gifted ruler, William III. But for their opposition to be successful, the Dutch needed strong allies, and they did not get them until the English had severed the connection that had existed between England and France under the later Stuarts and until Austria had modernized its administration and armed forces, contained the threat from the east, and regained the ability to play a role in the politics of central and western Europe. The Glorious Revolution of 1688 and the assumption of the English throne by the Dutch king moved England solidly into the anti-French camp. The repulse of the Turks at the gates of Vienna in 1683 marked the turning point in Austrian fortunes, and the brilliant campaigns of Eugene of Savoy in the subsequent period, which culminated in the smashing victory over the Turks at Zenta and the suppression of the Rakoczi revolt in Hungary, freed Austrian energies for collaboration in the containment of France. The last years of Louis XIV, therefore, were the years of the brilliant partnership of Henry Churchill, Duke of Marlborough, and Eugene of Savoy, a team that defeated a supposedly invulnerable French army at Blenheim in 1704, Ramillies in 1706, Oudenarde in 1708, and the bloody confrontation at Malplaquet in 1709.

These battles laid the basis for the Peace of Utrecht of 1713–1715, by which France was forced to recognize the results of the revolution in England, renounce the idea of a union of the French and Spanish thrones, surrender the Spanish Netherlands to Austria, raze the fortifications at Dunkirk, and hand important territories in America over to Great Britain. The broader significance of the settlement was that it restored an equilibrium of forces to western Europe and marked the return of Austria and the emergence of Britain as its supports. Indeed, the Peace of Utrecht was the first European treaty that specifically mentioned the balance of power. In the letters patent that accompanied Article VI of the treaty between Queen Anne and King Louis XIV, the French ruler noted that the Spanish renunciation of all rights to the throne of France was actuated by the hope of "obtaining a general Peace and securing the Tranquillity of *Europe* by a Ballance of Power," and the king of Spain acknowledged the importance of "the Maxim of securing for ever the universal Good and Quiet of Europe, by an equal Weight of Power, so that many being united in one, the Ballance of the Equality desired, might not turn to the Advantage of one, and the Danger and Hazard of the rest."

Meanwhile, in northern Europe, France's ally Sweden was forced to yield its primacy to the rising powers of Russia and Prussia. This was due in part to the drain on Swedish resources caused by its participation in France's wars against the Dutch; but essentially the decline was caused, in the first instance, by the fact that Sweden had too many rivals for the position of supremacy in the Baltic area and, in the second, by the lack of perspective and restraint that characterized the policy of Gustavus Adolphus's most gifted successor, Charles XII. Sweden's most formidable rivals were Denmark, Poland, which in 1699 acquired an ambitious and unscrupulous new king in the person of Augustus the Strong of Saxony, and Russia, ruled since 1683 by a young and vigorous leader who was to gain the name Peter the Great. In 1700, Peter and Augustus made a pact to attack and despoil Sweden and persuaded Frederick of Denmark to join them in this enterprise. The Danes and the Saxons immediately invaded Sweden and to their considerable dismay were routed and driven from the country by armies led by the eighteen-year-old ruler, Charles XII. The Danes capitulated at once, and Charles without pause threw his army across the Baltic, fell upon Russian forces that were advancing on Narva, and, although his own forces were outnumbered five to one, dispersed, captured, or killed an army of forty thousand Russians. But brilliant victories are often the foundation of greater defeats. Charles now resolved to punish Augustus and plunged into the morass of Polish politics. It was his undoing. While he strove to control an intractable situation, an undertaking that occupied him for seven years, Peter was carrying through the reforms that were to bring Russia from its oriental past into the modern world. When his army was reorganized, he began a systematic conquest of the Swedish Baltic possessions. Charles responded, not with an attempt to retake those areas, but with an invasion of Russia—and this, like other later invasions, was defeated by winter and famine and ultimately by a lost battle, that of Pultawa in 1709, which broke the power of Sweden and marked the emergence of Russia as its successor.

Sweden had another rival which was also gathering its forces in these years. This was Prussia. At the beginning of the seventeenth century, it

9

had, as the Electorate of Brandenburg, been a mere collection of territories, mostly centered upon Berlin, but with bits and pieces on the Rhine and in East Prussia, and was rich neither in population nor resources. Its rulers, the Hohenzollerns, found it difficult to administer these lands or, in time of trouble, defend them; and during the Thirty Years War, Brandenburg was overrun with foreign armies and its population and substance depleted by famine and pestilence. Things did not begin to change until 1640, when Frederick William, the so-called Great Elector, assumed the throne. An uncompromising realist, he saw that if he was to have security in a dangerous world, he would have to create what he considered to be the sinews of independence: a centralized state with an efficient bureaucracy and a strong army. The last was the key to the whole. As he wrote in his political testament, "A ruler is treated with no consideration if he does not have troops of his own. It is these, thank God! that have made me *considerable* since the time I began to have them"—and in the course of his reign, after purging his force of unruly and incompetent elements, Frederick William rapidly built an efficient force of thirty thousand men, so efficient indeed that in 1675, during the Franco-Swedish war against the Dutch, it came to the aid of the Dutch by defeating the Swedes at Fehrbellin and subsequently driving them out of Pomerania. It was to administer this army that Frederick William laid the foundations of the soon famous Prussian bureaucracy; it was to support it that he encouraged the growth of a native textile industry; it was with its aid that he smashed the recalcitrant provincial diets and centralized the state. And finally it was this army that, by its participation after the Great Elector's death in the wars against Louis XIV and its steadiness under fire at Ramillies and Malplaquet, induced the European powers to recognize his successor Frederick I as king of Prussia.

Under Frederick, an extravagant and thoughtless man, the new kingdom threatened to outrun its resources. But the ruler who assumed the throne in 1715, Frederick William I, resumed the work begun by the Great Elector, restored Prussia's financial stability, and completed the centralization and modernization of the state apparatus by elaborating a body of law and statute that clarified rights and responsibilities for all subjects. He nationalized the officer corps of the army, improved its dress and weapons, wrote its first handbook of field regulations, prescribing manual exercises and tactical evolutions, and rapidly increased its size. When Frederick William took the throne after the lax rule of his predecessor, there were rumors of an impending coup by his neighbors, like that attempted against Sweden in 1700. That kind of talk soon died away as the king's work proceeded, and it is easy to see why. In the course of his reign, he increased the size of his military establishment to eighty-three thousand men, a figure that made Prussia's army the fourth largest in Europe, although the state ranked only tenth from the standpoint of territory and thirteenth in population.

Before the eighteenth century was far advanced, then, the threat of French universal dominance had been defeated, a balance of power existed in western Europe, and two new powers had emerged as partners of the older established ones. It was generally recognized that in terms of power and influence, the leading states in Europe were Britain, France, Austria, Russia, and probably Prussia. The doubts on the last score were soon to be removed; and these five powers were to be the ones that dominated European and world politics until 1914.

II

Something should be said at this point about diplomacy, for it was in the seventeenth and eighteenth centuries that it assumed its modern form. The use of envoys and emissaries to convey messages from one ruler to another probably goes back to the beginning of history; there are heralds in the *Iliad* and, in the second letter to the Church of Corinth, the Apostle Paul describes himself as an ambassador. But modern diplomacy as we know it had its origins in the Italian city states of the Renaissance period, and particularly in the republic of Venice and the states of Milan and Tuscany. In the fourteenth and fifteenth centuries, Venice was a great commercial power whose prosperity depended upon shrewd calculation of risks, accurate reports upon conditions in foreign markets, and effective negotiation. Because it did so, Venice developed the first systemized diplomatic service known to history, a network of agents who pursued the interests of the republic with fidelity, with a realistic appraisal of risks, with freedom from sentimentality and illusion.

From Venice the new practice of systematic diplomacy was passed on to the states of central Italy which, because they were situated in a political arena that was characterized by incessant rivalry and coalition warfare, were always vulnerable to external threats and consequently put an even greater premium than the Venetians upon accurate information and skillful negotiation. The mainland cities soon considered diplomacy so useful that they began to establish permanent embassies abroad, a practice instituted by Milan and Mantua in the fifteenth century, while their political thinkers (like the Florentine Machiavelli) reflected upon the principles best calculated to make diplomacy effective and tried to codify rules of procedure and diplomatic immunity. This last development facilitated the transmission of the shared experience of the Italian cities to the rising nation states of the west that soon dwarfed Florence and Venice in magnitude and strength. Thus, when the great powers emerged in the seventeenth century, they already possessed a highly developed system of diplomacy based upon long experience. The employment of occasional missions to foreign courts had given way to the practice of maintaining permanent missions. While the ambassadors abroad represented their princes and communicated with them directly, their reports were studied in, and they received their instructions from, permanent, organized bureaus which were the first foreign offices. France led the way in this and was followed by most other states, and the establishment of a Foreign Ministry on the French model was one of Peter the Great's important reforms. The emergence of a single individual who was charged with the coordination of all foreign business and who represented his sovereign in the conduct of foreign affairs came a bit later, but by the beginning of the eighteenth century, the major powers all had such officials, who came to be known as foreign ministers or secretaries of state for foreign affairs.

From earliest times, an aura of intrigue, conspiracy, and disingenuousness surrounded the person of the diplomat, and we have all heard the famous quip of Sir Henry Wotton, ambassador of James I to the court of Venice, who said that an ambassador was "an honest man sent to lie abroad for the good of his country." Moralists were always worried by this unsavory reputation, which they feared was deserved, and they sought to reform it by exhortation. In the fifteenth century, Bernard du Rosier, provost and later archbishop of Toulouse, wrote a treatise in which he argued that the business of an ambassador is peace, that ambassadors must labor for the common good, and that they should never be sent to stir up wars or internal dissensions; and in the nineteenth century, Sir Robert Peel the younger was to define diplomacy in general as "the great engine used by civilized society for the purpose of maintaining peace."

The realists always opposed this ethical emphasis. In the fifteenth century, in one of the first treatises on ambassadorial functions, Ermalao

Barbaro wrote: "The first duty of an ambassador is exactly the same as that of any other servant of government: that is, to do, say, advise and think whatever may best serve the preservation and aggrandizement of his own state."

Seventeenth-century theorists were inclined to Barbaro's view. This was certainly the position of Abram de Wicquefort, who coined the definition of the diplomat as "an honorable spy," and who, in his own career, demonstrated that he did not take the adjectival qualification very seriously. A subject of Holland by birth, Wicquefort at various times in his checkered career performed diplomatic services for the courts of Brandenburg, Lüneburg, and France as well as for his own country, and he had no scruples about serving as a double agent, a practice that eventually led to his imprisonment in a Dutch jail. It was here that he wrote his treatise *L'Ambassadeur et ses fonctions,* a work that was both an amusing commentary on the political morals of the baroque age and an incisive analysis of the art and practice of diplomacy.

Wicquefort was not abashed by the peccadilloes of his colleagues, which varied from financial peculation and sins of the flesh to crimes of violence. He took the line that in a corrupt age, one could not expect that embassies would be oases of virtue. Morality was, in any case, an irrelevant consideration in diplomacy; a country could afford to be served by bad men, but not by incompetent ones. Competence began with a clear understanding on the diplomat's part of the nature of his job and a willingness to accept the fact that it had nothing to do with personal gratification or self-aggrandizement. The ambassador's principal function, Wicquefort wrote, "consisted in maintaining effective communication between the two Princes, in delivering letters that his master writes to the Prince at whose court he resides, in soliciting answers to them, . . . in protecting his Master's subjects and conserving his interests." He must have the charm and cultivation that would enable him to ingratiate himself at the court to which he was accredited and the adroitness needed to ferret out information that would reveal threats to his master's interests or opportunities for advancing them. He must possess the ability to gauge the temperament and intelligence of those with whom he had to deal and to use this knowledge profitably in negotiation. "Ministers are but men and as such have their weaknesses, that is to say, their passions and interests, which the ambassador ought to know if he wishes to do honor to himself and his Master."

In pursuing this intelligence, the qualities he should cultivate most assiduously were *prudence* and *modération*. The former Wicquefort equated with caution and reflection, and also with the gifts of silence and indirection, the art of "making it appear that one is not interested in the things one desires the most." The diplomat who possessed prudence did not have to resort to mendacity or deceit or to *tromperies* or *artifices,* which were usually, in any case, counterproductive. *Modération* was the ability to curb one's temper and remain cool and phlegmatic in moments of tension. "Those spirits who are compounded of sulphur and saltpeter, whom the slightest spark can set afire, are easily capable of compromising affairs by their excitability, because it is so easy to put them in a rage or drive them to a fury, so that they don't know what they are doing." Diplomacy is a cold and rational business, in short, not to be practiced by the moralist, or the enthusiast, or the man with a low boiling point.

The same point was made in the most famous of the eighteenth-century essays on diplomacy, François de Callières's *On the Manner of Negotiating with Princes* (1716), in which persons interested in the career of diplomacy were advised to consider whether they were born with "the qualities necessary for success." These, the author wrote, included

> an observant mind, a spirit of application which refuses to be distracted by pleasures or frivolous amusements, a sound judgment which takes the measure of things, as they are, and which goes straight to its goal by the shortest and most neutral paths without wandering into useless refinements and subtleties which as a rule only succeed in repelling those with whom one is dealing.

Important also were the kind of penetration that is useful in discovering the thoughts of men, a fertility in expedients when difficulties arise, an equable humor and a patient temperament, and easy and agreeable manners. Above all, Callières observed, in a probably not unconscious echo of Wicquefort's insistence upon moderation, the diplomat must have

> sufficient control over himself to resist the longing to speak before he has really thought what he shall say. He should not endeavour to gain the reputation of being able to reply immediately and without premeditation to every proposition which is made, and he should take a special care not to fall into the error of one famous foreign ambassador of our time who so loved an argument that each time he warmed up in controversy he revealed important secrets in order to support his opinion.

14

In his treatment of the art of negotiation, Callières drew from a wealth of experience to which Wicquefort could not pretend, for he was one of Louis XIV's most gifted diplomats and ended his career as head of the French delegation during the negotiations at Ryswick in 1697. It is interesting, in light of the heavy reliance upon lawyers in contemporary United States diplomacy (one thinks of President Eisenhower's secretary of state and President Reagan's national security adviser) and of the modern practice of negotiating in large gatherings, that Callières had no confidence in either of these preferences. The legal mind, he felt, was at once too narrow, too intent upon hair-splitting, and too contentious to be useful in a field where success, in the last analysis, was best assured by agreements that provided mutuality of advantage. As for large conferences—"vast concourses of ambassadors and envoys"—his view was that they were generally too clumsy to achieve anything very useful. Most successful conferences were the result of careful preliminary work by small groups of negotiators who hammered out the essential bases of agreement and secured approval for them from their governments before handing them over, for formal purposes, to the *omnium-gatherums* that were later celebrated in the history books.

Perhaps the most distinctive feature of Callières's treatise was the passion with which he argued that a nation's foreign relations should be conducted by persons trained for the task.

> Diplomacy is a profession by itself which deserves the same preparation and assiduity of attention that men give to other recognized professions. . . . The diplomatic genius is born, not made. But there are many qualities which may be developed with practice, and the greatest part of the necessary knowledge can only be acquired, by constant application to the subject. In this sense, diplomacy is certainly a profession itself capable of occupying a man's whole career, and those who think to embark upon a diplomatic mission as a pleasant diversion from their common task only prepare disappointment for themselves and disaster for the cause which they serve.

These words represented not only a personal view but an acknowledgment of the requirements of the age. The states that emerged as recognizedly great powers in the course of the seventeenth and eighteenth centuries were the states that had modernized their governmental structure, mobilized their economic and other resources in a rational manner, built up effective and disciplined military establishments, and elaborated a professional civil service that administered state business in accordance with the principles of *raison d'état*. An indispensable part of that civil service was the Foreign Office and the diplomatic corps, which had the important task of formulating the foreign policy that protected and advanced the state's vital interests and of seeing that it was carried out.

Bibliographical Essay

For the general state of international relations before the eighteenth century, the following are useful: Marvin R. O'Connell, *The Counter-Reformation, 1559–1610* (New York, 1974); Carl J. Friedrich, *The Age of the Baroque, 1610–1660* (New York, 1952), a brilliant volume; C. V. Wedgwood, *The Thirty Years War* (London, 1938, and later editions); Frederick L. Nussbaum, *The Triumph of Science and Reason, 1660–1685* (New York, 1953); and John B. Wolf, *The Emergence of the Great Powers, 1685–1715* (New York, 1951). On Austrian policy in the seventeenth century, see especially Max Braubach, *Prinz Eugen von Savoyen*, 5 vols. (Vienna, 1963–1965); on Prussian, Otto Hintze, *Die Hohenzollern und ihr Werk* (Berlin, 1915) and, brief but useful, Sidney B. Fay, *The Rise of Brandenburg-Prussia* (New York, 1937). A classical essay on great-power politics in the early modern period is Leopold von Ranke, *Die grossen Mächte*, which can be found in English translation in the appendix of Theodore von Laue, *Leopold Ranke: The Formative Years* (Princeton, 1950). The standard work on *raison d'état* is Friedrich Meinecke, *Die Idee der Staatsräson*, 3rd ed. (Munich, 1963), translated by Douglas Scott as *Machiavellianism* (New Haven, 1957).

On the origins and development of diplomacy, see D. P. Heatley, *Diplomacy and the Study of International Relations* (Oxford, 1919); Leon van der Essen, *La Diplomatie: Ses origines et son organisation* (Brussels, 1953); Ragnar Numelin, *Les origines de la diplomatie*, trans. from the Swedish by Jean-Louis Perret (Paris, 1943); and especially Heinrich Wildner, *Die Technik der Diplomatie: L'Art de négocier* (Vienna, 1959). Highly readable is Harold Nicolson, *Diplomacy*, 2nd ed. (London, 1950). An interesting comparative study is Adda B. Bozeman, *Politics and Culture in International History* (Princeton, 1960).

There is no modern edition of *L'ambassadeur et ses fonctions par Monsieur de Wicquefort* (Cologne, 1690); but Callières's classic of 1776 can be found: François de Callières, *On the Manner of Negotiating with Princes*, trans. A. F. Whyte (London, 1919, and later editions).

2

Eighteenth-Century Diplomacy

During the first half of the nineteenth century, a period in which the forces of nationalism were still relatively undeveloped, a book that enjoyed a considerable vogue among students of international politics was the Göttingen historian A. H. L. Heeren's *History of the Political System of Europe*. The author contended that for more than a century, the component states of Europe had been moving insensibly but inevitably toward federation, a process that was encouraged both by their similarities—the fact that they "resembled each other in manners, religion, and custom and were connected by reciprocal interests"—and by their diversity, which, he said, "preserved practically in circulation a greater compass of political ideas" and, more important, created a general repugnance to the idea of dominance by a single power.

Heeren did not hesitate to suggest that the creation of a European system had been all but consummated in the eighteenth century. He admitted that "a rightful condition among the several states, such as might be projected in theory, was at all times far from being established." Nevertheless, he added,

> As a gradual result of the progress of culture, a system of international law was developed, which, reposing not merely on express treaties, but also on silent agreements, enjoined the observance of certain maxims in peace, but more especially in times of war, and which, though often violated, were still eminently beneficial. Even the strict, and sometimes excessive, etiquette, mutually observed by states toward one another, was by no means a matter of indiffer-

17

ence on the part of states, often the most unlike in power and constitution.

The most important results of this, Heeren argued, were, first, the acknowledgment of the sacredness of rightful possession, which he said was "the support of the whole system," and, second, the recognition of the principle of the balance of power, "that is, the mutual preservation of freedom and independence, by guarding against the preponderance and usurpation of an individual." To Heeren, maintenance of the balance was "the constant problem of higher policy" and the principal preoccupation of the diplomats who made and executed it; and the consequences of this were beneficial, resulting in

> a constantly wakeful attention of the states to one another, and various consequent relations by means of alliances and counteralliances, especially of the more distant states; the greater importance of the states of the second and third order in the political system; and, in general, the preservation of a feeling of the value of independence, and the elevation of politics above gross selfishness.

Heeren's view that after centuries of conflict, the European states had succeeded in the eighteenth century in moderating their anarchic tendencies and forming a system based upon mutual respect and recognition of the balance of power was bound to arouse a certain incredulity in the mind of anyone who had studied the politics of that century. How could one speak of a European system when the principal powers were engaged in almost continuous warfare against each other? The eighteenth century is often called the Age of Enlightenment or the Age of Reason, and we know that its greatest thinkers, impressed by Isaak Newton's discoveries concerning the laws that ran the universe, were curious to discover rules of rational behavior for human society. Yet between these earnest efforts and the actualities of international politics there seemed to be no vital connection. La Bruyère wrote mockingly that the diplomats of the age "spoke only of peace, alliance, and public tranquillity . . . and thought only of their special interest," and the same thought was voiced by a contemporary statesman who described the conditions of his time as "a continuous quarrel between people without morals, intent on taking and perpetually hungry."

The gulf that existed between the Enlightenment and politics, and the duplicity and greed that characterized great-power diplomacy in the eighteenth century, may be illustrated by some reference to the early

18

policy of Frederick II (the Great) of Prussia. In many ways, Frederick was the quintessential product of the Enlightenment. To the distress of his father, the soldier-king Frederick William I, he appeared to spend his time as crown prince on matters that seemed remote from statecraft and the art of war. He corresponded with French *philosophes* like Voltaire, who was later his guest as Sans Souci; he studied poetry and music, becoming an excellent flutist; and he wrote a long treatise on politics in which he attacked the principles of Machiavelli on ethical and rational grounds, like any other advocate of the *Aufklärung*.

Yet the young Frederick's thoughts were not as remote from politics as his fretful father supposed. In 1731, in a letter to one of his aides, he wrote that Prussia occupied an exposed and defenseless position in the center of Europe and that it would be the plaything of the other major powers if it did not increase and consolidate its territory. The important thing was to *corriger la figure de la Prusse* (correct the shape of Prussia), a process which, given the nature of Prussia's scattered holdings, was a necessity required by the honor of the Hohenzollern house, so that its leaders "could cut a good figure among the great of this world and play a significant role." This letter was a curious blend of cold realism and youthful idealism, as when the prince talked of "Prussia's raising itself from the dust into which it has fallen" and bringing the Protestant faith to bloom in Europe and the Reich so that it could represent "the future for the oppressed, a refuge for widows and orphans, a support for the poor, and a terror for the unjust." On the whole, the realism was the stronger note, as the sequel showed.

In 1740, Frederick succeeded his father on the throne of Prussia. The same year saw the death of the Austrian emperor, Charles VI, an ineffectual ruler whose extravagance had weakened Austrian finances and whose wars in eastern Europe had decimated the army. With Charles the main male line died out, and the throne passed to his daughter Maria Theresia. The emperor had feared that her claim might be contested and had therefore asked the European powers to subscribe to a document called the Pragmatic Sanction, in accordance with which they engaged to observe and defend the integrity of the Austrian possessions under Maria Theresia's rule. Frederick of Prussia had signed this document along with most of the other rulers.

Nevertheless, neither his signature nor the arguments against immorality that he had used in his *Anti-Machiavel* treatise deterred him now from taking advantage of what seemed to be an ideal opportunity for aggrandizement—an opportunity which he seemed, indeed, to think it would be criminal to let slip. Without hesitation, he ordered his armies to invade and seize the rich Austrian province of Silesia, a territory to which Prussia had some vague historical claims that could give a screen of legal plausibility to what was quite patently an act of aggression and is, indeed, remembered as "the rape of Silesia."

Before embarking on this adventure, Frederick, in order to still the doubts of his ministers, wrote a remarkable memorandum that should be quoted *in extenso* for the light it throws on him and upon eighteenth-century diplomatic practice.

> Silesia is the portion of the Imperial heritage to which we have the strongest claim and which is most suitable to the House of Brandenburg. The superiority of our troops, the promptitude with which we can set them in motion, in a word, the clear advantage we have over our neighbors, gives us in this unexpected emergency an infinite superiority over all other powers of Europe. If we wait till Saxony and Bavaria start hostilities, we could not prevent the aggrandizement of the former which is wholly contrary to our interest. . . . [As for the other powers], England and France are foes. If France should meddle in the affairs of the empire, England could not allow it, so I can always make a good alliance with one or the other. England could not be jealous of my getting Silesia, which would do her no harm, and she needs allies. Holland will not care, all the more since the loans of the Amsterdam business world secured on Silesia will be guaranteed. If we cannot arrange with England and Holland, we can certainly make a deal with France, who cannot frustrate our designs and will welcome the abasement of the imperial house.
>
> Russia alone might give us trouble. If the empress lives . . . we can bribe the leading counsellors. If she dies, the Russians will be so occupied that they will have no time for foreign affairs. . . . All this leads to the conclusion that we must occupy Silesia before the winter and then negotiate. When we are in possession we can negotiate with success. We should never get anything by negotiations alone except very onerous conditions in return for a few trifles.

This memorandum really requires no comment. Here is a mind completely dominated by *Staatsräson,* a mind that admits no legal or ethical bounds to state ambition. That Frederick's relations with Maria Theresia had been wholly amicable up to this time, that he was bound by treaty to respect the integrity of her possessions were, in 1740, wholly irrelevant to him. The opportunity for gain was imperative, and Frederick began his invasion. In the event, his gamble paid off, and Prussia won and retained Silesia, a fact that had profound influence upon the structure and future of Germany. For when Austria lost Silesia, with its large population and important resources, the western half of the Austrian Empire ceased to be a predominantly German state and the whole balance of forces in Germany tilted in Prussia's favor. But this result was gained only as a result of two wasting wars in which the Silesian issue at times seemed to drop out of view. In the first of these, the so-called War of the Austrian Succession, which extended from 1740 to 1748, Prussia was joined by France, Spain, Bavaria, and Saxony (although Saxony changed sides in 1743), all of which saw an opportunity of gaining some territory in the Netherlands or Italy or Bohemia at Austria's expense, whereas Austria was supported by Great Britain, which sent some troops to the Low Countries but devoted more of its energies to attacking French and Spanish possessions in the New World. The second was the Seven Years War, which extended from 1756 to 1763, in which Prussia, as a result of the brilliant diplomatic revolution effected by the Austrian chancellor Kaunitz, found itself opposed by Austria, France, Russia, Saxony, Sweden, and (after 1762) Spain and supported only by Great Britain and Hannover. In this war too, both Frederick's opponents and his supporters were motivated by a lust for gain, and it is significant that some of the most important battles took place not in Bohemia and Moravia, the main arena for the confrontations of the Austrian and Prussian armies, but in North America and India. It is difficult to read of the casualties demanded by these titanic struggles, in which Frederick confirmed Prussia's title to great-power status by bleeding his country white, and in which the other powers changed sides without the guidance of any but the meanest of principles, without thinking of the eighteenth century as an age of anarchy and rapine.

And yet it is important to note that much of what Heeren said about the elements of an emerging European system was also true. Despite the wars that pitted the European states against each other, there was a general assumption that they were members of a comity of states that were bound together by common ties of family relationship, religion, and historical tradition. These connections, it was often argued, were more significant than their sporadic enmities, which were evanescent. Clausewitz, the military theorist, was speaking in the spirit of the eighteenth century when he later wrote:

> If we consider the community of states in Europe today, we . . . find major and minor interests of states and peoples interwoven in the most varied and changeable manner. Each point of intersection binds and serves to balance one set of interests against another.

21

> The broad effect of all these fixed points is obviously to give a certain amount of cohesion to the whole. . . . The fact that Europe, as we know it, has existed for over a thousand years can only be explained by the operation of these general interests.

Some eighteenth-century publicists did not hesitate to talk of the great powers of Europe as forming a society or a federation (a term that frequently occurs) or a concert. And although it was difficult to prove that such a concert actually existed, they were fond of pointing out that on certain principles or rules of the diplomatic game there was enough broad agreement to indicate that some kind of concerted thinking could be mobilized.

For instance, there was a general agreement that it was normal and right that there should be five great powers. The thought that one of them might disappear—that Prussia might actually be destroyed in the Seven Years War, for example—was resisted by all major powers. There seemed to be an unconscious feeling (it was Ranke who first used this comparison) that the disappearance of one of the great powers would have the same kind of disastrous effect as that caused by the death of the first violinist in a quintet that had played together for a long time.

In the second place, there was general agreement that although the powers might fight against each other, the way in which they fought should be subject to some regulation. The codification of the so-called laws of war, began in the sixteenth and seventeenth centuries, was carried further in the eighteenth. The laws were extended from such things as rules governing military booty and the treatment of wounded and prisoners to relations between the military and civilian society. Efforts were made to determine under what conditions of war it was permissible for a commander to order the destruction of crops or livestock, or to destroy civilian dwellings, or to take hostages. There was no authority to see that these rules were respected, and they were often violated, but by and large they were fairly effective, and they represented a general feeling that if it was at all possible, this was the way soldiers were to behave and that unless circumstances seemed to demand it, civilian society should be spared the horrors that accompanied any war. In the eighteenth century, this control or limitation of the effects of military action on society reached its peak when even Frederick the Great, who was a daring and single-minded practitioner of war, declared that he wanted to fight his wars without the peasant behind his plough and the townsman in his shop ever being aware of them.

Finally, there was a general recognition of the principle of the balance of power, which took two forms. The first was a general wariness about anything that looked like an attempt at universal domination by a single power. Consider once more the case of Frederick II in 1740. That the attack on Silesia was an act of aggression was palpable; but it should be noted that it was designed as a limited aggression. Frederick could even argue—indeed, he did argue—that he was not violating the principle of the balance of power by invading Silesia but vindicating it, by correcting it and making it sounder. He knew that that argument was plausible enough to appeal to third powers, many of which felt that Austria was too big anyway.

But Frederick also knew that if he carried his aggression to the point of seeking to destroy Austria or, even further, to the point of seeking an ascendancy over all Europe, he would be stopped by a coalition of all other powers. This was, of course, never his intention. Like other European rulers of his time, balance of power meant to him a denial of universal ambitions. It also meant something else in the eighteenth century, this century of reason and mechanical rules. It was generally agreed that for the balance of power to work properly, a territorial gain effected in war by one power should be balanced by compensatory gains for other major powers.

The application of this rule involved such elaborate territorial arithmetic that it is almost impossible to describe some of the arrangements. Consider the case of the War of the Polish Succession, which was fought in the years 1733–1735. Just as Turkey was the Sick Man of Europe in the nineteenth century, so did Poland, which in the seventeenth century had been potentially a great power, become the Sick Man of Europe in the eighteenth, with all powers anxious about its condition and eager to have a share in the spoils if it fell to pieces. In 1733, the Polish Diet, tired of being ruled by Saxons, elected a Pole, Stanislaus Leszczynski, as king. This annoyed both the Russians, who sent an army of thirty thousand men to Poland to protest, and the Austrians, who had got along well with the Saxon rulers and who also mobilized. The Russians succeeded in deposing Leszczynski and forcing a rump diet to elect August III of Saxony as king, but the French, whose young King Louis XV had married Leszczynski's daughter, would not accept this result and declared war on Austria with the support of Sardinia (the House of Savoy) and Spain. The war was fought mostly in Baden and Italy and went badly for the Austrians. When it threatened to grow and involve England, the French called a halt, and a peace settlement was made.

In the interests of the balance of power, everybody, except the Poles over whom the war had started, received some compensation. Leszczynski gave up the throne of Poland but kept the courtesy title king and was given the Duchy of Bar. Later, in 1740, when Duke Francis of Lorraine, the husband of Maria Theresia, became emperor of Austria and gave up Lorraine in order to acquire Tuscany, Leszczynski got Lorraine too. It was agreed, however, that when he died both Bar and Lorraine would pass to his daughter, the wife of the French king, and would thus become part of France. The Habsburgs not only, through Duke Francis, acquired Tuscany in Italy, but also Parma and Piacenza. The Spanish got Naples, and the king of Sardinia was fobbed off with some minor frontier rectifications. It was a big pie, and everybody got a piece.

In 1735, the Russians did not bother to claim a share in the spoils, for they were not interested in Italy or the Franco-German borders. But they had demonstrated their ability to depose one Polish king and put a creature of their own in his place. They had advertised the weakness of Poland, and they were willing to wait until the situation was ripe for a real land grab there. But they were prepared also to recognize the principle of sharing the booty when that time came. The most spectacular of the eighteenth-century applications of balance to territorial aggrandizement was to come with the division of Poland between Russia, Austria, and Prussia in the three partitions of 1772, 1793, and 1795.

It can be maintained, therefore, that the eighteenth century was not completely anarchic and that the great powers acknowledged certain rules of international intercourse, such as the necessity of the existence of the normal quota of five great powers, the view that the rigors of war should be ameliorated by restrictions upon the freedom of commanders in the field, and the belief that it was important to observe the balance of power as a limitation upon ambition and as a guide in territorial partition. But this hardly justifies Heeren's contention that a European system existed in the eighteenth century. The most that can be said is that the *idea* of a system of a European federation, of a concert of powers, was in men's minds. Writers on politics often talked of it as a desirable thing, in the sense that if it really existed, it might be able to develop the already recognized rules of international behavior into a more effective code of law that would restrain international violence and reduce the constant drain that war imposed upon state resources.

For the most part, this was publicists' talk, the discourse of philosophers and theorists. It was not reflected in the deliberations and activities of governments, which went their violent ways without bothering themselves with thoughts of federations and concerts. To make them concern themselves over such matters, something was needed that was capable of shocking and frightening them into real collaborative action, something that would force them to convert the dream of a European concert into an effective working concert.

That was supplied by the French Revolution and the foreign policy of the Republic and the Napoleonic Empire. Yet so entrenched were the European powers in their customary ways that the significance of the revolution was lost on them when it took place. Their first reaction was one of satisfaction—a feeling that the events in Paris would not last but that, while they did, France would be paralyzed and incapable of conducting foreign policy, a situation from which they would derive advantages. The idea that the revolution might threaten them never occurred to the powers. The same Kaunitz who had effected the diplomatic revolution of 1756 wrote a pamphlet called "Reflections on the Pretended Dangers of Contagion with Which the New Constitution of France Menaces Other Sovereign States," in which he scornfully dismissed the very idea of the revolution having external consequences.

This relaxed attitude almost proved fatal for them in the end, for it enabled the revolutionary forces in France to survive the awkward period when they might have been put down easily by foreign intervention. It gave the revolution a chance to consolidate itself and then to go on the offensive, as it did in 1792 with the decrees that declared its intention of liberating Europe from absolute rulers.

Even these decrees and the subsequent movement of French armies toward the Rhine did not unduly alarm the other powers. The Austrians and Prussians sent armies to block the French, but their efforts in the campaigns of 1793–1795 were uncoordinated and lamed by their nervous concern lest the Russians, while their backs were turned, decide to seize Poland. The war in the west was really a kind of Austro-Prussian competition for spoils in the east. In 1793, Prussia managed to participate in the second partition of Poland while Austria was left in the lurch and, in 1795, knowing that another partition was pending, the Prussian government did not hesitate to make a private deal with the French in order to extricate itself from the war before all Poland was gone. By the secret peace of Basel in 1795, the Prussians sold out their Austrian ally and promised the French that they could have the left bank of the Rhine (which Louis XIV had never been able to conquer) if they gave Prussia compensation in western Germany. Then they terminated hostilities and scrambled back eastward just in time to share in the third and final partition of Poland.

It is unnecessary to continue the story in any detail. This kind of selfish and self-centered behavior enabled the French republican armies to conquer the Rhineland and to penetrate into southern Germany, Switzerland, and Italy. When the Republic gave way to the Consulate of Napoleon Bonaparte and then to the Empire, this French imperialism gained in momentum and intention. As Ranke wrote later, "Everything that had happened in Louis XIV's time had now been far exceeded. The old liberties of Europe were submerged. Europe seemed about to be swallowed up by France. The universal monarchy, that had hitherto seemed only a remote danger, was almost realized."

Yet the other great powers still seemed incapable of understanding the dimension of the danger. Although England strove to form anti-French coalitions and received the support of Austria, the Russians were unreliable allies, and the Prussians remained neutral until 1806 and then, choosing the wrong moment to fight Napoleon, were smashed and rendered powerless for another seven years. Napoleon was well on his way to complete domination of Europe, having turned both Austria and Prussia into near satellites, when he overreached himself in Russia in 1812. And it was only in the wake of that setback that the other powers finally formed the Grand Alliance that would encompass his defeat.

When they had done so and when they had won their first great collaborative battle at Leipzig in 1813, quarrels and dissension threatened to divide their union. But their awareness of the danger that they had not yet fully escaped not only kept them together but, at long last, induced them to take the first real step toward converting the eighteenth-century aspiration for a concert into an effective working arrangement. In the French town of Chaumont on 1 March 1814, the governments of Austria, Prussia, Russia, and Great Britain, largely under the influence of the British foreign secretary, Castlereagh, signed a treaty in which they agreed not only to continue the war against Napoleon until a definitive victory had been gained, but also to continue their alliance after their victory. The language of the treaty is significant as showing their motivation. "The present Treaty of Alliance having for its object the maintenance of the balance of Europe, to secure the repose and independence of the Powers, and to prevent the invasions which for so many years have devastated the world, the High Contracting Parties have agreed among themselves to extend its duration for twenty years from the date of signature."

This treaty held the allies together until the Corsican was banned from Europe and until the great settlement of 1814–1815 was completed. And at the Congress of Vienna and in the Second Peace of Paris, the stipulations of the Treaty of Chaumont served as the basis for the first notable experiment in institutionalizing the principles of concert and balance in behalf of European peace.

Bibliographical Essay

Heeren's treatise is available in English: A. H. L. Heeren, *History of the Political System of Europe and Its Colonies,* 2 vols., trans. from the German by George Bancroft (Northampton, Mass., 1829). A fundamentally different view will be found in the classical account of eighteenth-century diplomacy, Albert Sorel, *L'Europe et la révolution française,* 8 vols., I, 4th ed. (Paris, 1897).

The years of relative peace are treated by Penfield Roberts, *The Quest for Security, 1715–1740* (New York, 1947); those of conflict in Walter L. Dorn's masterful *Competition for Empire, 1740–1763* (New York, 1940), which is particularly good on Kaunitz and his contemporaries. On Frederick II, see the account in Friedrich Meinecke, *Die Idee der Staatsräson;* Gerhart Ritter, *Frederick the Great,* trans. from the German by Peter Paret (Berkeley, 1968); and G. P. Gooch, *Frederick the Great: The Ruler, the Writer, the Man* (New York, 1947).

For the period of the American and French revolutions, see R. R. Palmer's classic *The Age of the Democratic Revolution,* 2 vols. (Princeton, 1959, 1964); Leo Gershoy, *From Despotism to Revolution, 1763–1789* (New York, 1944); and Crane Brinton, *A Decade of Revolution, 1789–1799* (New York, 1934). On the diplomacy of the Napoleonic age, see especially Enno E. Kraehe, *Metternich's German Policy: I. The Contest with Napoleon, 1799–1814* (Princeton, 1963) and C. K. Webster, *The Foreign Policy of Castlereagh, 1812–1815* (London, 1931). Geoffrey Bruun, *Europe and the French Imperium, 1799–1814* (New York, 1938) is still useful.

The best edition of Clausewitz's classic treatise is Carl von Clausewitz, *On War,* ed. and trans. by Michael Howard and Peter Paret (Princeton, 1976).

3
Balance of Power, 1815-1914:
Three Experiments

During the nineteenth century, the greatest challenge to statecraft was the task of devising a political system that would contain international violence and prevent war from threatening once more, as it had during the Napoleonic period, to assume its absolute form. Three generations of statesmen struggled with the problem of establishing a viable equilibrium of forces in Europe, and their efforts found expression in three quite different systems of balance of power, each of which reflected the characteristic tendencies of its time. The first of these experiments was made by the negotiators who gathered in Vienna in 1814 and 1815; the second by the German chancellor Otto von Bismarck at the end of the 1870s; the third by the harried diplomats in the years after 1890. In terms of effectiveness, the first came closest to fulfilling the purposes for which it was formed. The second embodied all of the ingenuity of its creator but was too complicated to have much inherent stability; and the third was little more than an exercise in desperation.

I

One of the most famous paintings ever made of a diplomatic conference is the one that the French portraitist Jean-Baptiste Isabey made of the Congress of Vienna. In the center of this large canvas, standing with a proprietary air and a look of satisfaction on his handsome face, is the host of the meeting, the Austrian chancellor Prince Metternich, while around him are grouped the chief representatives of the other powers:

Castlereagh, the British foreign secretary, with his legs crossed negligently; the king of Prussia, Frederick William III, looking gloomily at the phlegmatic Englishman; the czar of Russia, Alexander I, wearing a uniform with epaulettes so big that one wonders how he will be able to lift himself out of the chair in which he is sitting; and the representative of France, Talleyrand-Périgord, with his clubfoot, his badly powdered wig, his pendulous lips, and his sardonic eyes. In the background, in bestarred and bemedalled clusters, stand the lesser figures of the congress—resident ambassadors, diplomatic secretaries, military aides, and the like—all bearing on their faces that arch and condescending smirk that is worn by persons who wish to give the impression that they are privy to mysteries that they are pledged not to reveal.

It is well to consider the faces of these bedecked and bedizened statesmen, for they were pathbreakers. There had been other conferences and congresses before Vienna, like Münster and Osnabrück in 1648, and Utrecht in 1713. But those meetings had been for the purpose of ending hostilities and dividing spoils. The statesmen at Vienna had set themselves another task. Metternich made this clear when he said:

> No great political insight is needed to see that this Congress could not be modelled on any which had taken place. Former assemblies which were called congresses met for the express purpose of settling a quarrel between two or more belligerent powers—the issue being a peace treaty. On this occasion, peace had already been made [he was referring to the First Peace of Paris, which had ended hostilities] and the parties meet as friends who, though differing in their interests, wish to work together towards the conclusion and affirmation of the existing treaty.

What did he mean by "conclusion and affirmation"? Clearly, that the main task of this congress was to move from a mere ending of past hostilities to a settlement that would prevent future conflict. This was the assigned task, and it was accomplished.

This did not mean that the peacemakers of Vienna utterly neglected the kinds of things that had preoccupied their predecessors at Osnabrück and Utrecht. They made sure that the members of the Grand Alliance were rewarded in accordance with the degree of their sacrifice and their contribution to the victory, and they devoted considerable time also to the complicated business of restoring titles and territory to rulers who had been deprived of them by Napoleon. But they did not allow this attention to the principles of compensation and legitimacy to obtrude upon what Metternich had defined as their more important obligation—that of constructing a new international system that would be able to resist any renewal of the kind of subversion and aggression that Napoleon had practiced against them; and in seeking to fulfill that obligation, they refused to allow themselves to be distracted by the greed of petty princelings or the desire for revenge against France. They did not, for example, attempt to restore, in facsimile form, the Europe that Napoleon had destroyed. They did not clutter up the international landscape with scores of rehabilitated petty principalities. And they did not succumb to the temptation to be vindictive toward the French people. Wilhelm von Humboldt, the Prussian ambassador to Vienna, who was to play a leading role in devising the agenda for the congress, had been in Paris when the Silesian army of Blücher and Gneisenau had entered the conquered city, and he had been distressed when the Prussian soldiers had wanted to blow up all the bridges over the Seine because they were named after Napoleonic victories. This kind of pettiness Humboldt and his colleagues in Vienna succeeded in excluding from the deliberations. They had no desire to cripple France in any serious way, least of all to make it so weak that it could not play its appropriate role as a great power in the postwar period.

The two principal architects of the new order were Viscount Castlereagh, the British foreign secretary, and Prince Clemens von Metternich, the chief minister of the emperor of Austria. Both were convinced that the key to the new international settlement must be the principle of the balance of power. The core of this doctrine was to them, as it had been to their predecessors who had fought against Louis XIV in the seventeenth century, a readiness on the part of the powers to resist unilateral attempts at universal domination. But they also believed that there should be such an equilibrium of forces among the major powers as to discourage such attempts, and they did not think that the eighteenth-century procedure of allowing territorial aggression on the part of the individual states, provided everybody else received compensation, had been a good way of attaining that. In general, the eighteenth-century territorial equilibrium had, in their view, been too loosely defined and too full of dangerous imbalances (like the one that goaded Frederick into such bloody action in 1740).

Under their leadership, therefore, the negotiators at Vienna went through enormous efforts to adjust territory, resources, and population as equitably as possible among the major powers—balancing off Russian gains in Poland with Austrian gains in Italy and Prussian acquisitions in the Rhineland, constructing buffers between the great powers in the Low Countries (by joining Belgium and Holland into one state) and in the German states that lay between Prussia and Austria. Germany, one delegate said later, had to serve as a kind of shock absorber and hence had to remain disunited in the interests of peace, preserving the "balance through an inherent force of gravity." The labors expended upon this elaborate redrawing of the map of Europe were onerous and protracted, and the results were written into the final act of the Congress of Vienna.

The men who guided this work were not, however, so naive as to believe that they had insured themselves against future trouble by this elaborate exercise in cartography. They were well aware that a new Frederick or a new Napoleon might arise, and they believed that some executive body must be established that would be capable of dealing with threats to the balance as soon as they occurred. In the eighteenth century, no such body had existed; and although publicists like Voltaire were fond of writing articles in which they argued that the rulers of Europe were tied together by bonds of religion, common history, and intermarriage and thus constituted a European federation or concert of Europe, this was always an ideal rather than a reality. Metternich and Castlereagh and their colleagues now actualized it by building upon the Treaty of Chaumont of March 1814. The Quadruple Alliance of November 1815 (later broadened to include France) not only reiterated the key features of Chaumont but stipulated that the great powers would hold periodic conferences of their foreign ministers "for the purpose of consulting upon their interests, or for the consideration of measures which . . . shall be considered the most salutary for the purpose and prosperity of Nations and the maintenance of the Peace of Europe." Thus, the new order was in a sense given both a constitution and a constitutional watchdog—a balance of power (as defined by the final act) and a concert of powers to watch over it.

In the form in which it was conceived, the system did not last long. When Metternich and Czar Alexander of Russia became concerned over the threat that liberalism posed to existing thrones of Europe, they tried to turn the Quadruple Alliance into an agency that would automatically intervene in the affairs of any country in which there was a revolution or an agitation against the status quo and suppress by force the revolutionary or democratic or liberal movements. These attempts the British government viewed as a subversion of the true purpose of the

Quadruple Alliance; and in a powerful note of 19 October 1818, Castlereagh protested that "nothing would be more immoral or more prejudicial to the character of governments generally than the idea that their force was collectively to be prostituted to the support of established power without any consideration of the extent to which it was abused." The eastern powers were not, however, to be stayed, and the British felt compelled to refuse to attend further meetings of the foreign ministers.

This withdrawal from the concert was more apparent than real. In a note of 5 May 1820, protesting against the Metternich policy, Castlereagh made it clear that, while Great Britain could not countenance a policy of joint meddling in the internal affairs of small states, its cooperation could always be counted upon when there was a genuine threat to the peace of Europe and the balance of power; and his successors periodically repeated this pledge as late as the mid-century. In 1852, Lord John Russell said in the House of Commons:

> We are connected, and have been for more than a century, with the general system of Europe, and any territorial increase of one Power, any aggrandisement which disturbs the general balance of power in Europe, although it might not immediately lead to war, could not be a matter of indifference to this country and would, no doubt, be the subject of conference, and might ultimately, if that balance was seriously threatened, lead to war.

Nor were these only words. In every crisis that threatened the peace between 1815 and 1854, the British were represented and played a leading role in finding a solution short of war. This was true in the Belgian crisis of 1830, the Near Eastern crisis of 1838, and the first Schleswig-Holstein crisis of 1850, to mention only the uglier disputes of this period. In all those cases, and in others, the European concert was able, with British participation, to demonstrate its effectiveness in preserving the Vienna balance and the public order.

There can be little doubt that the balance-of-power system worked more effectively in the years from 1815 to 1854 than at any later period in the nineteenth century, and we must ask ourselves why this was so.

For one thing, statecraft in this period was not subject to certain pressures which subsequently caused governments, often reluctantly, to do things that were bound to arouse the suspicion and fear of other powers and to invite violent retaliation. For the most part, the governments of these years did not have to worry about public opinion as they set their course in foreign affairs. There were exceptions to this, of course. Turkish atrocities against Christians in the Balkans could and did cause popular agitation for reprisals in Russia; and French boulevard opinion got very worked up in 1840 about a minor setback in the Near East and almost stampeded the government into war. But in general, Metternich's view that "foreign affairs is not for the plebs" seemed to be reasonably sound, and foreign ministers did not concern themselves overmuch about what might be in tomorrow's headlines.

Governments were free also from pressure from organized economic interests. Industrialization and capitalism had not evolved to the point where business firms were forming lobbies and seeking to influence political decisions; in this period most businessmen were convinced that the best thing that the government could do for them was to leave them alone. The problem of reconciling desirable foreign policy initiatives with the desiderata of powerful private interests, which in our own time often makes the use of economic pressures ineffective (as was true in the case of the U.S. grain embargo against the Soviet Union in 1980–1981), did not plague foreign offices in the first half of the nineteenth century.

Again, there was no agitation on the part of military establishments for an increased rate or level of armament. Indeed, the country with the biggest army after 1815, Russia, actually proposed a general scaling down of armaments one year after the Congress of Vienna had completed its work. This proposal did not find favor with the other powers— the British said they believed that each power should be its own judge when it came to setting limits to its armed forces, although they added that they would be ready at all times to inform others of their force levels; the Austrians were not even prepared to go that far, because of what Metternich called "the perpetual difficulty of obtaining any true data from Russia"—but on the other hand, if they wouldn't disarm, there was no disposition on the part of any of the powers to launch a program of military expansion; and the war offices of the various powers seemed completely content with this situation. There were no military pressure groups, any more than there were economic pressure groups, to complicate the policy-making process and disturb international relations.

In the second place, there were no ideological differences of any importance between the powers. There were moments, to be sure, when it seemed that divisions of this kind were on the point of becoming real. After the revolutions of 1830, which brought a liberal regime to power in France, Europe seemed to be divided into two camps: a liberal one of England and France, and a conservative one comprising Russia, Prussia and Austria. The British foreign secretary, Lord Palmerston, admitted that this was the apparent drift of international politics when he said, "The three and the two think differently and therefore they act differently."

If one examines the record of the years 1830–1854, however, it is clear that the powers ignored their ideological differences more than they observed them. If cooperation with France was, as Lord Palmerston once said, the axle upon which British policy turned, he had no compunction about concluding agreements with the eastern powers in moments when he felt the French were threatening British interests; while on the French side, Louis Philippe showed a growing desire—once his regime was firmly established—to seek an accommodation with the eastern powers even at the expense of his entente with England. When Metternich became worried about the czar's policy in the Near East, he consulted the British about ways of restraining him; when the czar became annoyed with his Prussian ally's Baltic ambitions, he collaborated with the British to frustrate them. If Europe was divided after 1830 along ideological lines, they were not so rigidly drawn as to prevent a high degree of interpenetration of combinations and a considerable amount of collaboration between the eastern and western powers.

Finally, all differences between the powers were subordinated to the high degree of consensus among them. With the possible exception of France, which did not dare admit its uniqueness, all powers accepted the balance of power—that is, the territorial arrangements made at Vienna and the broader principle that no single state should be allowed to increase its possessions except with the consent of others. The acceptance of this implied certain other things: a high degree of restraint on the part of single powers (Czar Nicholas could probably have exacted a higher price for his aid to the Turks in 1833 but refused to do so because he feared such unilateral action might lead to emulation); a willingness to accept the validity of existing treaties (in no age in modern times was there greater respect paid to the principle *Pacta sunt servanda*); and a willingness when single powers seemed on the point of seeking unilateral aggrandizement (as was true of France in 1840) to participate in concerted action to restrain them.

This consensus was the essential strength of the international system of the years 1815–1854. Figure 1 is a reasonably accurate visual expression of the way in which the balance of power was maintained

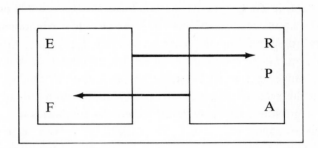

Figure 1

in the early nineteenth century. The inner squares represent the Anglo-French entente on the one hand and the combination of the northern courts on the other; the arrows signify the interpenetration and intercamp collaboration that went on throughout the period; and the outer square represents the consensus that held all of the major powers together in an effective concert that preserved the Vienna settlement in its major outlines and maintained the equilibrium of forces in Europe.

II

The strength of this Vienna system was seriously eroded by the revolutions that took place during the year 1848, a year of political convulsions that undermined confidence in all legal structures, including the international ones. After 1848, a new spirit prevailed in the chancelleries of Europe, one that found its strongest expression in the policies of a new generation of young men in a hurry who were ambitious for their own countries and no longer willing to abide by the collaborative principles and practices invented and followed by the statesmen of Vienna. These newcomers included Felix zu Schwarzenberg in Austria, Camillo di Cavour in Piedmont, Otto von Bismarck in Prussia, and Louis Napoleon in France. The event that opened the way to the fulfillment of the ambitions of these *Realpolitiker* (to use the term invented in the fifties by Ludwig von Rochow) was the outbreak of war between Russia and Britain (supported by France and Piedmont) in 1854. The two powers whose collaboration had prevented the revolutions of 1848 from degenerating into a major international conflict now slipped into one themselves—a senseless struggle that resulted not from any deliberate threat to the interest of either power, but from a series of escalating moves to ward off imaginary dangers. The Crimean War by itself caused more deaths than any conflict between 1815 and 1914; but more important, it left Europe in an anarchical situation in which more powers were interested in revising what was left of the balance than were interested in preserving it. After 1856, Russia, France, Prussia, and the rising power of Piedmont could all be considered as revisionist powers, and only Austria and Great Britain as supporters of the existing order, and the second of these, wearied by its exertions in the Crimea, was in a pronouncedly isolationist mood. In this situation, the European concert could not exert effective restraint against aggressors, and its failure was illustrated in the fact that within fifteen years, four major wars were fought in Europe: the Italian war of 1859, between Austria on the one hand and Piedmont and France on the other; the war between Denmark and the German states in 1864; the Austro-Prussian War of 1866; and the Franco-Prussian War of 1870. As a result, the old European balance was destroyed beyond recognition.

Moreover, the task of making a new balance and building an effective new international system to maintain it was much more difficult than that which had confronted the men of Vienna. There was no relaxation of tension after 1870, as there had been after 1815. The resentments and frustrations left by the wars of unification were great—the French unable to forget the annexation of Alsace and Lorraine by Germany, the Austrians seeking to make good their losses in Germany by a forward policy in the Balkans that aroused Russia's anger and distrust, the Italians dissatisfied with the extent of their new united kingdom and burning to despoil the Austrians of areas inhabited by Italian minorities.

The opportunities for friction between the powers were many after 1870, not only because all of the free territory in Europe, all of the buffers and shock absorbers, had disappeared with the completion of Italian and German unification (so that the great powers now had common borders and rubbed up against each other uncomfortably), but also because the age of free trade was coming to an end and the age of neomercantilism and imperialism dawning, so that tariff wars and colonial competition between powers would soon be the order of the day. The psychological mood of the years after 1871 was not one of appeasement, but rather one of hypersensitive nationalism and combativeness, which was fed by the widespread currency of Darwinism and by the sensationalism of a newspaper press that pandered to a gullible and excitable new reading public that had been created by the spread of free compulsory elementary education. Governments that were interested in following sensible collaborative foreign policies were no longer as free of external pressures as Metternich had been. Public opinion still exercised only a sporadic influence upon policy determination, but economic interests were now organized and were developing techniques for persuading governments to alter policies in their interest. Bismarck, for example, found that he could not simply ignore industrial and agricultural pressure for tariffs in the seventies and colonies in the eighties. Also, in an age in which warfare had become mechanized and increasingly technical, governments were discovering that they had to consult their military staffs more frequently and that it was increasingly difficult to disregard the advice they received, even when it had questionable political implications. In all countries, war offices now tended to become pressure groups for the increased armaments that were a feature of the age.

In view of all this—and of the increased incidence of ideological differences between powers that came with the growth of French *revanchisme,* Pan Slavism, Pan Germanism, irredentism, and integral nationalism—it is clear that there could be no real consensus between the powers as there had been in the period before the Crimean War; and, this being so, it was unlikely that the concert of Europe, even if it could be reassembled, would be effective in maintaining the uneasy balance of power that the wars of the sixties had created.

This was a source of concern to the leading statesman of the country that had been the principal beneficiary of those wars. Otto von Bismarck, who had contributed so powerfully to the destruction of the old European balance, was a changed character after 1870, a man who was determined to keep the gains his country had made but who wanted nothing more for it but peace, since he regarded Germany now as a sated power. It became rapidly apparent to Bismarck, however, as he became aware of the unreliability of old friends during the crisis of 1875 and of the possibility of an Austro-Russian conflict in the Balkans that would almost certainly involve Germany, that wishing for peace was not enough. When he acted as an honest broker in 1878, inviting the contentious powers to a congress in Berlin and successfully averting a war in the Near East, the Russian government took the line that the settlement was a blow to its vital interests and a betrayal of past friendship and began to talk of an alliance with France. It was clear to Bismarck that the traditional friendship between Prussia, Austria, and Russia, forged in the

37

war against Napoleon, could no longer be relied on. If the existing balance of power, and Germany's place in it, was to be preserved, it would have to be by some new means.

Bismarck reluctantly concluded that the only effective way of escaping from his dilemma would be the elaboration of a system of secret alliances that would, at a minimum, relieve Germany of potential isolation and might, if things went well, give him some measure of control over the policies of enough of the other powers to prevent their embarking upon actions that would threaten the general peace. Later on, he was to define his policy by saying that one must not lose sight of "the importance of being one of three on the European chess-board. That is the invariable objective of all cabinets and of mine above all others. Nobody wishes to be in a minority. All politics reduce themselves to this formula: to try to be one of three as long as the world is governed by an unstable equilibrium of five great powers."

This was probably a rationalization after the fact. After the Congress of Berlin, when Germany was in a state of near isolation, Bismarck had more limited objectives. He decided that Germany needed one reliable ally, and he reached out to Austria-Hungary, concluding a secret treaty that stipulated mutual defense in the event of an attack by Russia and benevolent neutrality if either ally were attacked by a power other than Russia. But this treaty of 1879 rather unexpectedly brought him the kind of control that was to secure the European balance for the next twelve years. For although the Austrian treaty was a secret, its conclusion was not, and it startled the Russians into changing their tune and asking for a renewal of the Three Emperors' League, which Bismarck granted. And that success brought the Italians, hat in hand, to Berlin, asking for protection against French attacks on their interests in North Africa—to which Bismarck agreed on condition that the Italians also make a treaty of accommodation with Austria. Assured by his Austrian treaty of assistance in case of a Russian attack upon Germany, Bismarck had, by means of his other new engagements, blocked the possibility of a Franco-Russian alliance and greatly reduced the chance of a war between Austria and Russia in the Balkans or a conflict between Austria and Italy in the Trentino. Simultaneously, his support of British interests in Egypt completed the isolation of France.

A graphic illustration of Bismarck's balance of power would be markedly different from that of the Vienna system. It would look something like Figure 2. Here there is no outer all-embracing consensual frame-

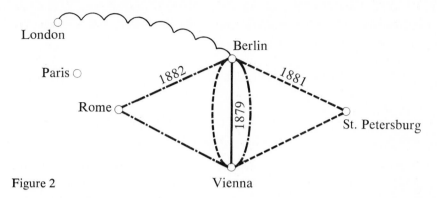

Figure 2

work. The suspicion between the powers was so great that consensus was impossible. At the same time, there are no opposing but interconnected subsystems. In this model, all powers, with the exception of France, are bound one way or another to Berlin, and bound on Bismarck's terms. The Austrians, for instance, were assured of German support in the event that their Balkan interests were subjected to Russian attack, but they were at the same time held on a very short leash by Bismarck's warning that he would not support them if they took the initiative in causing an Austro-Russian war.

The Bismarck way of maintaining the post-1871 equilibrium of forces was a complicated one, and that was its chief weakness. It operated by means of secrecy, constant maneuver, and a high degree of disingenuousness. During the tense Bulgarian crisis of 1886–1887, when a renewal of Austro-Russian antagonism in the Balkans dissolved the Three Emperors' League and a simultaneous wave of *revanchisme* in France made a Franco-Russian alliance seem possible, Bismarck was able to contain these dangers and repair his system only by the most questionable means: a deliberately manufactured war scare designed to intimidate the French and professed support of Russian objectives in the Balkans that was belied by covert connivance with third powers and stock market manipulations that rendered his promises meaningless. Bismarck's performance in this affair has often been described as a tour de force, but the course that he followed was so subterranean and devious that, while it is unnecessary to accept the judgment of a distinguished British scholar who held "that the old gentleman had slightly lost his head," it is difficult to avoid the suspicion that he was beginning to prefer tactical virtuosity to plain dealing. Certainly his methods in the Bulgarian affair saved his system only in a formal sense, while increasing the feeling of the Russians in particular that they had been lied to. As a result, the days of the Bismarckian model of balance of power were numbered. Even if the chancellor had remained in office after 1890, it is impossible to believe that it could have stood the strain of his manipulations much longer.

III

The third systematic form assumed by balance of power came in the years from 1907 to 1914, when all of the major European powers, including Great Britain, which had abandoned the "splendid isolation" upon which it had prided itself during most of the nineteenth century, were ranged in two hostile and highly armed coalitions. It was this manifestation of the politics of equilibrium that fastened itself upon the imagination of later generations and, because of its catastrophic end, made balance of power an opprobrious term in the postwar period, particularly in the United States.

It is possible—and not entirely unjustified—to place the blame for the emergence of the 1907–1914 system, with all of its deplorable consequences, upon the nature of German policy after Bismarck's dismissal in 1890. That event had been followed almost immediately by the German government's decision to simplify its foreign commitments by dropping the connection with Russia, which appeared to be incompatible with obligations assumed toward Austria in the Dual Alliance of 1879. This was a reasonable enough step to take and one that certainly did not justify the loud predictions of doom voiced by the Bismarck *fronde*. Had the German government maintained its aplomb when the Russians did the natural thing and began to move toward an accommodation with France, much later harm might have been avoided. Instead, the nervousness and tactical maladroitness of German policy destroyed what was left of Bismarck's system and left Europe in a much more unstable and fragile condition. This result the German government of William II, particularly in the period when Bülow was chancellor and Tirpitz chief of the imperial Naval Office, effected in two ways.

In the first place, it conducted an aggressive and offensive policy in the overseas areas of the world, interfering in the spheres of influence of other powers in Africa, the Pacific, and the Middle East in such a way as to annoy everybody and to convince old associates that the Germans were unreliable. The Russians, who tended still to be closer ideologically to the Germans than to the western powers and who regarded the British as their chief antagonist in the Middle East, were unpleasantly surprised, at the end of the nineties and the beginning of the next decade, to find the Germans moving into their sphere of interest in the Persian Gulf, and they began to revise their views. The British and the French, who were at loggerheads in Africa after 1882 and came uncomfortably close to war in the Sudan in 1898, discovered that Germany was becoming a nuisance and a potential threat to both of them and began to mend their fences. Meanwhile, Britain loosed its ties with Germany's junior partners out of irritation over German tactics.

In the second place, the stability of the German government at home and its security against socialism depended upon an alliance of conservative political parties and groups that derived financial support from heavy industry and big agriculture. Those economic interests had desiderata and knew how to combine their forces so as to get what they wanted. Specifically, their pressure was instrumental in persuading the German government to launch a heightened naval armaments program in 1900 which could not help but concern and worry the English and in the end to alienate them. And they were also able to mobilize enough votes in the Reichstag in 1902 to force the passage of a new tariff bill that virtually excluded Russian grain from German markets. This tariff struck a blow against the economic interests of that class in Russia that had always been the most friendly to Germany, and when that happened any chance of reconciliation between Germany and Russia came to an end. Since the early 1890s, there had been a military tie between France and Russia. This now became stronger, and both powers turned to Britain, which was waiting to receive them.

It would be a mistake, however, to think of this fateful course as having been caused solely by German clumsiness and impercipience. Even had William II, Bülow, and Tirpitz been wiser and more responsible leaders, it is difficult to believe the British apprehensiveness about Germany would have been different than it was. In his masterly study of the rise of Anglo-German antagonism, Paul Kennedy has pointed out that basically, it was the transformation of Germany from a cluster of second-rate states under insignificant princelings to a united empire with a population greater than Britain's, impressive industrial resources, and advanced technology that was the root cause of the deterioration of its relations with Great Britain. By the end of the nineteenth century, Germany was "not only growing out of its European 'skin' but also acquiring the early attributes of a world power. . . . All this necessarily implied a relative diminution in Britain's own commercial/colonial/maritime position unless it in turn was able to export more, colonize more, and build more ships so as to preserve the original relationship."

To the British this change brought new anxieties and new resentments. The nervousness characteristic of German policy after 1890 was no less pronounced in Great Britain. It was all too easy to believe that Germany was infringing upon British interests, even when this was more a question of perception than of actuality. British decision makers concerned about "saving the empire" slipped easily into the habit of regarding Germany not as a rival but as a future foe. Lord Esher was not alone in thinking "there is no doubt that within measurable distance there looms a titanic struggle between Germany and Europe for mastery. The years 1793–1815 will be repeated, only Germany, not France, will be trying for European domination. She has 70,000,000 of people and is determined to have commercial pre-eminence. To do this *England* has got to be crippled and the Low Countries added to the German Empire." It was this kind of deep-seated *Angst* that led the British governing class to conclude in the first years of the new century that Britain could no longer maintain its security by its own resources but must seek to contain the German threat by entering into partnership with Germany's antagonists.

The result was the Entente Cordiale with France in 1904 and the Anglo-Russian Agreement of 1907, which effected a radical transformation of the European balance and a confrontation between Triple Alliance and Triple Entente (see Figure 3). The salient characteristics of this new system were, as was true of the Bismarckian experiment in equilibrium, a lack of any consensus between the powers and a reliance

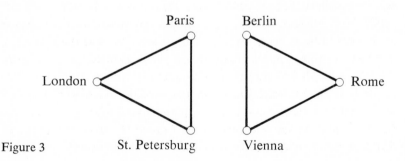

Figure 3

upon formal secret alliances rather than informal combinations. But this new variant was a bipolar system, in contrast to the Bismarck system, in which everything had centered upon Berlin; and this bipolarity made it as much more unstable than the Bismarck system as that system had been more unstable than the Vienna one. For there was no interpenetration here, as there had been in the Vienna system, and there was no control by a strong alliance leader, as there had been in the Bismarck system. In the years 1907–1914, the predominant characteristics of both parts of the new bipolar system were a constantly accelerating armament program and a growing fear in both coalitions of losing allies to the opposite camp and thus being placed at a dangerous disadvantage, or being encircled and destroyed.

The German government, aware that the Italians were unreliable (there was lots of evidence of this after 1900) came to fear isolation and to place an excess valuation upon the Austrian alliance (hence William II's talk about the necessity of Nibelungen loyalty). Because the Germans did so, they abandoned Bismarck's wise limitation upon his commitment to Austria, namely, that Germany would support it against Russia only if it were attacked by the latter power and not if it took the initiative itself. In 1909, during the last stages of the Bosnian crisis, the German chief of general staff, Moltke the younger, specifically told his opposite number in Vienna that he could rely upon German support, regardless of the origins of the conflict, an assurance that was patently dangerous but seemed necessary in the circumstances. The British and the French began to have similar apprehensions about losing the Russians to the Germans (this was the constant fear of the permanent undersecretary of the British Foreign Office, Sir Arthur Nicolson), and they tended, in consequence, to give them a dangerous degree of freedom of action, instead of warning them that, if they were foolhardy, they would have to stand alone. The details of the various crises from the Bosnian affair of 1908–1909 to the Sarajevo crisis of 1914 need not be spelled out. It is enough to say that in the simplest terms, the First World War resulted from the inflexibility of the alliances and the lack of control by the senior members over the most irresponsible of their partners. Once more the result can be shown schematically (see Figure 4), the triangles indicating the opposed alliances and the arrows indicating the irresponsible drives of the two junior partners, which drew the whole family of nations into war after the murder of the heir to the Austrian throne in Sarajevo on 28 June 1914.

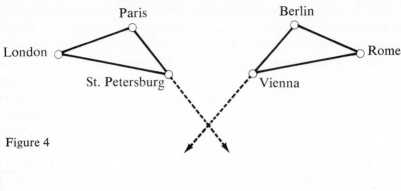

Figure 4

IV

The three experiments contrived by European statesmen in the nine-teenth century to construct and operate a viable balance-of-power system differed, as noted, in significant respects. The earlier variant of that system, described in chapter 2, was even more competitive and less regulated by common conventions, practices, and institutions and, perhaps partly for that reason, more vulnerable to Napoleon's drive to replace it by a hegemonic system. These differences notwithstanding, all variants shared certain essential features to a greater or lesser extent, and these general characteristics of the multipolar European balance-of-power system deserve brief mention.

The major "rule" of the European balance-of-power system was that each of the five great powers should cooperate as necessary to preserve the balance, for this was the principal means for discouraging any one state from seeking hegemony. It was understood that considerable flexibility in making alliances and shifting alliance partners was necessary to this end. Permanent, rigid alliances were to be avoided, a rule violated with disastrous consequences in the variant of the system that came into being during the years 1907 to 1914. Similarly, to ensure that the five major actors remained of roughly equal power and to dampen the competition among them, several other rules and practices were institutionalized as necessary means for the operation and maintenance of the system. One of these, the principle of compensation, as already noted, worked as follows: when one of the great powers acquired—or wished to acquire—additional territory or resources, it was understood that the other powers also had to receive appropriate payoffs of territory, population, or resources—usually at the expense of weaker states inside or outside of Europe.

Another rule of the system that operated to maintain balance and stability was the understanding that war involving the great powers should be fought for strictly limited objectives. A related rule was that punitive peace terms were to be avoided in terminating such wars and that the great power that was defeated in such a contest had to be re-admitted to the system as a regular member to participate once more in the balancing process. In these and other ways, the competition and con-flicts among the great powers were regulated in the interest of preserving the balance-of-power system and, in turn, the essential security and sur-vival of each of them.

The European balance-of-power system of the eighteenth and nine-teenth centuries displayed a number of distinctive characteristics that are not found in hegemonic international systems, such as that centered on Manchu China during roughly the same period, or in systems of world government that have been advocated from time to time. Thus, the Euro-pean system was a *decentralized, self-regulating system*—one in which power and responsibility remained in the hands of the constituent state actors. There was, in other words, no supranational political or govern-mental authority at the apex of the system to keep the major powers in line, to regulate their quarrels, to ensure that international politics did not become too anarchic, to act in order to enforce the rules of the sys-tem. All these were, indeed, important requirements for the mainte-nance of the European system, but they had to be achieved by the great powers themselves by coordinating and regulating their own behavior.

Furthermore, the management of the European system in the interest of maintaining the balance was understood to be a responsibility that all of the great powers should assume. Awareness of the responsibility emerged with greater clarity and conviction particularly after the nearly disastrous experience with Napoleon. Before that, there was a tendency to assume that the balancing and equilibrium the system required would follow more or less automatically from unrestrained competition among them—a reflection, one is tempted to say, of the Smithian and physio-cratic belief regarding the virtues of perfect, unregulated competition. Afterward, European statesmen felt the need to create an institutional framework and practices—embodied in the concert of Europe—to pro-mote the kind of cooperation and coordination of foreign policies needed to ensure the workings of a balance-of-power system. When the concert proved to be ineffective in the decade after 1871, Bismarck attempted to fill the vacuum by developing a different variant of the system in which he arrogated to himself unilateral responsibility for "managing" the system.

A third characteristic of the European system was that the competition among the major actors was not conceived of, or pursued, in terms of a "zero-sum" game. That is, the great powers did not perceive each other as implacable enemies engaged in an elimination contest, one in which any gain for one side could only be at the expense of the other. Rather, the actors viewed each other as "limited adversaries": not only was a gain for one not necessarily a loss for the other, but the principle of compensation was invoked as a means of moderating the competitiveness of the game.

Efforts to preserve the character of a non–zero-sum game were facilitated by another feature of the European system, which can be highlighted by invoking the colorful distinction in economic analysis between the "constant pie" and an "expanding pie." For much of the eighteenth and nineteenth centuries, the amount of territory and resources available to be contested and divided up among the great powers was not fixed and finite. The struggle over "who gets what" was alleviated because the European powers were competing for an expanding pie. Thus, the competition did not (and was not permitted to) jeopardize the vital interests of any of the great powers. Rather, it was conducted in good part at the expense of third parties—that is, weaker European states, declining major powers (such as Spain and the Ottoman Empire), and non-European territories in Africa, Asia, and America. Toward the end of the nineteenth century and in the decade before the outbreak of World War I, however, opportunities for further expansion at the expense of third parties narrowed, and some statesmen began to view the competition with their great-power rivals in terms approaching a constant-pie analogy, a development which contributed to the rigidification and polarization of the two alliance systems.

Finally, it should be noted that the European balance-of-power system did *not* aim at eliminating war as an instrument of foreign policy. Instead, a distinction was made between permissible and impermissible wars. War and the threat of military action were often regarded as permissible if the objectives were limited and did not threaten the stability of the balance-of-power system. Thus, one could make war, or threaten it, in order to achieve useful marginal gains (or to avoid irksome losses) that did not threaten the vital interests of other major powers or undermine their status as such; but wars were impermissible if they aimed at, or created the possibility of, drastically weakening any of the great powers or their essential allies. On the other hand, resort to threats of war and actual war were legitimate, indeed in a sense became necessary, if one state attempted to achieve predominant power and domination of the system, for this would destroy the balance-of-power system itself and replace it with a hegemonic international system. With the passage of time, and particularly in the rigid bipolar version of the system at the turn of the century, the distinction between permissible and impermissible war faded. This was nowhere more evident than in July 1914, when the great powers for a variety of reasons could not agree whether the Austrian declaration of war upon Serbia was permissible or not.

Bibliographical Essay

The literature on the reconstruction of Europe after the Napoleonic wars is very rich. Most useful on the Vienna negotiations are C. K. Webster, *The Congress of Vienna* (London, 1937) and Harold Nicolson, *The Congress of Vienna* (London, 1945). Illuminating on the men who made the settlement are C. K. Webster, *The Foreign Policy of Castlereagh, 1815–1822*, 2nd ed. (Oxford, 1937); A. Duff Cooper, *Talleyrand* (London, 1932); Henry L. Kissinger, *A World Restored: Metternich, Castlereagh and the Problems of Peace, 1812–1822*, new ed. (New York, 1964), an excellent account; and the biographies of Metternich by H. Ritter von Srbik, 4 vols. (Munich, 1925ff.), H. du Coudray (London, 1935), G. Berthier du Sauvignon (London, 1962), and Algernon Cecil (New York, 1933). On the Austrian statesman, see also E. L. Woodward's provocative essay in *Three Studies of European Conservatism* (London, 1930). On the congress system, the old but still useful authority is G. Allison Phillips, *The Confederation of Europe*, but see also H. G. Schenk, *The Aftermath of the Napoleonic Wars: The Concert of Europe—an Experiment* (New York, 1947). For the course of international politics before 1848, H. W. V. Temperley, *The Foreign Policy of Canning, 1822–1827* (London, 1925) and Paul W. Schroeder, *Metternich's Diplomacy at Its Zenith, 1820–1823* (New York, 1962) give interesting contrasting views; and C. K. Webster, *The Foreign Policy of Palmerston, 1830–1841*, 2 vols. (London, 1951) is essential. For general coverage of the middle years, see Gordon A. Craig, "The Great Powers and the Balance of Power, 1830–1870," in *New Cambridge Modern History*, 10 (Cambridge, 1960), 246–73; and on disarmament, see Gordon A. Craig and Peter Paret, "The Control of International Violence: Some Historical Notes," in *Stanford Journal of International Studies*, 7 (1972), 1–21; E. L. Woodward, *War and Peace in Europe* (London, 1929); and J. Headlam-Morley, *Studies in Diplomatic History* (London, 1930).

For the second half of the century, see especially A. J. P. Taylor, *The*

Struggle for Mastery in Europe, 1848–1918 (Oxford, 1954), sometimes a bit sweeping in its judgments; R. C. Binkley, *Realism and Nationalism, 1852–1870* (New York, 1935), a brilliantly executed study; W. L. Langer, *European Alliances and Alignments,* new ed. (New York, 1950) and *The Diplomacy of Imperialism,* 2nd ed. (New York, 1951). Bismarck's diplomacy is treated in the biographies of A. J. P. Taylor (New York, 1955), Erich Eyck, 3 vols. (Zurich, 1941–1944), and Lothar Gall (Frankfurt am Main, 1980); but see also W. N. Medlicott, *Bismarck, Gladstone and the Concert of Europe* (London, 1956) and George F. Kennan, *The Decline of Bismarck's European Order: Franco-Russian Relations, 1875–1890* (Princeton, 1979). On the deterioration of the balance of power after 1890, see the first chapters of the much discussed Fritz Fischer, *Griff nach der Weltmacht* (Dusseldorf, 1961), translated in abbreviated form from the German as *Germany's Aims in the First World War* (New York, 1967); Zara S. Steiner, *The Foreign Office and Foreign Policy, 1898–1914* (Cambridge, 1969) and *Britain and the Origins of the First World War* (London, 1977); and Paul Kennedy, *The Rise of the Anglo-German Antagonism, 1860–1914* (London, 1980), a masterly study.

Two useful general works are F. H. Hinsley, *Power and the Pursuit of Peace: Theory and Practice in the History of Relations Between States* (Cambridge, 1963), which concentrates upon the nineteenth-century system, and E. V. Gulick, *Europe's Classical Balance of Power* (Ithaca, N.Y., 1955).

4

System-Building, 1919-1939

In 1814–1815, after almost twenty-five years of intermittent warfare, representatives of the European powers had been able to sit down together—in Metternich's phrase, "as friends"—and to lay the foundations for a diplomatic system that worked effectively for thirty-five years and, after a period of reorganization by war between 1854 and 1871, reasonably effectively for another forty. The war that brought that system to its calamitous end lasted only four years, but when it was over at last and the statesmen of the belligerent nations came together in another great diplomatic congress, this time in Paris, their achievement fell far short of that of their predecessors at Vienna. No viable system emerged from their labors and, although they tried at times to pretend that it had, the fact that a greater war than that of 1914–1918 broke out within twenty years was proof of their failure.

The peacemakers of 1919 were, to be sure, confronted with a situation of unprecedented difficulty. For one thing, the conflict that had just come to an end had not been contained and completed by the powers that began it, nor did some of them survive the fighting of it. That the war had expanded from its European center to every part of the world was not, of course, surprising. We have seen that that happened even in the wars of the eighteenth century, and that then, and during the great age of imperialism in the nineteenth century, the great powers often sought to regulate their intra-European relations by means of action in colonial areas. But in this war, the former colonial areas came into their own as independent actors in world politics, and they emerged from the

49

war with policies and objectives of their own. Canada, Australia, New Zealand, and South Africa, as well as Japan and the United States, had played a secondary and sporadic or discontinuous role in international affairs before the war; their part was to be greater from now on. But how much greater it was still difficult to say; and the question of how to fit them into his political calculations confronted the system maker with grave structural problems.

Moreover, there was not much left after the war of the known entities of international relations. Of the five great powers that had dominated the old system, three—the German Empire, the Russian Empire, and the Austro-Hungarian Empire—had succumbed to revolution, and the third of these had dissolved into its component parts. How was one to work into any new system such untried elements as the Bolshevik state of Russia and the new German and Austrian republics, to say nothing of such nations as Hungary and Czechoslovakia, Yugoslavia and the revived Poland?

Any attempt to do so was bound to be complicated by political passions that had been unknown in 1814. There was no question now of former friends and foes sitting down together to lay the foundations of peace, as they had at Vienna. The war of 1914–1918 had far exceeded the conflicts of the nineteenth century in duration and ferocity, and in other senses it was revolutionary: it was not a limited but a total war that involved the whole of the resources at the command of the participants, and it broke down the old division between the military and civilian parts of society. Indeed, there were really no noncombatants in this war, and the suffering of civilian populations was greater than it had been since the horrors of the Thirty Years War. That war, as we have seen, started as a religious conflict and ended as a political one. One could say of the First World War that it marked a reversal of that process, beginning as a political conflict and ending as a religious one, in which each side began to view the other not as an opponent who must be defeated, but as a kind of anti-Christ who must be extirpated. This transition, which was much more marked in the case of civilian populations than in that of the fighting men themselves, was the result of suffering and sacrifice on the one hand and wartime propaganda on the other, and it had serious results, turning the war for many people into what has been called above a zero-sum game. When it was over, there was little sentiment among the victors for reconciliation with the beaten foe. The impulse was rather to punish him, to place burdens upon him that would prevent his recovery or delay it for an indefinite period.

This is why events at Paris in 1919 took a different course than they had a hundred years earlier in Vienna. In 1814–1815, the settlement had been a two-stage process. The war was ended by the First Peace of Paris, and certain arrangements were made to establish a government in the defeated country with which the others could have relations. Only after that was done was a congress held for the purpose of making a comprehensive and viable peace settlement and, during the negotiations for this, the former enemy was allowed to participate on equal terms with the victors. The original intention in 1919 was to have a similar procedural model: a preliminary conference to make peace and some tentative decisions about new territorial arrangements, as well as about penalties and compensations, followed by a second conference, with the participation of the defeated powers, to consider these and other matters and to draw up the definitive settlement. But the peacemakers never got to the second stage, and many decisions that were tentative and made in the expectation that they would be revised in a followup conference became definitive by default, with grave consequences later on.

This was due partly to the failure of the victorious powers to realize how complicated a task it would be to make peace after so protracted a war, or how long it would take, a discovery that led them in the end to abandon their original intention. But the deeper reason lay in the passions engendered by the war. Too many of the participants were unreconciled and bent solely upon the most draconian forms of punishment against the Germans or the Austrians or the Turks. The enemy powers were not given the chance to express their views during the deliberations, and in the end they were simply handed peace terms that were in large part vindictive, and told to accept them. When the victors' will to revenge seemed to falter or when they sought to moderate their treatment of the enemy, their representatives were attacked by their own newspapers and threatened with reprisals at the next elections. During the whole of the peace conference, the *Daily Mail* in Great Britain carried a box on its first page that read "The Huns will cheat you yet!" This was meant as a warning to British negotiators, and it persuaded them to be unforgiving in their attitude and savage in their demand for reprisals. The head of the British government in 1919 was David Lloyd George, and his election slogan of 1918 is indicative of the temper of the times. It was "We will squeeze the orange till the pips squeak!"

During the peace conference and afterward, the former enemy powers were relegated to a kind of limbo. It should be remembered, for instance, that Germany—although it was no longer the same Germany that had caused the war, but a new republic—was not allowed to become a member of the League of Nations until 1926. If one recalls that Russia, in its new form as a union of Socialist Soviet states, was also excluded, since it was considered to be a subversive threat to the Western nations, which had only intermittent relations with it and generally regarded it as lying outside the comity of nations, one can understand that it was extremely difficult to construct an international system that promised to be as effective as the one that had been destroyed in 1914; and it became more difficult when the United States, despite its leading role in the years 1917–1919, voluntarily withdrew into isolation.

This became clear even before the future course of the United States was determined. One of the problems confronting the peacemakers was to find a theoretical basis for a new international order. The negotiators in Vienna a hundred years earlier had invoked the principle of the balance of power, and there were statesmen in Paris, particularly the French, who continued to think in those terms, as also in terms of treaties of guarantee and of alliance, the traditional support of the balance. But this idea found an eloquent and powerful antagonist in the president of the United States, Woodrow Wilson, who like many Americans before him believed that balance-of-power politics was a contrivance of states that had always been prone to absolutism, militarism, and antidemocratic behavior and that the coming of the war in 1914 was rooted in its acrobatics and intrigues. He had made his determination to eliminate the old system abundantly clear in his speech to the United States Senate on the essentials of peace on 22 January 1917, in which he had called for "a peace without victory" and declared:

> There must be not a balance of power but a community of power.
> . . . I am henceforth proposing that all nations henceforth avoid
> entangling alliances that draw them into competitions of power,
> catch them in a net of intrigue and selfish rivalry, and disturb
> their own affairs with influences intruded from without. There is
> no entangling alliance in a concert of power. When all unite to act
> in the same sense and with the same purpose, all act in the com-
> mon interest and are free to live their own lives under a common
> protection.

One month after the Armistice, he made the same point clear to his associates in the peacemaking process. In his speech at the Guild Hall in London on 28 December 1918, he said that the soldiers of the Allied armies had fought to do away with an older order and to establish a new one, and the center and characteristic of the old order was that venerable thing which we used to call the "balance of power"—a thing in which the balance was determined by the sword which was thrown in the one side or the other; a balance which was determined by the unstable equilibrium of competitive interests; a balance which was maintained by jealous watchfulness and an antagonism of interests which, though it was generally latent, was always deep-seated. The men who have fought in this war have been the men from free nations who were determined that that sort of thing should end now and forever.

This was, of course, a biased view, and Wilson's picture of the balance-of-power system was a restricted one, based entirely upon the unstable post-Bismarckian model. But in these speeches, the president was less a historian than a visionary, inspired by a conviction held by many Americans since the beginning of their nation that relations of the peoples of the world should be regulated not by the outworn standards of Europe, but by democratic principles. "The old nonsense about balance of power," an American journal had announced in 1852, "is wholly out of date, and the doctrine of the solidarity of mankind is beginning to spread; popular sovereignty is on the point of overcoming legitimacy quickly; every day the system, which is now restricted to Europe and America, is expanding; and soon it will embrace Asia, Africa and Oceania." This vision had persisted in American thinking about foreign affairs, although challenged by realists like Alfred Thayer Mahan and Theodore Roosevelt; and after the debacle of 1914–1918 it inspired Wilson and the members of the U.S. delegation to the peace conference. They came to Paris in a militant mood, as suspicious of European motives as the founding fathers had been—(John Adams once said, "It is obvious that all the powers of Europe will be continually maneuvering with us, to work us into their real or imaginary balances of power")— and intent, as Walter Lippmann wrote at the time, upon "teach[ing] the European mind . . . that back of all our physical display lies a purpose which strikes at the roots of the old European system."

In its place, Wilson desired to establish a community of free nations that would adjust their relations with each other without resort to the modalities of the old European order, and the basis of this was to be a League of Nations, with permanent institutions for the discussion of matters of interest to the international community, for the revision of the peace treaties when inequities became apparent, and for the regulation of disputes. The establishment of this body was the president's principal objective during the Paris negotiations, but the potential advantages that he claimed for it proved to be less than attractive to the representatives of the Allied powers. Premier Clemenceau of France remained an intransigent supporter of the balance-of-power system, convinced that history had shown it to be the most effective regulator of relationships between nations; and he was not prepared to abandon it because of sermons by a man whom he regarded as an idealistic schoolmaster from a country with no experience in world affairs. The British and the Italians and the Poles were inclined to agree. They wanted to punish the enemy, to be compensated for their sacrifices, and to construct a new system on the basis of treaties and guarantees.

The Paris Peace Conference became, therefore, the scene of a protracted conflict between President Wilson and his former associates. In the end, he gained his major objective, the establishment of the League of Nations, but only at the expense of so many compromises that vitiated his own declared principles—particularly the Fourteen Points of the peace program that he had announced in his address to Congress on 8 January 1918—that it was difficult to talk any longer of a peace without victory and with justice for all parties. The discrepancies between what the Fourteen Points had promised and what the Treaty of Versailles stipulated were so palpable that Wilson's critics in the United States had no difficulty in mounting a powerful offensive against the settlement. In the debate over the treaties in Congress, the League was attacked not only as a tool in the hands of selfish and greedy powers, rather than a symbol of a new international order, but as a conspiracy to involve Americans in the corrupt old system of secret treaties and irresponsible commitments. Membership in such a body would, in the view of one elder statesman, "entangle the American nation in a European-Asiatic balance of power"; and in the end the Senate rejected the treaties and forbade American membership in the League.

This was a fatal blow to Wilson's dream of a new international system. The League survived until the coming of another world war, but it was weakened irreparably by American abstention at the outset, as well as by the fact that two other major powers stood outside its membership, namely, Germany (until 1926) and the Soviet Union (until 1934). Nor did it show any capacity for growth, since the British and French governments could not agree upon its right to apply sanctions in moments of aggression by single powers. The French tried periodically to put teeth into the League covenant by having its members sign guarantees to act automatically when peace was threatened; this was the purpose of the Draft Treaty of Mutual Assistance of 1923 and the Geneva Protocol of 1924, the latter of which was intended to bind League members to take action against states that refused to arbitrate disputes or were designated as aggressors by the League Council. The British consistently defeated these attempts, taking the line that the League would not survive if too great a strain were placed upon it and that it would be advisable to regard it, not as a body that took punitive action against wrongdoers, but as a clearinghouse for differences.

The British attitude was perhaps influenced by a veiled resentment over the equality rule in the League Assembly. From Salisbury's time to the Sudeten crisis of 1938, the British showed periodic disrespect for the pretensions, and even the rights, of small powers; and it was said of Austen Chamberlain that when he spoke in the Assembly, he sometimes seemed to be saying, "We are perfect. We are British. And yet you, you dagoes, dare to come here and criticize US!" To vest too much authority in a body that listened as intently to the speeches of Benes of Czechoslovakia and Titulescu of Rumania as it did to those of their own representatives must, to the British, have seemed injudicious. Finally, even if they had been more receptive to arguments for something like the Geneva Protocol, the British government would have been restrained by the attitude of the Dominions, which now claimed the right to be consulted on policy matters and were firmly opposed to any new European commitments by the home country. In consequence, the British steadfastly opposed reform of the League, which tended as time passed to become a mere debating club.

In exasperation, the French began to build up their own security system by concluding alliances with Belgium and, since Russia lay outside the new international system, with Poland and the so-called Little Entente (Yugoslavia, Rumania, and Czechoslovakia). But France's resources were not sufficient to support these eastern allies unless the British were prepared to give some assistance; and the British were not ready to do any such thing. In 1925, when the British government, in order to encourage an alleviation of tension, signed the Rhineland Pact at Locarno guaranteeing the common boundary between Germany on the one hand and France and Belgium on the other, it made it clear that it was unprepared to enter into any similar engagements with respect to eastern Europe. In private, the British were brutally frank about this. Sir Austen Chamberlain told the Committee of Imperial Defence that the Rhineland Pact would actually reduce British liabilities on the continent, for "by making it perfectly clear that we were prepared to make our maximum effort . . . in the case of one frontier . . . it was implied that in the case of the other frontier we were not." This, Chamberlain suggested, would eventually make France see that it would be advisable to reduce its commitment to Poland, since it could not now count upon British support in a Franco-German conflict that had resulted from a French attempt to prevent Germany from overrunning its eastern ally. Weakened by this British attitude and by the high cost of military assistance to its eastern members, the French system lost even more credibility after the conclusion of the Nazi-Polish Pact in 1934; and the French government cast doubt upon its own confidence in the system by its subsequent efforts to complete the Maginot Line, a gigantic defensive rampart along its eastern frontier from the Swiss border to Belgium, and, as we shall see, by the nature of its commercial policy in the 1930s.

A word more should be said about the British attitude toward eastern Europe. In 1925, when it became clear that the British government was going to oppose the Geneva Protocol because that arrangement would oblige it to intervene anywhere in Europe where aggression occurred, the historical adviser to the Foreign Office, Sir James Headlam-Morley, struck a dissenting note. It would be a mistake, he wrote, for Britain to dissociate itself from European problems, nor was the argument that the Dominions did not desire new involvements in Europe compelling. In the future, the danger point in Europe was likely to be not the Rhine but the Vistula, and consequently no security pact would be effective if it were not European rather than regional in scope. These were prophetic words and intended as a warning that the principle of the European balance of power had always been central to Great Britain's foreign policy. They were, however, disregarded, and the British government not only restricted itself in European affairs to a regional arrangement (the Rhineland Pact) but for the rest sought to create a system of its own that was essentially non-European in nature, based upon the closest possible political and, after 1932, economic relations with its empire and upon cooperation with the United States in the Far East to protect their joint interests against Japanese ambitions.

These French and British experiments in system-making did not restrain the aggressive tendencies of Fascist Italy and National Socialist Germany after 1935 or of Japan after 1937. In the face of these new totalitarian threats, both the French security system and the League system crumbled, while the British gave themselves over to an increasingly dangerous policy of seeking peace by appeasing the dictators. These tendencies found their ultimate form in the belated attempt by Neville Chamberlain to ignore both the League and the Soviet Union (which after 1934 was a League member and a supporter of collective security) and to settle European affairs at least (Far Eastern affairs were by then in a hopelessly dangerous condition) by means of a Four Power Directorate of Britain, France, Germany, and Italy. Created at the Munich Conference in September 1938, this experiment was, to all intents and purposes, dead by March 1939, when Hitler's troops marched into Prague, at which time the world was only six months away from another great war.

In large part, the failure to build an effective international system after 1919 was due to the absence of any real measure of collaboration between the powers that had won the war. The British and the French pursued separate, and at times antagonistic, lines of policy, while the United States withdrew itself as far as possible from the world arena. Yet a major complicating factor in this, as in all aspects of diplomacy in these years, was what has been called in the introduction to this volume the diplomatic revolution, the complex of technological, socioeconomic, and political changes that impinged upon the behavior of members of the international community, the most dramatic of which—beginning during the war and continuing until the present—were the steady growth in the number of active members in the international community and the simultaneous breakdown of its internal homogeneity.

Before 1914, there were only about a dozen nations in the whole world that took a continuous interest and share in world affairs, and most of these were European. The Paris Conference was the first clear demonstration of how radically that condition was changing, and from that time onward the number of states that were determined to play independent roles upon the world stage increased steadily until the Second World War, which brought an explosive acceleration in its train, so that today there are about 130 nations with permanent delegations at the United Nations. Long before that result was achieved, it had become apparent that it was more difficult to convert the larger community into a working system than it had been when the participating states were fewer in number.

Along with the numerical expansion went another fateful change. An important reason for the relative effectiveness of the nineteenth-century system was that its members were bound together by a common historical tradition, by cultural and religious ties, and by familial relationships. Its statesmen spoke the same language and, in general, played the game of diplomacy according to the same rules, and all of this greatly facilitated communication and cooperation. This kind of homogeneity did not survive the war, largely because of the intrusion into international politics of new ideologies unknown in the nineteenth century. The victory of bolshevism in Russia in 1917, of fascism in Italy in 1922, and of national socialism in Germany in 1933 put an end to the commonly accepted norms of behavior. The Chicherins and Mussolinis, as we shall see, did not accept the rules of the club; they were constantly experimenting with the possible advantages of rule-breaking. This had subversive effects. It is difficult to play chess with someone who insists upon moving his bishops like rooks; and it was equally hard to reach agreement in negotiation with a vis-à-vis who employed all of his diplomatic guile to make agreement impossible. The British permanent under secretary of foreign affairs in the 1930s, Lord Vansittart, once summed up his experience of dealing with diplomats from totalitarian regimes by saying in exasperation, "I have 'done' many conferences in my life but never went into one without some hope of a fairly quick result. No one could say the same today. Results are often not expected and often not even desirable." In an ideological age—and such an age opened in 1919—the possibility of creating an effective international system was remote.

Bibliographical Essay

On the organization and procedures of the peace conference, see especially F. S. Marston, *The Peace Conference of 1919* (Oxford, 1944); on the problems caused by them, Harold Nicolson, *Peacemaking 1919*, new ed. (New York, 1939) and Paul Birdsall, *Versailles Twenty Years After* (New York, 1941); and on the broader problems of the conference and the interests of the participants, Arno J. Mayer, *Politics and Diplomacy of Peacemaking: Containment and Counterrevolution at Versailles, 1918–1919*, an informative study although tendentious. The literature on Wilson is almost unmanageable in bulk, but an excellent guide is provided by the editor of the Wilson papers, Arthur S. Link, in *Wilson the Diplomatist* (Baltimore, 1957). See also Arno J. Mayer, *Political Origins of the New Diplomacy* (New Haven, 1959) and Gordon A. Craig, "The United States and the European Balance," *Foreign Affairs,* 55 (1976), 189–98. Important also is Alexander L. George and Juliette L. George, *Woodrow Wilson and Colonel House: A Personality Study* (New York, 1956).

On Anglo-French differences after the war, there are three important books: Arnold Wolfers, *Britain and France Between the Wars: Conflicting Strategies of Peace* (New York, 1940); Piotr Wandycz, *France and Her Eastern Allies, 1919–1925* (Minneapolis, 1962); and W. M. Jordan, *Great Britain, France and the German Problem, 1918–1939* (London, 1943). On the League of Nations, the standard history is F. P. Walters, *A History of the League of Nations,* 2 vols. (London, 1952); while Jon Jacobson, *Locarno Diplomacy* (Princeton, 1972) is a sound work. On the diplomatic revolution, see Gordon A. Craig, "The Revolution in War and Diplomacy," in *War, Politics and Diplomacy: Selected Essays* (New York, 1966); and, in general, Gordon A. Craig and Felix Gilbert, eds., *The Diplomats, 1919–1939* (Princeton, 1953).

5

Public Opinion
and Foreign Policy

One of the salient features of the interwar period was the heightened influence that public opinion exercised upon the formulation and execution of foreign policy. Particularly in democratic countries, this manifested itself in an excessive preoccupation with the mood of the electorate and a consequent tendency of governments to follow rather than lead opinion. It also had the effect of changing the conduct and forms of diplomacy in ways that were not always conducive to efficiency.

This deference to public opinion would have seemed strange to nineteenth-century statesmen. Otto von Bismarck did not allow the vagaries of the mass mind to influence his policy, although he was adroit in manipulating it through his controlled press and was not above explaining that actions that he had taken for other reasons (the refusal to allow France to annex the Grand Duchy of Luxemburg in 1867, for instance, the seizure of Alsace and Lorraine in 1871, and the beginning of German colonialism in 1884) were demanded by public opinion. The British government paid lip service to the principle of popular sovereignty in the realm of foreign affairs, and Benjamin Disraeli told the House of Commons in August 1880 that "any human conclusion that is arrived at with adequate knowledge and with sufficient thought is entitled to respect, and the public opinion of a great nation under such conditions is irresistible, and ought to be so."

He was quick, however, to add a caveat, with the words, "But what we call public opinion is generally public sentiment," and it was clear that in his view, public expressions of opinion about foreign affairs were generally emotional and ill-informed and hence unworthy of attention. Salisbury, Lansdowne, and Grey tended to agree. Indeed, one of the most striking characteristics of the men who molded British policy in the fateful days before the outbreak of war in 1914 was their lack of interest in what the public might be thinking about the drift of affairs and their irritated contempt for press views. Sir Arthur Nicolson, the permanent undersecretary for foreign affairs, complained that "the public are as a rule supremely indifferent to and very ignorant of foreign affairs," although—as Zara Steiner has written—neither Nicolson nor anyone else in the Foreign Office ever took any special pains to enlighten it. As for the press, the Foreign Office view was that its members were not gentlemen, their views were unsound, and their meddling in foreign affairs was deplorable. The "enlightened public," which was the only public that counted, didn't need the press in any case and could be counted on to agree with the professional elite in the Foreign Office.

Attitudes like these could not be maintained after the world war. The sacrifices caused by that conflict made the man in the street more insistent upon his right to express an opinion about what the foreign policy of his country should be, and politicians or officials who appeared to disregard this ran the danger of being swept away by public indignation, even when they could claim that they had acted in the national interest. During the interwar period, there were any number of distinguished victims of this kind, and their example served *pour encourager* (or rather *décourager*) *les autres*. Woodrow Wilson was one such, a man hailed as a world savior in 1918 and then forced to see his design for a democratic world system rejected by an American electorate whose ardor for a role in the world community cooled when its prospective costs were realized and which then retreated precipitately toward the supposed blessings of what Warren G. Harding called "normalcy." Aristide Briand, an earnest worker for conciliation with Germany, fell before a similar wave of irrational feeling when rumors spread after the Cannes Conference of 1922 on reparations that he had become a pawn in the hands of Lloyd George, an accusation that seemed to be corroborated by newspaper photographs showing him apparently receiving golfing lessons from the British prime minister. Lloyd George himself, who had been the author of victory during the Great War, was the victim of a public outcry against his handling of a crisis in the Middle East (the so-called Chanak crisis of September 1922). The objections were based not on a reasoned understanding of his policy, which was undoubtedly questionable, but rather on a supposition that he was really trying to drag Britain into another war.

Moral indignation sometimes played an important part in public sentiment, and the case of Sir Samuel Hoare, British foreign secretary in 1935, is instructive in this regard. Hoare was driven from office by a surge of public indignation whose violence astonished seasoned political observers after he had, with Pierre Laval of France, worked out a plan for ending the war in Ethiopia. This involved the loss to the ruler of that country of about two-thirds of his empire, part of which would go to Italy outright, the rest being reserved as a sphere of Italian economic interest. The thought of Haile Selassie being thus despoiled and left with a mere fragment of territory connected to the sea by a narrow passage that the *Times* called "a corridor for camels" revolted the public conscience. In an able speech, Hoare sought to defend himself by pointing out that Great Britain was the only country that had placed military and naval units on alert for possible support of League action in defense of Ethiopia; no one else was stirring; and, since Britain could not carry the burden of war alone, the Hoare-Laval plan was not unreasonable. No one listened to this argument, and Hoare fell; but no one called, or at least not for very long, for real sanctions against Italy, certainly not after Hitler had taken advantage of the continuation of the war to move his troops into the Rhineland. Ethiopia was forgotten after that, and the emperor lost not only two-thirds of his realm but all of it.

The retribution that public feeling could wreak upon statesmen and diplomats seeking to deal with complicated international problems in accordance with the rules of *raison d'état* or national interest was, therefore, real, and this was intimidating. It tended to make the people who were charged with the conduct of foreign policy more cautious than their nineteenth-century predecessors had been. It induced them to alter the way they did their business. And in several ways, it made them less effective than their predecessors.

Examples of governmental timidity in the face of a possibly vindictive public opinion are not hard to find. In Great Britain, the fall of Lloyd George in 1922 had a depressing effect upon his successors, and the Bonar Law, MacDonald, and Baldwin governments all showed a nervous tendency to seek to appease the public at any cost, even if this meant reversing positions regardless of the effect upon ongoing negotiations and the ultimate cost to the national interest. During the ticklish Lausanne negotiations of January and February 1923, which finally liquidated the Chanak crisis and arranged a settlement with Turkey, the chief British negotiator, Foreign Secretary Lord Curzon, was handicapped at every turn by a fearful and bitterly critical public opinion and a cabinet that seemed more than once on the verge of disavowing him. By brilliant diplomacy, Curzon gained all of his objectives, but he wrote: "I found Bonar [the prime minister] longing to clear out of Mosul, the Straits, and Constantinople, willing to give up anything and everything rather than have a row, astonished at the responsibility I have assumed at Lausanne, and prepared for me to back down everywhere."

The passage of time did not make British governments more willing to place national interest above public mood, as the story of the peace ballot of 1935 makes clear. Sponsored by the League of Nations Union, this was intended to determine the public attitude toward the League and collective security in general. Five questions were asked: (1) Should Britain remain a member of the League? (2) Were respondents in favor of all-round reduction of armaments by international agreement? (3) Did they favor general abolition of national military and naval aircraft by international agreement? (4) Should the manufacture and sale of armaments for private profit be prohibited by international agreement? and (5) Did respondents believe that if a nation attacked another, the other nations should compel it to stop by economic and non-military measures or, if necessary, by military means?

Eleven and a half million people voted, and of these the great majority voted affirmatively on the first four questions and the first part of the fifth. On the question of military sanctions, however, only six and three-quarter million votes were affirmative.

It was clear that a lot of thought had gone into the voting—the ballot came close to satisfying Disraeli's criteria of reflective public opinion—but the discrepancy between the 11,090,387 votes for League membership and the 6,784,368 for military measures to preserve its principles was striking; and to the government in power, and its prime minister Stanley Baldwin, it seemed clear that this reflected a strong aversion to war and to building up the armaments to support it. Baldwin was aware that Great Britain's armed strength was dangerously low, too low for it to go beyond its present modest effort to persuade Mussolini to withdraw from Africa. What line should he, as a responsible leader, take in the forthcoming parliamentary elections? With an eye to public feeling, he took all lines. He declared that the League of Nations would continue to be the cornerstone of British foreign policy and that, in the dispute over Ethiopia, there would be "no wavering in the policy we have hitherto pursued." (The Hoare-Laval plan was still months away.) Gaps in the national defense would be filled, but the prime minister pledged his word that "there will be no great armaments" and that the government would continue to work for general disarmament.

With this trimming of sail to catch every breath of popular feeling, Baldwin sailed to an easy victory in the parliamentary elections. A year later, when many things had gone wrong, when disarmament was dead, Ethiopia conquered by Italy, Hitler in the Rhineland, and the arms gap wider than ever, Winston Churchill accused Baldwin of irresponsibility in failing to call in 1935 for a heightened armaments effort. The prime minister answered in a speech in the House of Commons: "Supposing I had gone to the country and said that Germany was rearming and we must rearm, does anyone think that this pacific democracy would have rallied to that cry at that moment? I cannot think of anything that would have made the loss of the election from my point of view more certain."

In Britain's sister democracy across the Atlantic, the government was no more eager to risk offending public sentiment by adopting firm positions in foreign affairs. In 1932, when the disarmament conference opened in Geneva, hope of a successful conclusion was weak from the outset because the French government refused to consider any real reduction of armaments or any kind of concession to Germany on the question of equality unless it were given additional guarantees of security by the other powers. There were two ways in which the United States government might have tried to persuade the French to modify this negative stance, and both, at various times, were suggested. The first would have been to agree to a consultative pact—that is, a commitment to consult with other signatories of the Pact of Paris if there were a crisis caused by some state that threatened to resort to war. The second would have been to offer to reduce or abandon war debts owed to the United States if the beneficiaries of that action would scale down their armaments. President Hoover rejected both ideas because he believed that they would be politically unacceptable in the United States. Like Baldwin, he was afraid of losing the election.

Hoover's successor proved during his first term to be equally reluctant to defy the isolationist temper of American voters. During his second, however, Roosevelt became increasingly concerned about the deterioration of the world situation and convinced that the United States should be doing something to check it. He said this plainly for the first time in a speech in Chicago on 5 October 1937: "The epidemic of world lawlessness is spreading. When an epidemic of physical disease starts to spread, the community approves and joins in a quarantine of the patients in order to protect the health of the community against the spread of the disease." He suggested that the peace-loving nations must act in the same way against the current epidemic and said, "There must be positive endeavors to preserve peace." The response to this appeal was immediate, massive, and negative. The White House was flooded with mail from groups of veterans, pacifists, and mothers and from church congregations and organized isolationists, deploring this apparent attempt to involve the United States in the morass of world intrigue and war; and the administration felt it expedient to disavow the true intent of the speech and to retreat into an inactivity that lasted until the very eve of the European war.

In addition to its tendency to lame the resolution of governments, particularly in critical situations where risks of war were involved, the power of public opinion had a significant effect upon the conduct of diplomacy itself. For one thing, it ended the virtual monopoly of the professionals. One of the striking features of postwar opinion about foreign affairs in the democratic countries was the unanimity of the view that professional diplomats and their way of doing business had been largely responsible for causing the recent conflict and that the sooner their control was broken the better. Diplomats, the French ambassador Jules Cambon wrote sadly, were not regarded with any affection. Indeed, in the United States they were, both in Congress and in the press, ridiculed as social butterflies and attacked as persons of ambiguous loyalty, while in England the Labour party regarded the whole diplomatic establishment as a consciously aristocratic instrument, dedicated to the defeat of truly democratic policy.

In the face of this feeling, political leaders thought it wise to reduce the public role of the professionals, which generally meant that they took over their functions themselves. The fashion was set by Lloyd George, who shared the popular prejudice against the professionals and who also believed, as he once said, that "diplomats were invented simply to waste time. . . . It is simply a waste of time to let [important matters] be discussed by men who are not authorized to speak for their countries." During the peace conference and the three years that followed, Lloyd George bypassed the Foreign Office and to a large extent ignored the

65

missions abroad and traveled about Europe with his own staff, conducting negotiations with other heads of state on complicated matters that he did not always perfectly understand. The meager and sometimes disconcerting results of these methods did not discourage others from imitating them. Instead of letting chiefs of mission abroad do what they were trained to do, foreign ministers and secretaries of state took to doing their business for them, either by telephone, the enemy of reflection, which was generally accepted as a means of diplomatic communication in the 1930s, or by traveling themselves to their posts to take over the conduct of negotiations. The latter practice was to become increasingly frequent after World War II, particularly in the United States, where people spoke of Secretary of State John Foster Dulles's infinite capacity for taking planes and asked, with reference to his most distinguished successor, "I wonder where's Kissinger now?"

The results of this diplomatic activity by political leaders, ministers, and special missions of prominent politicians or private citizens (another device much resorted to in the United States) was disappointing. After World War II, a commission established by the French Constituent Assembly to investigate the political, economic, diplomatic, and military events that contributed to the defeat of 1940 did not hesitate to underline the deficiencies of the so-called new diplomacy. Its report noted that

> after the conclusion of the treaties of 1919, ministers had the habit of multiplying their contacts with their colleagues in other countries. The abuse of direct conversations opens the door to numerous dangers. Engagements are taken too easily. They are often improvised. It is better to define the course of a negotiation by a note which has matured in the silence of the ministry than by chance exchanges that are likely to be imprecise.

There were many ministerial meetings during the interwar period that testified to the truth of that statement and were the cause of subsequent confusion and misunderstanding—Stresemann's meeting with Briand at Thoiry in 1926, for example, and that of Pierre Laval with Mussolini in January 1935. Nor was imprecision the only danger inherent in this kind of diplomacy. When politicians engaged in the process of negotiation, they were apt to feel that their reputations were at stake and that a successful result was imperative. Some of Lloyd George's negotiations ended with ringing declarations that were plainly designed to convince a credulous public that great objectives had been achieved which later, however, proved to be insubstantial. A striking example of this kind of disingenuousness can be seen in the case of the negotiations for an Anglo-Soviet agreement in 1924. The salient issue was the question of compensation for British properties confiscated and debts repudiated by the Bolsheviks, and when the Soviet representatives showed no inclination to give any assurances on this point, the British Foreign Office decided that the talks should be broken off. At this point, a deputation from the Labour party, which had itself been in contact with the Russians, intervened, arguing that failure to reach a result would have unacceptable political results and producing a compromise that conveniently papered over all the irreconcilable differences between the parties. This the MacDonald government accepted, and a treaty was signed.

Along with the changes in the personnel charged with the conduct of important foreign business went a change in format. During the war, Woodrow Wilson had called for "open covenants openly arrived at," and it soon became an article of public faith that "open diplomacy" was the only acceptable procedure for any state that claimed to be a democracy. This was, of course, based upon a misconception, since government action in the Western democracies had long been controlled by the people, working through their elected representatives and by means of their power to change governments by periodic elections and dismiss those whose performance in office had not been satisfactory. In such a system, foreign relations, like all other aspects of policy, were subject to periodic review. To the advocates of open diplomacy, this was not enough. In effect, they were demanding the right to watch over policy as it emerged, to have a window into the rooms where the negotiators were at work, to know what was going to be said tomorrow and what their government intended to do if the other side did not like its proposals. This was a demand that Metternich or Bismarck would have regarded as preposterous and which Disraeli would have described as palpably dangerous.

It was, however, widely granted, and the result was a rapid growth of diplomacy by conference. This took two basic forms: large meetings, in which many states participated in discussions of matters of general interest, like the Genoa Conference of 1922, the disarmament conference of 1932, and the world economic conference of 1933; and what came in time to be called summit conferences, meetings of the foreign ministers or heads of state of great powers to deal with particular crises or opportunities, like the Locarno Conference of 1925, the Bessinge meeting of 1932, the Stresa meeting of 1935, and the Munich Conference of 1938.

Such meetings gratified the public desire for openness, but that was their greatest weakness. The large conferences often met, as in the case of the disarmament conference, under the pressure of public impatience and without adequate preliminary talks to lay a basis for fruitful negotiation. They often, indeed, seemed to be planned more for their public effect than for the substantive issues at stake. There were too many newspapermen and photographers on hand, and too many press conferences, inspired leaks, and other inventions of modern public relations. Because of the presence of the journalists, all conferences began with public statements by the heads of the various delegations, in which they made their objectives clear. This often had the effect of so fixing their positions that they had no subsequent room for maneuver or concession, since an alteration of position might seem, to a vigilant public, to be a humiliating retreat. In these circumstances, not much could be expected, except a final communiqué that sought to record a success where none existed.

As for summit conferences, surely the most unfortunate invention of the new diplomacy, even when they were successful, they were apt to have unfortunate results. What Richard Nixon wrote about the Peking and Moscow summit meetings of 1972 could be applied with equal force to the Locarno Conference of 1925. "Creation of a willowy euphoria is one of the dangers of summitry," Mr. Nixon wrote. "Many people embraced the naive notion that . . . we would all live happily ever after. . . . The euphoria also made it more difficult to gain support for the decisive actions and strong military forces that were needed to make détente succeed." So in 1925, the apparent success of the Locarno Conference diverted public attention from the problems that had not been solved there and that soon undermined the accord.

More often than not the summit meetings failed for reasons once outlined by a shrewd critic of diplomatic practice, Sir Harold Nicolson. The participants in summits were always, he pointed out, particularly busy men. "The time at the disposal of these visitors is not always sufficient to allow for patience and calm deliberation. The honors which are paid to a minister in a foreign capital may tire his physique, excite his vanity, or bewilder his judgment." In 1932, during the first phase of the disarmament conference, there was what was in effect a loosely structured summit meeting in the villa of U.S. Secretary of State Henry Stimson at Bessinge, in which Prime Minister Ramsay MacDonald of Great Britain, Premier André Tardieu of France, Chancellor Heinrich Brüning of Germany, and Foreign Minister Dino Grandi of Italy met with Stimson. Nothing but confusion resulted from their conversations. Secretary Stimson concluded from them that Brüning was so conciliatory in temperament and so modest in his demands for concessions that a Franco-German agreement was imminent. Tardieu went back to Paris with the feeling that Brüning "wouldn't commit himself to anything." Brüning claimed later that MacDonald had agreed to support the German claim for equality of treatment in armament. The British prime minister did not believe that he had said anything of the sort. There was no way of resolving the discrepancies, since no record was made of the conversations, and the Bessinge summit had a negative effect upon the hope of reaching a disarmament agreement.

Lack of precision also marked the Stresa summit of 1935. This meeting had been called in order to decide what response the Locarno powers would make to Hitler's repudiation in March of the arms clauses of the Versailles Treaty. Failing to discover an effective means of retaliation, the participants drew up a statement expressing their determination to oppose any further acts of aggression. Into this statement, Mussolini proposed the insertion of the words "in Europe," a suggestion that Prime Minister MacDonald accepted without any attempt to clarify Italian motives. The duce interpreted this silence to mean that he need fear no British opposition to his already well-matured plans to acquire an empire in Africa, and the Stresa Conference, which had been designed to build a front against Hitler, turned out to be a kind of prologue to the Italian aggression in Ethiopia.

As for the Munich summit, which resembled more a dictated peace than a negotiating situation, it produced a classic illustration of the folly of taking seriously hastily drafted and ill-considered agreements. This was the so-called Anglo-German Declaration which Neville Chamberlain scribbled with his own fountain pen on the morning after the conference proper and which Hitler, after a moment's hesitation, signed. It was this loosely stated pledge of future cooperation that Chamberlain waved to the welcoming crowd at Croydon Airport as proof that he had secured "peace for our time" and which sustained his faith in the appeasement policy until Hitler showed the unreliability of pledges that are not guaranteed by invading rump Czechoslovakia in March 1939.

A final result of the heightened importance of public sentiment in the interwar period was a new emphasis upon what might be called diplomacy by public declaration. This was the technique of using a public address to send a message, not to another government, but to public opinion in another country, in the hope of influencing it to bring pressure upon its own government in the interest of the message's initiator. Generally speaking, democratic states were less effective at this sort of thing than totalitarian ones, because they had to worry about both the foreign audience and the one at home. Woodrow Wilson, whose appeals to other peoples during the war had an exciting effect, and who in some ways could claim to have dissolved the Austro-Hungarian Empire by his eloquence, was singularly unsuccessful in his attempt to appeal to peoples over the heads of their governments during the peace conference, partly because of mounting evidence that he had lost the support of his own. When Heinrich Brüning was chancellor of the Weimar Republic, he sought desperately to gain a foreign policy success—a further scaling down of reparations or the grant of parity, at least in principle, in armaments—that might shore up his position at home, and for this end he used public diplomacy to convince the Western governments and their public that he was a man of good will who believed in peace and international collaboration, and one to whom they could safely make concessions. But for every speech that Brüning made in this vein for foreign consumption, he had to make another in order to appease domestic opinion by sounding the nationalist strain, talking about Germany's grievances, and promising to be unyielding in his demands for rectification.

Herbert Hoover, who believed that the world of the 1930s was suffering from mass insanity, tried to cure this by appealing to "world opinion" in various ways; but if such a thing existed, it didn't seem to be listening.

The past master of this kind of diplomacy was Adolf Hitler. Whenever he did something particularly outrageous, such as casting off the arms restrictions of the Versailles Treaty or declaring that he no longer recognized the provisions of Locarno, he could be counted on to make a major address in which he appealed to the uneasy conscience of the West by recalling the harsh provisions of the peace settlement. He would explain that far from being a provocative or aggressive action, what he had just done was a means of opening up opportunities for a sounder peace, in preparation for which he was ready to enter into any kind of treaty the Western powers might desire, providing that it was a bilateral one. (He never bothered to explain that bilateral treaties are the easiest ones to break.)

These speeches were remarkably effective, principally because people in the West did not want war; and they helped to dissuade Western governments from proposing active resistance to his aggressions. After all, what could they do about the Rhineland invasion, when Hitler's speeches and sympathetic reaction in their own newspapers, some of which were secretly financed by German agencies, had persuaded a good part of their electorate that Hitler was "only going into his own backyard"? What could they do about the *Anschluss,* when many of their voters had been persuaded that Austria was German anyway?

There is no doubt that the emergence of public sentiment as an important factor in foreign policy made Western governments in the 1930s vulnerable to German and other propaganda that worked on the feelings of their peoples in such a way as to jeopardize national interest. The fact that most people felt more than they thought and had strong hostilities and fears that could be easily mobilized increased this vulnerability. This was most apparent in France in 1938 and 1939, when an appreciable number of people became convinced that to resist Hitler was to invite Stalin to Paris and, for that matter, that a Hitler victory was preferable to a government by Léon Blum, which would involve France in an unwinnable war.

Bibliographical Essay

Details about the impact of public opinion upon postwar American foreign policy can be found in the rich literature on the fight over the League of Nations. See, among many works on the subject, Thomas A. Bailey, *Woodrow Wilson and the Lost Peace,* new ed. (Chicago, 1963) and *Woodrow Wilson and the Great Betrayal,* new ed. (Chicago 1963). On the British susceptibility to public moods, compare Zara S. Steiner, *The Foreign Office and Foreign Policy, 1898–1914* (Cambridge, 1969) with Gordon A. Craig, "The British Foreign Office from Grey to Austen Chamberlain," in *The Diplomats, 1919–1939,* ed. Gordon A. Craig and Felix Gilbert (Princeton, 1953) and "The Professional Diplomat and His Problems, 1919–1939," in *War, Politics and Diplomacy, Selected Essays* (New York, 1966). On the League of Nations Union peace ballot, see Winston S. Churchill, *The Gathering Storm* (Boston, 1948); Harold MacMillan, *The Winds of Change, 1914–1939* (New York, 1966); and Keith Middlemas and John Barnes, *Baldwin, A Biography* (London, 1969); and on the Hoare-Laval Pact and its effects, Anthony Eden, *Facing the Dictators* (Boston, 1962) and Middlemas and Barnes, *Baldwin.*

On conference diplomacy and summitry, see the comments of Charles W. Thayer, *Diplomat* (New York, 1959) and Richard Nixon, *The Real War*

(New York, 1980). On the Genoa Conference, see J. Saxon Mills, *The Genoa Conference* (New York, 1922), Harry Kessler, *Walter Rathenau, His Life and Work* (New York, 1930), and Jane Degras, ed., *Soviet Documents on Foreign Policy: I, 1917–1924* (Oxford, 1952); on Locarno, Gustav Stresemann, *Vermächtnis,* 3 vols. (Berlin, 1932–1933); on the disarmament conference and the Bessinge meeting, the articles of Michael Geyer and Gordon A. Craig, in *Internationale Beziehungen in der Weltwirtschaftskrise 1929–1933,* ed. Josef Becker and Klaus Hildebrand (Munich, 1980); and on the Munich Conference, John W. Wheeler-Bennett, *Munich: Prologue to Tragedy* (New York, 1948) and Telford Taylor, *Munich: The Price of Peace* (New York, 1979).

6
Economics
and Foreign Policy

In the failure of the collective security system in the years from 1919 to 1939, economic problems and the way in which the various powers reacted to them played a major part. Without attempting to deal with this subject as comprehensively as it deserves, we will argue here that the powers that won the war and wrote the peace settlement were the chief culprits in the process. First, the economic tactics that they used against the most important of their recent antagonists were unrealistic and uncoordinated and fatally weakened the possibility of genuine appeasement in the early postwar years. Second, after the international system was already in grave jeopardy, they underestimated the purpose and effectiveness of German economic diplomacy and thus lost the ability to maintain by economic means a viable balance of forces between the status quo and the revisionist powers.

This sorry story had its origins in the decision of the Allied powers at Paris in 1919 to impose upon the beaten foe a burden of reparations. It is understandable enough that they should have done so. The war had cost them heavy losses of life and property and had consumed their financial resources and foreign investments. In the postwar temper, democratic leaders felt it impossible to ask their own people to assume these liabilities, and it seemed logical to conclude that their former antagonists should be made responsible.

Even so, the decision was taken without a rigorous examination of its potential results. It overlooked previous experience with the use of reparations, which was not exactly heartening, Napoleon's financial exactions in Prussia after 1806 having been a major factor in inflaming the powers of resistance in that defeated country, and the reparations paid by France after its defeat in 1870 having contributed to the speculative boom in Germany that culminated in the financial crash of 1873. It ignored the psychological effects that were bound to flow from the unhappy notion of attributing to Germany and its allies the sole responsibility for having caused the war, an arguable and needlessly provocative hypothesis which John Foster Dulles, a member of the United States delegation at Paris, later believed was one of the principal causes of Germany's turning to Hitler. And it failed to appreciate the lack of logic in a procedure that set out to punish not the imperial government that had been in power in 1914 (which it might have done by being more insistent upon the surrender of its leaders), but rather the new republican regime that had been founded in 1919 and was guiltless as far as the war was concerned.

Moreover, the way in which the decision was implemented flew in the face of Woodrow Wilson's Fourteen Points, which had promised "the removal as far as possible of all economic barriers" between nations, and ignored the advice of the British economist John Maynard Keynes that the first order of business at Paris should be to restore the freely functioning world economy that had brought general prosperity before 1914. The reparations burden bore no relation to Germany's ability to pay. Because the British government insisted that the liability should include, not only shipping losses and damages to property, which the Germans themselves were resigned to paying, but the cost of pensions and disability payments made to British citizens during and as a result of the war, the resultant total was twice as large as the original estimate. In other parts of the treaty, the Allies also deprived Germany of all of its colonial empire, some of its richest mining districts, and its merchant marine, deprivations that would make it difficult if not impossible for the new German government to raise and transfer the sums demanded. In face of these conditions, there was no question that Germany was separated by very formidable barriers from normal economic activity.

This in turn posed the question of the purpose of the reparations. Were they intended merely to pay the costs of the war and to enable the Allies to liquidate the debts that they had contracted to the United States during the course of the conflict, or did they mask a political purpose, a desire not merely to punish Germany but to keep it in a position of economic and hence political weakness for a long period? During the negotiations at Paris, there was no discernible clarity of motive. The American expert Norman Davis wrote: "Some of the delegates wanted to destroy Germany, some wanted to collect reparations, and some wanted to do both. Some wanted to collect more than Germany had agreed to pay or could pay; and others wanted to take all her capital, destroy her, and then collect a large reparation bill." In the years that followed, this muddle disappeared and, among the principal powers, a basic difference emerged between the French, who quite clearly regarded reparations as a political weapon, and the British, who deplored this and felt that even the financial motive had become dubious. The United States, which had not signed the treaty, occupied a detached position.

It was over the question of treatment of Germany that the disarticulation of Anglo-French policy, which soon had unfortunate effects in other areas, particularly the Near East, first became pronounced. At Paris, the French had been denied the territorial compensation along the Rhine that they felt they had deserved and had been forced to be content with an Anglo-American pledge of support in the event of a future German attack. But in consequence of the American decision not to accept the treaty, that guarantee had never been ratified, and the French felt cheated of their legitimate security requirements. They found it necessary, therefore, to insist upon the strict observance of the Versailles Treaty, and particularly of those articles that called for the disarmament of Germany and its liability to pay reparations. The strongest advocate of this position was Raymond Poincaré, the dominant figure in French foreign policy from 1921 to 1924. A representative of the Conservative-Nationalist tradition in French politics and the wartime president of the Republic, Poincaré had been convinced of Germany's aggressive tendencies well before 1914. After the war, his suspicion was not modified, and he believed that the Germans must be kept down by a program of treaty enforcement, military alliances, and a strong army. As R. D. Challener has written, he was known for his impassioned orations during dedications of war memorials, which always culminated with the insistence that the Germans could and must pay every sou of their reparations obligation.

The British had increasing reason to doubt the possibility and even the advisability of full repayment. The first effect of reparations upon the British economy had not been fortunate. The acquisition of the German merchant marine had contributed to the postwar slump of the domestic shipping industry, and German reparations in coal were destroying Britain's European markets for that commodity. In addition, the British had a keener appreciation than the French of the transfer difficulties confronting the Germans and of the dangers implicit in the course that they were compelled to take in order to keep up with their financial liabilities—namely, resort to the printing presses with resultant depreciation and inflation.

From 1920 until his fall from office in 1922, therefore, Lloyd George sought to convince the French of the advisability of revising the treaty terms in Germany's favor. He called a series of conferences for that purpose, at Spa in 1920, at Cannes in 1922, and—a larger meeting, designed to discuss the European economy in general, including relations with the Soviet Union—at Genoa in the same year. He had no success in persuading the French to moderate their attitude, partly because of the maladroitness of the Germans themselves. At Spa, their delegation included not only General von Seeckt, in uniform, but the industrialist and banker Hugo Stinnes, the first of a long series of businessmen who played an important role in interwar diplomacy. On this occasion, he destroyed any possibility of the Germans receiving a sympathetic hearing by berating the Allies and accusing them of suffering from "the disease of victory." At Genoa, perhaps in a desperate attempt to break out of their isolation, the Germans absented themselves from conference business long enough to make a pact of friendship with the Soviet Union. Such an action could only confirm the French in their suspicion of German intransigence, the more so because it was soon rumored that there were secret military arrangements between the two new partners.

Lloyd George's efforts thus came to nothing, and the hard line followed by the French was allowed to take its ultimate and self-defeating form. This came in January 1923, when French and Belgian troops entered the Ruhr, Germany's last productive mining area. The reason for this invasion, which had been authorized over British objections by the Reparations Commission, was a German reparations default in coal and timber deliveries, but Poincaré had for some time suspected that the German government, by doing nothing to control the mounting inflation in its country, was steering toward a fraudulent bankruptcy as a means of escaping from the reparations obligation. He believed that an occupation of the Ruhr and the seizure of its mines and forests as "productive guarantees" was the only way that France could be assured of German compliance with the treaty. His action was strongly supported by the French steel industry, which wanted to secure a reliable supply of coke, and by soldiers like Marshal Foch and War Minister Maginot, who saw an opportunity of gaining permanent possession of the area.

Stephen Schuker has called the Ruhr invasion and the passive resistance with which it was met a renewal of war between France and Germany by economic means. This is the way Marshal Foch saw it and, in September 1923, when the German government was forced to call off the policy of passive resistance, he said, "Armistice! Von Hoesch [the German *chargé d'affaires* in Paris] at the Quai d'Orsay is like Erzberger coming to my railway car in the Rethondes station." There was really no reason for jubilation. The costs of supporting passive resistance had compelled the German government to resort to the printing presses in earnest, and the resultant runaway inflation, by victimizing the bulk of the German *Mittelstand,* had struck a fatal blow to the stability of the Republic and enormously strengthened the nationalist, anti-Weimar, anti-Versailles elements in the country. This could be a source of satisfaction for no one who believed in peace and collective security.

Moreover, even if regarded in narrower and more selfish terms, it was difficult to think of the French operation in the Ruhr as a victory. Certainly its objectives had not been attained. There was no assurance that German reparations payments would be resumed soon or would ever reach the proportions that a too-optimistic French legislature had hoped would relieve them of the responsibility for recasting an inefficient financial structure and devising a system of taxation capable of reducing France's dangerously swollen burden of debt. Four months after the German capitulation, in January 1924, belated realization of the true weakness of the French fiscal situation came to the financial community, and the franc collapsed with a bang that shook Poincaré's government to its foundations. In the weeks that followed, panic was widespread and bankruptcy was near, and in the end the currency was saved only by the government's ability to float loans with the banking houses of J. P. Morgan in New York and Lazard Brothers in London.

This desperate expedient was of more than economic significance. The British government, unwilling to leave the Ruhr in French possession, had revived a suggestion originally made in 1922 by U.S. Secretary of State Charles Evans Hughes that an independent committee of business and financial experts inquire into all of the ramifications of reparations. Under British and American pressure, Poincaré had consented in December 1923. Whatever such a commision might recommend, he was resolved to fight for the retention of productive pledges in the Ruhr and even of some form of military control. After the onset of the financial crisis in Paris, however, this became impossible. France's dependence upon foreign loans that had to be approved by the United States and British governments sharply reduced the bargaining power of both Poincaré and Herriot, who succeeded him in May, when dealing with the findings of the experts, which were ultimately incorporated in the Dawes Plan of 1924.

The consequences became clear at the London Reparations Conference, which met in July 1924 to amend and put into effect the provisions of the Dawes Plan. In the history of postwar diplomacy, this conference was notable for being the first European diplomatic gathering since 1919 in which the United States government participated formally and the first at which the Germans appeared as equals. But more interesting—and illustrative of the enhanced diplomatic presence of financiers in a period when governmental decisions were so heavily influenced by economic considerations—was the role played at the meeting by bankers, particularly Sir Montagu Norman of the Bank of England and Thomas W. Lamont of J. P. Morgan and Company. Since the resumption of reparations payments in accordance with the new and less onerous schedules devised by the experts could only be effected by means of a loan to Germany that was floated in the United States through the house of Morgan, the New York bankers insisted that all possibility of another Ruhr invasion be eliminated, for reasons summed up in the *Wall Street Journal:* "The average investor is disinclined to 'buy into a quarrel,' and, if there is no assurance that France will not reenter the Ruhr at some future date with the avowed purpose of compelling Germany to live up to the letter of the law in connection with its reparation payments . . . a German loan offering in this country will fall flat."

At the conference, Lamont pushed this point vigorously from behind the scenes, with the at first hesitant support of the American delegation and the more enthusiastic backing of the MacDonald government, prompted by the virulently anti-French Norman and by the Foreign Office, which had long felt that French fears of security were exaggerated. Uncertain of their own financial future, the French did not dare antagonize what again might be their only sources of support. In the end, although minor concessions were made to save Herriot's face, the powers of the Reparations Commission were amended so as to make impossible reprisals in the case of any but the most flagrant future reparations default (although dispassionate observers of the German scene believed that the nationalist passions inflamed by the French action in January 1923 would not be appeased by the Dawes Plan and that new defaults were bound to come sooner or later). Since at the same time the French were forced to give up their productive pledges and to agree to withdraw their troops from the Ruhr within a year from the implementation of the plan, their ability to compel the Germans to observe the terms of the Versailles Treaty had been seriously diminished, although not perhaps so fatally as to warrant Stephen Schuker's statement that at the London Conference, "the era in which France could lay claim to great power status also effectively came to an end."

The conference widened the already significant differences that marked Anglo-French attitudes toward the Germans. In the period that followed, despite the apparent rapprochement reached at the Locarno Conference in 1925 and the close relationship that came to exist between Aristide Briand and Gustav Stresemann, French suspicion of Germany and disinclination to make further concessions in the question of reparations or that of the military occupation of the Rhineland remained strong. The British, on the other hand, inclined increasingly to the view that everything possible should be done to strengthen the faltering German Republic by restoring its full sovereignty in foreign affairs. In the last years of the Weimar Republic, this divergence of view became particularly acute over the question of armaments, the British taking the position that the arms clauses of the Versailles Treaty should be modified to give Germany equality of status and, in time, equality in substance, the French adamantly refusing any change unless it were accompanied by formal guarantees of French security by the other great powers. This failure to agree prevented any scheme of arms control based upon general reductions from emerging from the disarmament conference of 1932, and that failure in turn led, after Hitler's accession to power, to Germany's departure from the conference and from the League of Nations in October 1933 and its subsequent repudiation of the arms clauses of the Versailles Treaty in March 1935.

The disarmament conference of 1932 brought the United States back temporarily to European councils and raised the possibility that it might use its financial resources to effect a favorable diplomatic result. President Herbert Hoover had long been a personal advocate of disarmament and was aware of the strong popular support that it enjoyed in the United States. He was convinced, moreover, that reduction of armaments was the best way of promoting recovery from the world depression and, in a speech before the International Chamber of Commerce in May 1931, had recited figures to show how heavily armaments bore on the economies of the principal powers. He concluded with the words, "Of all the proposals for the economic rehabilitation of the world, I know of none that compares in necessity or importance with a successful result of the [forthcoming disarmament] conference."

When it became clear in preconference talks that the French were disinclined to agree, some of the president's advisers urged him to use economic weapons to gain his point. His ambassador in Paris, Walter E. Edge, wrote: "It is my conviction that France will continue to throw monkey wrenches in the gear box until she is forced by such colossal and general pressure that even she will find difficulty in resisting." The time was probably coming, he suggested, when the deepening depression would cause a repudiation of both reparations and the war debts owed to the United States. Why not anticipate that and, while the debts still offered some leverage, provide remission or reduction as a reward to those powers willing to cut back their armaments, a form of pressure that the French would surely be unable to resist?

The president had no great sympathy for the French, and the idea of using debts as a weapon was not new to him. In 1924, when he was secretary of commerce in the Coolidge administration, he had been disappointed when the State Department had failed to withdraw its approval for further private lending to countries like France, Belgium, and Italy that had not made debt-funding arrangements with the United States. He then said that the "financing operations of those governments were merely covert schemes of finding money for unproductive purposes, largely for military purposes." In 1931, however, Hoover was unwilling to follow the logic of his earlier position, because he knew that any suggestion of debt reduction, even as a means of pressure to promote disarmament, would arouse a storm in the Senate and in the general public, where there was no inclination to dissolve the European obligation and widespread agreement with the sentiment attributed to President Coolidge, "They hired the money, didn't they?" Nor, when Edge repeated his suggestion, did it appeal to Hoover's secretary of state, Henry L. Stimson, who seemed shocked at the thought of using such an unconventional and even ungentlemanly method of diplomacy. "Other countries," Stimson wrote, "would flare up at being asked to sell their independent right to fix their own armaments by a bargain with another nation." As a result of the president's reluctance to jeopardize his electoral chances and the secretary of state's distaste for economic arm-twisting, American statecraft proved incapable of breaking the impasse in the Geneva Disarmament Conference and preventing the fateful consequences that flowed from it.

The American example of 1931–1932 suggests that economic diplomacy was not congenial to the diplomatic establishments of the Western democracies and not a weapon that they used effectively. This is borne out by a comparison between Adolf Hitler's use of economic diplomacy in eastern Europe and that of Great Britain and France.

Even before the coming of the National Socialist regime, the Germans had evinced a lively awareness of the political goals that could be achieved by economic means. The ill-fated Customs Union plan of 1931 with Austria, which failed because of clumsy diplomatic preparation and spirited French and Polish opposition, may have been regarded by Chancellor Heinrich Brüning, who authorized it without ever being deeply committed to it, as a means of recouping his political fortunes after the electoral setback of September 1930 and as a useful way of combating the depression. But in the Foreign Office, State Secretary Bülow, who was to survive Brüning and continue in office in Hitler's first years, had no doubt about its wider political significance. In a memorandum of January 1931, he wrote:

> Once the German-Austrian customs union has become a reality I calculate that the pressure of economic necessity will within a few years compel Czechoslovakia to adhere to it in one way or another. I would see in this the beginning of a development which would be likely to lead to a solution, scarcely conceivable by other means, of vital political interests of the Reich. In this I am thinking of the German-Polish frontier problem. If we should succeed in incorporating Czechoslovakia in our economic bloc, and if meanwhile we should also have established closer economic relations with the Baltic States, then Poland with her unstable economic structure would be surrounded and exposed to all kinds of dangers; we should have her in a vise which could perhaps in the short or long run make her willing to consider further the idea of exchanging political concessions for tangible economic advantages.

Once Hitler had taken power, the integration of economic diplomacy with political objectives became both closer and more successful. From 1934 onward, Germany's economic life was based upon *Wehrwirtschaft* (war economy), and in August 1936, in the long memorandum that

81

formed the basis of the Four Year Plan, Hitler made this more explicit. Those charged with making economic decisions should remember, he said, that their sole duty was to enable the German people to assert itself in the world of politics. The time was past for fruitless debates over economic theory and for irresponsible suggestions for solving shortages of foodstuffs and raw materials at the cost of the national armament program. The task confronting the nation was to find provisional solutions for the problems of food and raw materials and to create the basis for "the struggle for self-realization." Hitler called for an economic mobilization comparable to the military one, which would maintain living standards without jeopardizing the military effort and would attain self-sufficiency in strategic materials. "The German army must be operational in four years. The German economy must be capable of supporting war in four years."

German success in achieving these goals was due in part to the skillfulness of economic strategy in eastern Europe. Because of the weakness of the Reichsmark on international exchanges, the Germans were forced to institute exchange controls and to reserve hard currency for purchases of strategic materials in short supply. But this weakness did not handicap them in eastern Europe, where the currencies were also weak and controlled, where there was a willingness to accept the Reichsmark for sales made to Germany, and where—most important—there was an ardent desire for weapons. German penetration of eastern Europe proceeded on the basis of these facts and took the form of exchanges of foodstuffs and raw materials for arms made in Germany, a trade that not only kept the German people well fed until the war began but protected the German arms industry from the alternative dangers of overproduction and stagnation. This German strategy was so successful that by 1938, the Western powers were ready to acquiesce in German economic hegemony in the area.

This was, however, a victory by default. In his informative study of economic diplomacy before World War II, David E. Kaiser argues that the British and French never shared the German belief in the primacy of foreign policy and that under the pressures of the world depression, they allowed economic considerations to take precedence over basic principles of foreign policy that were vital to their future security. Between 1931 and 1934, the British government made a conscious decision to stimulate domestic and empire production at the expense of trade with foreign countries, a decision that was implemented by the abandonment of the traditional policy of free trade and by the Ottawa Agreement of 1932. The consequences of this were foreseen in a Foreign Office memorandum of December 1931, which stated that "a high protective tariff, combined with Empire preference, implies a measure of dissociation from Europe, a corresponding diminution of our influence over European affairs, and possibly a growth of economic nationalism." Despite these risks, the new policy was not only adhered to but elaborated upon with other features that were bound to make trade with Europe, and especially eastern Europe, difficult: an agricultural marketing bill that empowered the Board of Trade to restrict European imports of selected commodities in the interest of British agriculture, and a stubborn resistance by the Treasury and the Bank of England to clearing agreements that might have facilitated trade with countries with managed currencies.

France showed the same short-sighted parochialism as Great Britain, although one might have thought that the fact that it had allies in eastern Europe might have counselled a more reflective coordination of foreign and economic policy. Yet tariff and quota policies continued to favor the French empire over foreign markets throughout the thirties, and although France imported between 1.0 and 1.5 million tons of cereals annually and hundreds of millions of francs worth of timber, relatively small amounts of these came from eastern Europe. An attempt to change the pattern and to follow the German example of trading weapons for grains was prevented by the slow pace of French rearmament, which started only in 1936 and took another two years to get into high gear.

Particularly after the extent of German penetration of eastern Europe became clear, there were people in the foreign offices of both countries who tried to galvanize their governments into meeting the German challenge. In Great Britain, Laurence Collier of the Northern Department and his colleague in the Southern Department, E. M. B. Ingram, argued the need for a more aggressive commercial and foreign policy. In a strong memorandum in 1938, Ingram wrote:

> It has always been the traditional policy of His Majesty's Government to prevent one Power from attaining a predominant position on the Continent. It is true that conditions change and that England no longer stands in exactly the same relation to Europe as she did either in the 18th or 19th centuries. Nevertheless it will no doubt be generally conceded that it remains very much to her in-

terest—indeed, it will be argued in some quarters that it is vital to her interests—that Germany should not attain a virtual hegemony in Europe.

With a reference to the recent extension of credit to Turkey, Ingram continued:

> That the situation is not hopeless is shown by the fact that we have already managed, so we hope, to prevent one power at least in this part of Europe from falling under German influence . . . and the success we have had in this direction leads us to hope that it may not be impossible to take similar action in respect to other minor European states. Even where it is not possible to prevent German influence playing a very large part, it might be all-important to convince the countries concerned that they are not completely abandoned by the Western Powers and that the latter still offer them a loophole of resistance to the German stranglehold which they dread.

In France, the political director of the Quai d'Orsay, René Massigli, had long shared the same views. In July 1936, he wrote a strong appeal to the government, in which he warned that

> already partially dependent on the Reich economically, Central and Eastern Europe is now menaced by its military influence. Having begun its intensive rearmament, Germany can offer arms in payment of its commercial debts. By doing so she can also keep her arms factories running and improve her own materiel. She is also interested in assuring her supplies of raw materials from the neighboring countries, which are not separated from her by the sea— which she does not command—and which are in fact her commercial creditors.

It was high time, he argued, that France had an economic plan to meet the German hegemonial drive. Despite its current economic troubles, "the moment has come to furnish our allies with tangible proof that we intend to put our economic relations in harmony with our political ones, and practise our alliances."

That these arguments fell on deaf ears was due in part to the administrative disarticulation of policy and the high degree of bureaucratic jealousy in the Western democracies. In economic matters in particular, policy had been allowed to fall into the hands of agencies other than the Foreign Office—the Board of Trade and the Treasury and the Bank of England in Great Britain, the ministries of Finance, Commerce, Agriculture, and Public Works in France—and these bodies were frequently blind to the broader aspects of the policies they managed and resentful of any interference with their sphere of activity. The lack of any proper machinery for coordinating views aggravated the situation and made it possible for individual ministries to veto trade policies of political significance, as the French Ministry of Agriculture was able to do in 1938–1939 in the case of trade concessions to the Danubian states.

Had the Foreign Office and the Quai d'Orsay possessed the prestige that was theirs before 1914, this bureaucratic competition might have been reduced. But in both Britain and France, the traditional ministries for the conduct of foreign relations fell upon evil days in the 1930s. Even during the Baldwin years, Foreign Office advice was both neglected and resented, since it appeared to invite conflict with the dictators when nothing of the sort was desired; and once the appeasement policy had triumphed with the accession of Neville Chamberlain as prime minister, the Foreign Office was considered to be too pro-French and anti-German to be trusted on any matter of importance. After 1936, the same attitude prevailed on the French ministerial level, and it was no accident that uncomfortable views about competing with the Germans were not welcomed and that René Massigli lost his post in 1938.

The failure of the French and British governments to devise an effective economic diplomacy for eastern Europe underlined the lack of any French determination to make a vigorous attempt to support its own eastern alliance system. It also provided striking evidence of how completely Great Britain abandoned in the years from 1919 to 1939 the principle of the European balance of power that had guided nineteenth-century British foreign policy. The beneficiary of this failure was Adolf Hitler.

Bibliographical Essay

The reparations debate began with John Maynard Keynes, *The Economic Consequences of the Peace* (London, 1920) and has continued ever since. See, for example, Etienne Mantoux, *The Carthaginian Peace* (New York, 1952); Gustav Stolper, *The German Economy, 1870–1940* (New York, 1940); Sally Marks, "Reparations Reconsidered," *Central European History,* 5 (1972), 358–61; and Charles J. Maier, *Recasting Bourgeois Europe: Stabilization in France, Germany and Italy in the Decade After World War I* (Princeton, 1975). On Anglo-French differences and their diplomatic consequences, see W. M. Jordan, *Great Britain, France and the German Problem, 1918–1939* (London, 1943); Harold Nicolson, *Curzon: The Last Phase, 1919–1925,* new ed. (New York, 1939); the brilliant study by

Stephen Schuker, *The End of French Predominance in Europe: The Financial Crisis of 1924 and the Adoption of the Dawes Plan* (Chapel Hill, N.C., 1976), upon which the account of the London Conference above is based; and, for the period after Locarno, Jon Jacobson, *Locarno Diplomacy* (Princeton, 1972), J. W. Wheeler-Bennett, *Information on the Reparation Settlement, Being the Background History of the Young Plan and the Hague Agreements, 1929–1930* (London, 1930), Philip Snowden, *An Autobiography*, 2 vols. (London, 1934), and Gustav Stresemann, *Vermächtnis*, 3 vols. (Berlin, 1932–1933).

On economic aspects of the disarmament conference, see Gordon A. Craig, "Die Regierung Hoover und die Abrüstungskonferenz," in *Internationale Beziehungen in der Weltwirtschaftskrise 1929–1933,* ed. Josef Becker and Klaus Hildebrand (Munich, 1980); and Heinrich Brüning, *Memoiren, 1918–1934* (Stuttgart, 1970).

On German economic diplomacy, see Edward W. Bennett, *Germany and the Diplomacy of the Financial Crisis, 1931* (Cambridge, Mass., 1962), which has the most satisfactory explanation of the Austro-German customs union plan; Hjalmar Greeley Schacht, *Confessions of 'the Old Wizard'* (Boston 1956); Dieter Petzina, *Autarkiepolitik im Dritten Reich: Der nationalsozialistische Vierjahrsplan* (Stuttgart, 1968); and, especially, David E. Kaiser, *Economic Diplomacy and the Origins of the Second World War: Germany, Britain, France and Eastern Europe, 1930–1939* (Princeton, 1980), from which the quotations from Ingram and Massigli are taken.

7
Totalitarian and Democratic
Diplomacy, 1919-1939

In September 1938, when Neville Chamberlain went to Godesberg, carrying his allies' approval of the terms for a settlement of the Sudeten question that Hitler and he had agreed on at Berchtesgaden two weeks earlier, he was disagreeably surprised to find that his host had changed his mind and had drafted much more draconian conditions for the Czechs. When Chamberlain was handed a paper embodying these, he is reported to have said angrily, "This is an ultimatum, not a negotiation!" Pointing to the title page, Hitler replied mildly, "It says memorandum."

This incident illustrates how faulty real communication was apt to be between the democracies and the totalitarian states in the interwar period. Indeed, these diplomatic conversations and negotiations often resembled what the French call a *dialogue des sourds,* a conversation between deaf people, or more properly a conversation in which one side misheard what was being said while the other side wasn't really listening.

The basic reason for this condition was a profound difference in values and aspirations. Great Britain, France, and the United States had developed in the liberal-democratic tradition, and their approach to international relations after 1919 was strongly influenced by the faith in the primacy of reason that is part of that tradition and the repugnance to war that is common to liberal-democratic societies. Western diplomats regarded great-power politics as a rational pursuit and assumed that it would, as in the past, operate according to reasonable and generally accepted rules of procedure and accommodation. They believed that in an age that followed the most terrible war in history, any person competent enough to rise to the leadership of a great nation would be intelligent enough to see that war was not to anyone's advantage. And they assumed that the task of diplomacy would continue to be one of seeking the peaceful settlement of disputes without the sacrifice of one's own interest and security. In contrast, from the beginning of their existence, the totalitarian states rejected these values and assumptions and operated according to rules of their own.

In the case of the Soviet Union, this rejection was recognized and resented in the West, and Soviet-Western relations were consequently so heavily burdened by distrust and hostility that even when both sides were confronted with a common danger in the 1930s, no *modus vivendi* between them was possible. In contrast, Western statesmen long failed to recognize the true nature of fascism and national socialism and to appreciate how different the basic values of those movements were from their own. This misunderstanding and the persistence with which the West sought an accommodation with the dictators was the source of much frustration and tragedy.

I

If the West had fewer illusions about relations with the Soviet Union than about those with Fascist Italy and Nazi Germany, this was largely because the new regime in Russia had quickly made its own position abundantly clear. It did this not only by repudiating the debts owed by the czarist government to its Western allies and by confiscating all foreign properties in Russia without compensation to the owners, but by officially rejecting all of the forms and usages of traditional diplomacy. When Leon Trotsky assumed the office of commissar for foreign affairs, he announced that it was his intention "to issue a few revolutionary declarations to the peoples and then shut up the joint [the Foreign Office]"; and, when he led a delegation to the Brest-Litovsk Conference of 1918 to make peace with the Germans, he flatly refused to observe any of the amenities of the old diplomacy. He insisted that the Bolshevik delegation dine alone, that it accept no invitations of any kind from its hosts, that the forms of courtesy customary in diplomatic intercourse be dispensed with, and even that the word "friendship" be deleted from the preamble to the draft treaty. "Such declarations," he stated, "copied from one diplomatic document into another, have never yet characterized the real relations between states."

When this defiance didn't work and the revolutionary regime began to realize the true extent of its weakness and vulnerability to external pressures, it reconsidered its attitude toward diplomatic formalities and began to cultivate the traditional usages in order to be able to maintain contact with the bourgeois states. This seemed to be the best way of detecting and even influencing their behavior and of securing the loans and credits that Russia sorely needed. But the damage had already been done and was compounded by the activities of the Comintern—that "general staff of the world revolution of the proletariat" that Lenin had founded in 1919 with the mission of coordinating the activities of Communist parties abroad and encouraging subversion against non-Communist governments—and Soviet approaches to the West were regarded with lively suspicion. In August 1920, U.S. Secretary of State Bainbridge Colby wrote in a note to the Italian government:

> It is not possible for the Government of the United States to recognize the present rulers of Russia as a government with which the relations common to friendly governments can be maintained. This conviction . . . rests upon . . . facts . . . which none dispute [and which] have convinced the Government of the United States, against its will, that the existing regime in Russia is based upon the negation of every principle of honor and good faith, and every usage and convention underlying the whole structure of international law, the negation, in short, of every principle upon which it is possible to base harmonious and trustful relations, whether of nations or of individuals. . . . There cannot be any common ground upon which [the United States] can stand with a Power whose conceptions of international relations are so entirely alien to its own, so utterly repugnant to its moral sense. There can be no mutual confidence or trust, no respect even. . . . We cannot recognize, hold official relations with, or give friendly reception to, the agents of a government which is determined and bound to conspire against our institutions.

Other governments were not so adamant, and in the case of Great Britain both Lloyd George and Ramsay MacDonald sought agreement with the Soviet Union on the basis of economic collaboration, the former because he was convinced that the Bolsheviks could be "tamed" in this way, the latter because of the strong sentiment in his party for rapprochement with the great revolutionary country of the east. The history of these attempts was not happy, for they did not satisfy Western desires concerning debts and confiscations, and they brought no cessation of Comintern activities, which the Soviet government always disavowed as emanating from an independent organization for which it bore no responsibility.

It was clear, from the very beginning of contacts with the Soviet Union, that Soviet negotiators had a fundamentally different approach toward diplomacy from that of their Western colleagues. To them it was more than an instrument for protecting and advancing national interest; it was a weapon in the unremitting war against capitalism. Diplomatic negotiations could not, therefore, aim at real understanding and agreement. On the eve of the signature of the Anglo-Soviet Trade Agreement of 1921, L. B. Kamenev said, "We are convinced that the foreign capitalists, who will be obliged to work on terms we offer them, will dig their own graves."

In Soviet practice, negotiations were often intended not to reach settlements but to block or delay them until the situation elsewhere had changed in such a way as to improve the Russian position. Sometimes they were entered into in a spirit of speculation or in an effort to test the objectives and will of the other side; sometimes they were designed for propaganda purposes, in order to ingratiate the Soviet Union with third parties. In large conferences in particular—this was true of the Genoa Conference of 1922 and the Geneva Disarmament Conference of 1932—the Soviet delegation was apt to follow a line that, in the Western view, was neither practical nor conducive to progress in the discussions. The Soviets' favorite ploy was to universalize their position in the hope that the peoples of colonial areas and significant parts of the populations of Western nations would identify themselves with it. This was in accordance with the advice given by Marx and Engels in *The German Ideology* where they held that since "increasingly abstract ideas hold sway" in the modern world, the revolutionary class was compelled "to represent its interest as the common interest of all the members of society, put in an ideal form; it will give its ideas the form of universality and represent them as the only rational, universally valid ones," and it will seek to speak "not as a class but as a representative of the whole society."

In pursuing this tactic, Soviet negotiators kept the conversations on the level of general principles as long as possible, knowing that this made for endless debate and gave frequent opportunities for rhetorical fireworks. At the same time, they tried to place the Western states on the defensive by questioning their good faith and inserting into the record statements by public figures in Western countries which, they claimed, showed a fixed determination to resist peaceful agreement. Refutations of these allegations they blandly disregarded and, in general, they admitted no obligation to answer rational arguments.

Even when they desired a settlement, Soviet negotiators made accommodation difficult. They did not subscribe to the view, common to Western diplomacy since the Renaissance, that negotiation was a bargaining process in which agreement was reached through mutual concession, what Callières had called a *commerce d'avis réciproque.* After World War II, Nikita Khrushchev once called this "a huckster's approach" and said that Soviet negotiators did not have "to make any concessions because our proposals have not been made for bartering. We act on the principle that sensible solutions must be found that would not damage any country. . . . Those who really strive for peace must not use methods of petty bargaining in the talks." In the interwar period, Soviet diplomats like Chicherin, Litvinow, and Molotov were guided by similar principles, and Soviet negotiators, bound by rigid directives that allowed little flexibility, regarded the freedom of maneuver permitted to their Western counterparts with suspicion. Proposals from the other side of the table met with automatic opposition, followed by persistent and uncompromising advocacy of the Soviet point of view.

The tactic of initial rejection was carried at times to ridiculous extremes, as it was in September 1929, when British Foreign Secretary Arthur Henderson presented the Soviet envoy Dovgalevsky with a list of questions that he felt should be discussed and settled before the resumption of formal relations between their two countries was considered. Dovgalevsky came to the second meeting with his own list, on which the same questions appeared in different order, and proceeded to fight tenaciously for his proposed agenda. So also, in December 1929, the British minister in Moscow complained that "anyone accustomed to dealing with M. Litvinow will remember how he frequently appears to be on the point of agreeing to suggestions made to him, but in practice, when pressed for any definite statement, he invariably reverts to his original point of view."

These methods reinforced the conviction that it was difficult under any conditions to carry on political discussions with the Soviet Union and impossible to rely on any agreements made. The belief proved to be a heavy handicap to any revision of view in the years when the Soviet Union, alarmed by the threat of National Socialism, placed the Comintern under restraint and began to seek agreements with the West that might strengthen the system of collective security. This shift in policy was marked by a new spirit of accommodation in Soviet diplomacy, and it had some success: diplomatic recognition by the United States in 1933, Soviet admission to the League of Nations in 1934, and the negotiation of the Franco-Soviet Pact in 1935. Even so, Western suspicion of Soviet motives remained unabated.

Recognition by the United States did not, for instance, lead to any effective collaboration against the totalitarian states until after the war had broken out; nor did Soviet membership in the League diminish the British government's growing disenchantment with that body. The strongest man in the National government, Neville Chamberlain, was not impressed by Litvinow's eloquent speeches at Geneva in behalf of collective security or by Soviet proposals for the containment of Hitler before it was too late. He dissuaded the French from seeking to elaborate their flimsy pact with the Soviets by means of military engagements, and he brushed aside Soviet proposals for four-power talks after Hitler had seized Austria in March 1938, stating that "the Russians [were] stealthily and cunningly pulling all the strings behind the scenes to get us involved in war with Germany." During the Sudeten crisis, Chamberlain discouraged those who believed that the Soviet Union might play a positive role; and the exclusion of the Soviet Union from the Munich Conference was in full accordance with his view that the security of Europe could be maintained by a directory of great powers, but not one that included the Soviets.

Even when that experiment collapsed and English voices were raised in behalf of attempts to secure an Anglo-French-Soviet alliance, Chamberlain remained unmoved. "I must confess," he wrote on 26 March 1939, "to the most profound distrust of Russia. I have no belief whatever in her ability to maintain an effective offensive, even if she wanted to. And I distrust her motives, which seem to me to have little connection with our ideas of liberty, and to be concerned only with getting every one else by the ears."

It would be a mistake to blame the British prime minister for driving the Soviet Union into Hitler's arms and making the Second World War inevitable. There is no assurance that, had he been eager to forget the past and enthusiastic about an alliance with the Soviets, their course would have been any different than it was. Soviet policy was animated by its ideological hatred of all bourgeois regimes; its diplomatic strategy, however, was determined by considerations of relative danger, which

92

made it necessary for Russia to throw its support to one or the other of its ideological opponents.

Chamberlain's attempt to exclude the Soviet Union from his own plans for the consolidation of European peace, however, probably persuaded the Soviet government that the Western powers were not serious about opposing Hitler but hoped to turn his aggressive tendencies toward the east. This made Russia anxious to make its own deal with Hitler. Vice Commissar Potemkin's words to the French ambassador Coulondre after Munich were revealing in this respect. "My dear friend," he said, "don't you see what you have done? You have made a fourth partition of Poland inevitable."

Absent from that worried remark was any intimation of recognition that Soviet behavior from 1919 onward may have contributed to this unhappy state of affairs. Criticism of Western policy toward the Soviet Union before 1939 must be tempered by an awareness of how sharp the memory was in Western capitals of Soviet deviousness and double-dealing. This distrust, even more than the practical difficulties that the negotiations of 1939 revealed, was the main obstacle to a last-minute marriage of convenience in the face of the threat of Adolf Hitler.

II

In contrast to the West's attitude toward the Soviet Union, Western views of the other principal totalitarian states were remarkably tolerant, and London and Paris seemed for a long time eager to excuse Hitler's and Mussolini's breaches of treaty law without recognizing the threat posed to their own national safety. The explanation is to be found, in the first place, in the stubbornness with which the British government adhered to the policy of appeasement and compelled its French ally to go along. But the fallacies of British policy would have become apparent long before 1939, even to its authors, if it had not been for the diplomatic skills of Adolf Hitler, who proved to be adroit in playing to the prejudices and partialities of the British and French governments and in postponing the time when the scales finally fell from their eyes.

The appeasement policy was the invention of Neville Chamberlain, who as chancellor of the Exchequer during the last years of Stanley Baldwin's prime ministership had become steadily more dismayed by what he considered to be the mistaken premises of British foreign policy. A politician who had made his way to cabinet rank by distinguished service in a number of domestic ministries, Chamberlain had no experience with foreign affairs before becoming prime minister in 1937 and, indeed, had once been interrupted while airing his views on foreign subjects by his brother Austen, one of the authors of the Locarno treaties, who said, "Neville, you must remember you don't know anything about foreign affairs."

This was proved in the end to be tragically true. But Neville Chamberlain was a strong-willed and self-confident man in a government of ministers weaker than himself. As early as May 1934, he was writing in his diary, "Unhappily it is part of my nature that I cannot contemplate any problem without trying to find a solution for it. And so I have practically taken charge of the defence requirements of this country." A year later, he was confiding to his sister that he had become "a sort of acting P.M.," telling the indecisive Baldwin what he should do; and in June 1936, he showed that he did not exclude foreign affairs from the sphere of his intervention by calling in the House of Commons for an end to the policy of sanctions against Italy for its aggression in Ethiopia, in a speech which he had not bothered to clear with Foreign Secretary Anthony Eden because he was sure that Eden would beg him not to make it. Shortly before he became prime minister, he told Lady Astor that "he meant to be his own Foreign Minister."

The statement implied a fundamental change in the direction and methods of British foreign policy. In a Europe in which the power balance had been sensibly altered by Hitler's repudiation of the arms clauses of the Versailles Treaty, by the Ethiopian and Spanish conflicts, and by the remilitarization of the Rhineland, Chamberlain felt it idle to go on talking as if the Versailles system could be maintained and the League of Nations revivified. In a moment of brutal candor, he said, "We must not try to delude small weak nations into thinking that they will be protected by the League when we know that this will not be the case." The time had come to find a new basis for European order, and the way must be paved by a vigorous attempt to appease the revisionist powers in the interest of détente. Instead of invoking outworn ideals, one should bring into play the practical virtues of realism and accommodation. Like a good businessman seeking to make a deal, one should try to find out what the true objectives of the dictators were and then use this knowledge as the basis for a bargain that would bring them back into the international comity by satisfying their wants. That this might involve the recognition of Mussolini's African conquests and an end to demands that he withdraw his "volunteers" from Spain, that it could probably be effected only by giving Germany back its colonies and making adjustments in the boundaries of eastern Europe, Chamberlain acknowledged and accepted, on the ground that the détente that would follow would be to everyone's advantage.

There was no dearth of critics of these ideas. Foreign Secretary Anthony Eden, the permanent undersecretary for foreign affairs Lord Vansittart, Winston Churchill, the former ambassador in Berlin Sir Horace Rumbold, and other persons of wide European experience pointed out at various times that the basic flaw of appeasement was its assumption that the dictators could be appeased. They argued that on the contrary Hitler was still animated by the desire for *Lebensraum* that he had articulated in *Mein Kampf* and that Mussolini would, as far as possible, model his behavior on the Führer's; that an attempt to buy them off could only be made at the expense of small states; and that it was a mistake to think that they placed as high an evaluation on peace as Chamberlain did himself. These were shrewd arguments (and the last was corroborated by no less a person than Hermann Goering, who once said to Lord Halifax, "I should like to discuss these things with Mr. Chamberlain some time, but I suppose all he would want to talk about is peace"). But Chamberlain was too headstrong to take these criticisms seriously, and he resented the fact that they were made. His feelings were reflected in his kicking Vansittart upstairs and forcing Eden's resignation and his subsequent preference for bypassing the Foreign Office as much as possible. Like other outsiders, Chamberlain resented professionals, and he convinced himself that the Foreign Office was too pro-French and anti-German, too bound to the old Versailles system, and too unrealistic. He preferred to choose for advisers and associates people whose views agreed with his own, like Sir Horace Wilson, who came from the Treasury Department and had little prior knowledge of foreign affairs, and his ambassador in Berlin, Sir Nevile Henderson, who had none of the objectivity and skepticism of his predecessors Rumbold and Sir Eric Phipps.

In the end, Chamberlain's critics were proven to be right, and the appeasement policy helped to bring on the war that the prime minister was seeking to avoid. This was not, however, due solely to his gullibility. Hitler's gifts of persuasion were considerable, and Chamberlain was not the only European statesman who was deluded by his ability to mask his true intentions until he felt strong enough to be able to disregard potential opposition.

In the uses of diplomacy, Hitler was easily the most skillful of the totalitarian leaders. The Soviets often showed technical competence but were always handicapped by ideological rigidity and a tendency to alienate their negotiating partners by their inveterate suspicion, the tediousness of their tactics, and their deviousness. Mussolini and his diplomats brought nothing new to the art of negotiation, and Fascist diplomacy, after the duce's son-in-law Galeazzo Ciano had taken over the Palazzo Chigi, was characterized by an emphasis upon the sensational rather than the substantive, an inordinate degree of posturing and bombast (that was what the *tono fascista* on which Ciano insisted really amounted to), and a not inconsiderable amount of slipshodness in detail, as in the drafting of the Pact of Steel with Germany in May 1939, which imposed rigid conditions upon Italy without defining the *casus foederis,* providing escape clauses, or stipulating the necessity of consultation. In contrast, Hitler showed both skill and inventiveness in using the resources and techniques of diplomacy to advance his purposes.

For the sake of brevity, one can speak of Hitler's diplomacy as going through four distinct phases. The first of these, which followed immediately upon his accession to power, may be called the diplomacy of concealment or obfuscation, for it was designed to convince the other powers that the *Machtübernahme* would bring with it no fundamental change in German foreign policy. The personnel in the Foreign Office and the embassies remained unchanged; intensive propaganda was beamed abroad to convince other governments and peoples that the unpleasant things going on inside Germany (the *Gleichschaltung* process that was destroying all of the elements of potential resistance to the new regime) had no foreign political connotations; *Mein Kampf* and its arguments were played down; and every possible attempt was made to stress common bonds with the West by means of cultural exchanges and inducements to Western tourism. All of this was intended to prevent external interference while Germany was vulnerable and until *Gleichschaltung* was completed and secret rearmament was begun.

In the second phase, which began at the end of 1933 and extended through the next year, Hitler's diplomacy was intended to disengage Germany from obligations assumed by previous governments and to protect the country from the possible consequences of doing so. This began with Germany's departure from the disarmament conference and the League of Nations in October 1933, an action which Hitler carefully prepared by playing upon the bad conscience of the West with regard to Germany's remaining disabilities under the Versailles Treaty and the resentment that existed in some countries over France's reluctance to make concessions. He also used with effect tactics that were to be employed again during the Sudeten crisis of 1938, constantly raising the level of his demands at the disarmament conference so that a settlement became impossible and then withdrawing from the conference and the League on the grounds that the German people would no longer tolerate an imposed inequality. As in 1938, he subsequently held a plebiscite in Germany to demonstrate that he had full public support.

During the year that followed, Hitler's main diplomatic efforts were devoted to avoiding any attempt to punish him for his actions. This took the form of a flurry of public and private assurances that Germany was willing to make new engagements and enter into new pacts with any power. His promises had such a ring of sincerity that they reassured Western statesmen; even as late as the spring of 1939, Neville Chamberlain was telling journalists that he expected Hitler to return to the League and disarmament talks before the end of the year. To escape from diplomatic isolation, Hitler himself (for it was his own idea rather than that of the Foreign Office) negotiated a pact of friendship with Poland in January 1934, an arrangement that proved its worth later in the year, when his new partner helped scuttle French Foreign Minister Louis Barthou's plan to contain Germany by means of an eastern Locarno.

The third phase, which extended from the beginning of 1935 until the end of 1937, was characterized by a diplomacy of testing, designed to discover how much resistance could be expected once Hitler had unmasked his plans for expansion in the east. It began with the Saturday Surprises of March 1935, when, on successive Saturdays, Hitler announced that Germany had a new air force and that it would no longer be bound by the arms clauses of the Versailles Treaty. It continued, when no retaliatory spirit evinced itself (the Stresa front of April 1935 collapsed, and the British government proved perfectly willing, despite Hitler's violation of the treaty, to sign a naval accord with him in June) with the remilitarization of the Rhineland and the intervention in the Spanish Civil War.

It was during this period of testing that Hitler showed how skillful he could be in disarming potential antagonists. When Foreign Secretary Sir John Simon and Anthony Eden went to Berlin in late March 1935 to remonstrate with him concerning his recent actions, he managed to persuade Simon that his behavior had been actuated by a sense of honor and a desire to regain the kind of equality that would enable Germany to return to the League with pride; and on 21 May 1935, in a brilliant example of public diplomacy, he offered to conclude bilateral agreements with his neighbors, to recognize the independence of Austria and refrain from interfering in its internal affairs, and (less than a year before he unashamedly reversed himself) to observe the Locarno treaties, including the demilitarization of the Rhineland. Even the usually skeptical Phipps, then ambassador in Berlin, was won over, as his advice to his government showed. He wrote:

> His Majesty's Government may decide that it is now undesirable to conclude any convention with this country. . . . I earnestly hope that they will not allow themselves to be deterred by the mere contemplation of Herr Hitler's past misdeeds or breaches of faith. After all, he now leads nearly 70 millions of industrious, efficient and courageous, not to say pugnacious people. He is, like most men, an amalgam, and he may, like many men, have evolved since the old, somewhat gangster-like days at Munich. His signature, once given, will bind his people as no other could. It need not bind Great Britain to any state of undue weakness; it need not blind her to the undoubted dangers lying ahead. And if the worst befall, and Hitler decide to break his freely-given solemn pledge, surely our battleground would be all the firmer for having put him to the test?

The fourth phase was the period of aggression, heralded by Hitler's secret meeting with his military and diplomatic advisers on 5 November 1937 and by the reorganization of the army command and the appointment of Joachim von Ribbentrop as foreign minister in February. These actions were implemented by the *Anschluss* in March, the acquisition of the Sudetenland in September 1938, the absorption of rump Czechoslovakia in March 1939, and the preparations for war with Poland. Although the emphasis was now shifting to military action, diplomacy was still important to Hitler. By its means, he reassured Mussolini that the loss of Austria was tolerable in view of the other advantages that the duce would gain from their collaboration; and it was indispensable in carrying the British and French with him, despite momentary flashes of resistance in London and Paris, until the invasion of Prague proved the bankruptcy of appeasement. Not the least of Hitler's achievements was his ability to exploit Chamberlain's naive belief in his own realism. No word bulked larger in the German diplomatic vocabulary during the months when Hitler was explaining the reasonableness of his claims in central Europe, the irresponsibility of people like Schuschnigg and Benes who opposed them, and the wisdom of accepting the inevitable. Scarcely veiled threats and references to the invulnerability of German arms now began to mingle with the reassurances, but these did not become obtrusive until March 1939, when Hitler tired of the game and sent his tanks into Prague.

Even after that, however, and the beginning of the agitation against Poland, Hitler did not rely entirely upon the military weapon. Indeed, his most stunning diplomatic stroke came in August 1939 when, after a long period of careful sounding, he suddenly made up his mind to make an alliance with the Soviet Union and carried this plan through with blinding speed literally under the noses of French and British negotiators who were, clumsily and belatedly, seeking the same end. With that treaty in his pocket, Hitler had no further use of the diplomatic art. In contrast to his opposite numbers in London and Paris, he had never regarded it as a means of preserving peace but merely as an instrument for preparing the way for the war that he had always wanted. "After all," he said once the war had begun, "I did not raise the army in order *not* to use it." The statement underlines the fact that all of his diplomatic intercourse with the Western governments, upon which they had placed such high hopes, had been nothing but a deliberately contrived *dialogue des sourds,* in which the words he used had secret meanings that the other side could not hear.

Bibliographical Essay

This chapter is based in part on Gordon A. Craig, *On the Diplomatic Revolution of Our Times* (The Haynes Foundation Lectures, University of California, Riverside, April 1961) and on his essay "Totalitarian Approaches to Diplomatic Negotiation," in *War, Politics and Diplomacy: Selected Essays,* ed. Gordon A. Craig (New York, 1966).

On Soviet diplomacy, see Theodore von Laue, "Soviet Diplomacy: G. V. Chicherin, People's Commission for Foreign Affairs, 1918–1930," in *The Diplomats; Russian Foreign Policy: Essays in Historical Perspective,* ed. Ivo J. Lederer (New Haven, 1962); George F. Kennan, *Russia and the West Under Lenin and Stalin* (Boston, 1960); and Adam B. Ulam, *Expansion and Coexistence: The History of Soviet Foreign Policy, 1917–1964* (New York, 1968).

On the appeasement policy, there is much background material in Keith Middlemas and John Barnes, *Baldwin, A Biography* (London, 1969) and Anthony Eden, *Facing the Dictators* (Boston, 1962); and Keith Feiling,

Life of Neville Chamberlain (London, 1946) is still essential. J. R. M. Butler, *Lord Lothian* (London, 1960) and A. L. Rowse, *All Souls and Appeasement* (London, 1961) tell us much about the assumptions of Chamberlain and his associates; and *The History of "The Times,"* IV, Pt. 2 (London, 1952) is even more revealing. Special studies of value are Martin Gilbert, *The Roots of Appeasement* (London, 1966) and Martin Gilbert and Richard Gott, *The Appeasers* (London, 1963). Telford Taylor charts the course of Chamberlain's policy in detail in *Munich: The Price of Tragedy* (New York, 1979).

The rich literature on Hitler's foreign policy is summarized and reference is made to the principal works in chapter 19 of Gordon A. Craig, *Germany, 1866–1945* (Oxford, 1978). Special reference should be made to A. J. P. Taylor, *The Origins of the Second World War* (New York, 1962), an ingratiating but unsound book; Eberhard Jaeckel, *Hitler's Weltanschauung,* trans. from the German (Middletown, Conn., 1972); and Gerhard L. Weinberg, *The Foreign Policy of Hitler's Germany:* I, *Diplomatic Revolution in Europe, 1933–1936* (Chicago, 1970) and II, *Starting World War II, 1937–1939* (Chicago, 1980). Also of interest is Andreas Hillgruber, *Germany and the Two World Wars* (Cambridge, Mass., 1981).

8

Franklin D. Roosevelt's Plans
for a Postwar System of Security

The war that began when Hitler's columns sliced into Poland in September 1939 lasted for almost six years and, long before it was over, it had revealed itself to be more truly global than its predecessor, more total in its demands upon the resources and its impact upon all classes of society, more sophisticated in its weaponry, and more destructive in its results. At least seventeen million soldiers, sailors, marines, and airmen died in action during the conflict, and eighteen million noncombatants met their deaths; and, as if that were not enough, the war ended with the revelation of a terrible new system of weapons that promised to multiply these dreadful statistics beyond the limits of human comprehension if interstate conflict was ever renewed on a major scale.

Even before this last discovery was made, it had become clear to Allied statesmen that in this war victory was not enough. They realized that they must succeed where their predecessors after the First World War had failed, in establishing effective barriers against a repetition of the cataclysm. This was a task that the wartime president of the United States, Franklin D. Roosevelt, approached with particular dedication. At the end of the First World War, he had been inspired by Woodrow Wilson's dream of an international comity that was free of the scourge of war, and he had not abandoned his ideal, although he was realist enough to be conscious of the difficulties that lay in the way of its realization. Aware of the mistakes that had been made in 1918 and 1919, he was mindful also that circumstances had changed radically since then, and that the possibility of establishing a successful international system would

101

depend upon the continued collaboration of the Grand Alliance against Nazism and especially upon the relations between the United States and the Soviet Union, its strongest members. But an even more basic pre-requisite was a domestic one, the support of public opinion in the United States.

I

Relations with the Soviet Union have been a troublesome element in United States foreign policy ever since 1917, but since the end of the Second World War they have tended to be the dominant problem. The difficulties with which Franklin D. Roosevelt and his colleagues strug-gled in the last stages of the war have not disappeared. Just as his efforts to develop a cooperative relationship with the Soviet Union eventually encountered a crisis of credibility and became involved in domestic con-troversy, so did the similar effort of Richard Nixon and Henry Kissinger thirty years later, while the failure of President Carter to formulate a rationale for his attitude toward Moscow that could command public support was one of the principal reasons for the disarray of his foreign policy.

No one who reviews American foreign policy since the Second World War can fail to be impressed by the importance of domestic political constraints on the president's choice of a long-range policy toward the Soviet Union and on his ability to implement that policy over time. The term *domestic restraints* refers to all of the pressures on policy makers that arise directly or indirectly from the nature of domestic influences on foreign policy in industrialized democratic political systems. Democratic control of foreign policy is, of course, traditional and indispensable in the American system. But the forces of public opinion, of Congress, of the mass media, and of powerful interest groups often make themselves felt in ways that seriously complicate and hamper presidential ability to pursue long-range foreign policy objectives in a coherent and consistent manner. Under these circumstances, it is not surprising that presidents and their advisers have responded not only by seeking to inform and educate public opinion but also at times by attempting to manipulate and control it. Efforts to manipulate and deceive the public or to bypass the accepted procedures of shared responsibility in foreign policy mat-ters with the Congress cannot be condoned, but the fact that they are sometimes resorted to highlights the difficulty of the fundamental problem: that of attaining enough understanding and support for a particular policy to prevent domestic pressures from taming or distorting it.

To achieve this, a president must achieve a fundamental and stable national consensus that encompasses both members of Congress and the interested public. He cannot develop and maintain such support simply by adhering scrupulously to constitutional-legal requirements for the conduct of foreign policy, or by following the customary norms for consultation with Congress, or by conducting an "open" foreign policy that avoids undue secrecy and deceptive practices, or by attempting to play the role of broker mediating the competing demands and claims advanced by the numerous domestic interest groups. Neither can the president get durable public support for his policy merely by saying that he is acting in the "national interest" or by issuing appeals that politics should stop at the water's edge.

How then can a broad and stable domestic consensus be achieved? When we try to answer this question, the concept of *policy legitimacy* is useful. A president can achieve legitimacy for his policy only if he convinces enough members of Congress and the public that the policy is well thought out and soundly conceived. To do this, he must first convince them that his objectives and goals are desirable and worth pursuing; in other words, that his policy is consistent with fundamental national values and contributes to their enhancement. This is the *normative* or moral component of policy legitimacy. Second, the president must persuade and assure the public that he knows how to achieve these desirable long-range objectives. This requires him to convince people that he understands the Soviet Union and the evolving world situation and that he and his advisers have the competence to utilize available resources to enable them to influence the course of events in the desired direction. This is the *cognitive* basis for policy legitimacy.

Thus, policy legitimacy requires both a normative-moral component and a cognitive basis. The normative component establishes the *desirability* of the policy; the cognitive component its *feasibility*. Why is this valuable for the conduct of foreign policy, particularly in a democracy? If the president does gain legitimacy for his long-range policy toward the Soviets (indeed, for other aspects of his foreign policy as well), then the day-to-day actions he takes in order to implement the policy will become much less vulnerable to the many pressures and constraints on his freedom of action associated with "democratic control," pressures and constraints that could otherwise prevent him from pursuing his policy in a consistent manner. Incidentally, a durable bipartisan foreign policy is possible only on the basis of a broadly shared feeling that the president's foreign policy enjoys normative and cognitive legitimacy.

All presidents since World War II have had difficulty in achieving, and even more difficulty in maintaining, legitimacy for their long-range policies toward the Soviet Union. This became evident for the first time in the case of President Roosevelt's plan for a postwar security system based upon cooperation with the Soviets.

II

Roosevelt's "Great Design," as he himself called it, for the postwar world was based to a remarkable extent on lessons of the past that he and his closest advisers—indeed many others as well—had drawn from various failures of policy after the First World War which had led to the Great Depression, to the emergence of aggressive totalitarian governments in Germany, Italy, and Japan, and finally to another great war.

As Roosevelt and others saw it, one of the mistakes made by the Allies in 1918 was to enter into an armistice with the existing German government without completely defeating its armed forces and occupying the entire country. As a result, German nationalists could afterward claim that Germany had not really been defeated but that the army had been "stabbed in the back" by the new liberal democratic government in Berlin that came into power at that time. The first lesson for Roosevelt, therefore, was that it was essential this time to defeat completely, disarm, and occupy those countries which had started World War II. This was one of the first things Roosevelt, Churchill, and Stalin discussed and quickly agreed upon as their joint war aim, and they succeeded in carrying it out. But, as we will note, it had important consequences for the structure of the postwar world and for the task of creating a viable new security system.

Other important lessons from the failure of peacemaking after World War I also had to be kept in mind. The total defeat and occupation of Germany, Italy, and Japan would amount to little in the long run if economic conditions of the kind that had helped bring totalitarian governments into power in the 1930s were allowed to occur again. Hence a second requirement for a more lasting peace was to develop economic policies and cooperation that would avoid future depressions. Reconstruction of the world's economy on a durable basis was a prime objective in American planning during the war for the postwar era. Plans were made to remove or sharply reduce barriers to trade among nations. American postwar planners also took up the important matter of reforming the international monetary system. They developed detailed plans for creating mechanisms and institutions that would stabilize international currencies and facilitate the flow of capital across national boundaries in order to expedite postwar reconstruction and economic development.

There was, as one would expect, a strong element of national self-interest behind these economic measures. Roosevelt and his advisers knew perfectly well that his New Deal policies before the war had not solved the problem of unemployment in the United States. It took the war to do that. And there was real concern that, once the war was over and the stimulus of war production to the economy removed, large-scale unemployment would reemerge. Roosevelt wanted to stimulate free trade and healthy economies elsewhere in the world, not only because he believed this essential for developing a viable international system, but also because he hoped that foreign markets would absorb the vast amount of goods American industry would have to continue to produce to maintain employment at a high level at home. We need not go into the details of these economic plans, except to say that with some modifications they were put into effect after the war and were for a number of years generally successful.

Perhaps the most important lesson Roosevelt and his advisers drew from the bungling of the peace after the First World War had to do with the fact that the United States not only had failed to join the League of Nations but had also pursued a generally isolationist foreign policy. American isolationism and unwillingness to cooperate with other peace-seeking countries had indirectly contributed to the worldwide Great Depression of the 1930s and to the rise of the totalitarians. This time, Roosevelt felt, it was essential that the United States should not return to an isolationist foreign policy once World War II ended. But by no means could he take it for granted that American public opinion and Congress would not press for a return to the traditional American policy of avoiding "entangling alliances."

Thus, even while the war was going on, Roosevelt had to lay the groundwork to ensure a postwar internationalist policy. He had to define such a policy, at least in broad outlines, and to gain legitimacy and public acceptance for it. Roosevelt did so by conducting the war and justifying it in ways that would lead naturally to an internationalist foreign policy thereafter. In this he was successful in general terms, but less successful in important specifics, which should be considered in some detail.

III

The isolationists had been strong before America entered the war, but Pearl Harbor changed opinion and galvanized the nation. A great deal of support developed for the idea that the United States would have to participate actively in the effort to create a peaceful international system after the war. But those who opposed a return to isolationism were divided as to just what type of internationalist policy was best. There were many articulate and influential supporters of the old Wilsonian concept of collective security who favored a new and stronger League of Nations with United States participation. Roosevelt himself, however, rejected this as too idealistic and impractical. His approach to constructing an international security system was based on the realities of power. In Roosevelt's view, it was important that the states which possessed preponderant military power agree to cooperate to preserve the peace.

Roosevelt's thinking was very much influenced by his concern about the situation that would confront the peacemakers when the war was over. Once Nazi Germany was defeated, there would be an important power vacuum in Central Europe. The question of *who* and *what* would fill this vacuum would pose the most serious implications for the vital interests of both the Soviets and the Western powers. If the two sides could not quickly find a mutually acceptable approach to the power vacuum, then they would almost certainly enter into the sharpest kind of competition and conflict over the control of Central Europe.

Such an ominous prospect was all the more likely because the weak and divided international system of the interwar years had collapsed with the outbreak of World War II. The military alliance between the Western powers and the Soviet Union had been forced upon them by circumstances—the danger of defeat at the hands of Nazi Germany and its allies. After the enemy was beaten, all the mutual suspicion and the long-standing differences in ideology between the West and the Soviet Union would have an opportunity to emerge once again. Roosevelt was aware that the postwar world would contain only victors and vanquished; there would be no international system to provide a framework within which the Western powers and Russians could work out a solution to the power vacuum created by their victory. So Roosevelt had to tackle two important and difficult tasks at the same time—to create a new international system and find a way of preventing dangerous competition for control of Central Europe.

What were the various ways to accomplish these critical tasks? One approach was to try to recreate a new balance-of-power system in which there would be a great deal of competition among the major powers. Such a system had existed during the eighteenth century and had failed to deter Napoleon from trying to achieve hegemony; it had also failed for many years to form the kind of coalition needed to bring him down. Roosevelt believed that that kind of system for the postwar period would be neither desirable nor feasible. England would be too weak by itself to provide a military counterweight to Russia on the European continent. In Roosevelt's view, the United States, even with all its military power, would not want, or be able, to bolster England for the purpose of balancing Soviet pressure in Europe. One must keep in mind that Roosevelt operated on the premise—which seemed completely justified at the time—that American public opinion would not tolerate leaving large American military forces in Europe very long once the war ended. So the grim prospect he had to contend with, and to avoid if possible, was that the Soviet Union could end up dominating Europe unless the Russians were brought into a different kind of balance-of-power system.

Another possibility was to try to reduce the potential for conflict in a new balance-of-power system by giving each of the major powers generous spheres of influence in areas of special interest to them. This approach was favored by Winston Churchill, the British prime minister during the war. At his private meeting with Stalin in Moscow in October 1944, Churchill attempted to work out a mutually acceptable understanding that would take into account both the interests of the two sides in the Balkans and the power realities. Churchill provides a vivid description in his memoirs of one of his meetings with Stalin, which began at ten o'clock on the evening of October 9: "The moment was apt for business." Churchill took out a sheet of paper and wrote behind the name of each of the Balkan countries the percentage of influence each side should have there: Rumania—90-percent Russian; Greece—90-percent British; Bulgaria—75-percent Russian; Hungary and Yugoslavia—50 percent—50 percent. Churchill pushed the paper across the table to Stalin who looked it over and then proceeded to make a check mark to signify his approval. Churchill then said, "Let us burn the paper." Stalin replied, "No, you keep it." Although Churchill did obtain Stalin's approval for a spheres-of-influence agreement between their two countries covering the Balkans, Roosevelt—though initially sympathetic—felt he could not approve of such an arrangement.

For several reasons, Roosevelt rejected both the model of a highly competitive balance-of-power system and the idea of minimizing its potential for conflict by creating spheres of influence. First of all, he doubted—and in this he was unquestionably right—that domestic public opinion, given its historic antipathy to the European balance of power, would agree to American participation. Besides, for Roosevelt to endorse or to participate in a spheres-of-influence agreement would have directly contradicted the principle of self-determination and other historic American ideals that he had written into the Atlantic Charter. This document had been issued by him and Churchill early during the war and the Soviet Union had later given it a qualified endorsement. The Atlantic Charter was the major statement of Allied war aims and a major means by which Roosevelt secured public support for an internationalist U.S. foreign policy. Having done so, he could not turn around and support postwar plans that violated those principles.

Furthermore, Roosevelt did not believe that a traditional balance-of-power system or spheres-of-influence arrangement would really eliminate competition among the major powers for very long. He thought any such arrangement would be unstable and that the world would soon become divided into two armed camps—a Western democratic one and a Soviet-led one. An arms race would ensue that would result, at best, in a dangerous armed truce; at worst it would lead to another world war. Roosevelt, one might say, foresaw the possibility of the Cold War unless some alternative could be devised.

The only alternative, as Roosevelt saw it, was a version of the balance-of-power system modeled on some aspects of the concert system established by the European powers in 1815 after defeating Napoleon. Roosevelt hoped to maintain the unity and cooperation of the Allies after the defeat of the totalitarian states. This was the option the president favored from an early stage during the war—he called it his "Great Design," and he persuaded Churchill and Stalin to cooperate in trying to bring it about.

Roosevelt's Great Design deserves closer attention. The president wanted to establish a postwar security system in which the United

States, Great Britain, and the Soviet Union—and, it was hoped, eventually also China—would form a consortium of overwhelming power. These major powers, forming an executive committee, would cooperate in meeting threats to the peace, from either the defeated powers or any other states. The four would have a monopoly of military power; all other states would be prevented from having military forces that could pose a serious threat to others. Quite appropriately, Roosevelt called his idea "the Four Policemen"—but notice that the concept would certainly have encroached on the principle of the sovereign equality of all states, great or small.

The Great Design also called for the United States, Britain, and Russia to work out mutually acceptable settlements of the important territorial issues and political problems in Europe. These would be reached through joint consultation and agreement, that is, through a system of collective rather than unilateral decision-making. Once again, this was reminiscent of the *modus operandi* of the old European concert system. (Roosevelt also hoped that the Russians would participate in arrangements to deal with trade, currency stabilization, and other economic problems.)

Whatever the merits of the president's design, the problem remained of winning public support for this kind of realism. It is worth noting that Roosevelt himself was most cautious about attempting to publicize his Four Policemen concept, largely because he felt it necessary, if he was to maintain a domestic consensus for an internationalist foreign policy, to blur the differences between his own plan and the desire of the idealists for a system of collective security based upon another, stronger League of Nations. The president spoke about his own plan with a number of influential opinion leaders; but when he launched a trial balloon in order to publicize the idea, in an interview with Forrest Davis that appeared in the *Saturday Evening Post* in April 1943, there was a sharply negative reaction. As a result, Roosevelt backed away from further efforts to educate public opinion in order to gain legitimacy for his Four Policemen concept.

Indeed, in the end, his sensitivity to public opinion weakened his originally strong opposition to a revival of the League of Nations. Despite his private view that the task of enforcing the peace would have to be left to the strongest powers, in order to avoid political trouble at home, Roosevelt yielded to the pressure of the vocal groups who were calling for the establishment before the war was over of the United Nations organization promised in the Moscow Declaration of October 1943. He went along when his secretary of state, Cordell Hull, gradually transformed the Four Policemen idea into what became the Security Council of the United Nations. The president consoled himself with the thought that what was critical was not the early establishment of that organization, or the precise format of the Security Council, but rather that the United States and the Soviet Union should preserve a friendly and cooperative relationship, and that they should settle all important issues between them outside the Security Council and work together to maintain the peace.

Roosevelt, as mentioned earlier, could not approve a spheres-of-influence arrangement in Europe. He feared Americans would perceive it as another example of how the cynical, immoral European powers periodically made secret arrangements to divide up the spoils at the expense of weaker states, and hence as a violation of the principle of national self-determination and independence. Such a development in American opinion, Roosevelt foresaw, could jeopardize his postwar plans right from the beginning. At the same time, however, he recognized that the Soviet Union's legitimate security needs in Eastern Europe would have to be satisfied. Since the Red army was occupying Eastern Europe and would likely move into Central Europe as well, the Soviet Union could do as it wished there in any case. The United States was not going to employ force or threats of force to prevent or dissuade the Soviets from creating friendly regimes and making territorial changes in Eastern Europe. This was understood and accepted even by those of Roosevelt's advisers who were most negative in their attitude toward Soviet communism.

From the standpoint of maintaining domestic support for his postwar policy, it was terribly important for Roosevelt that the Soviet Union define its security needs in Eastern Europe in *minimal* terms, and that it go about securing friendly regimes in Eastern Europe in ways that the United States and Britain could agree to and that would not flagrantly conflict with the principles of the Atlantic Charter. At stake for Roosevelt was the legitimacy of his entire plan for a postwar security system based on cooperating with the Soviet Union. If the American public saw Russian behavior in Eastern Europe as contradicting the principle of national self-determination and independence, it would create the image of an expansionist and untrustworthy Soviet Union.

Roosevelt hoped, perhaps somewhat naively, that the potential conflict between Soviet security requirements and the principles of the Atlantic Charter could be avoided or minimized. He attempted to persuade Stalin that the complete defeat and disarming of Germany and the arrangements the Allies were making to weaken and control postwar Germany would do more to guarantee Soviet security than would the imposition of tight-fisted Soviet control over Eastern Europe. He also tried to make Stalin understand the difficult problem that would face his administration if the Soviet Union imposed arrangements in Eastern Europe that flagrantly conflicted with the charter commitments. In effect, Roosevelt was pleading for Stalin to show self-restraint; he hoped that Stalin would cooperate at least to the extent of providing a "cosmetic" facade to the creation of pro-Soviet regimes in Poland and other Eastern European countries by going through the process of "free elections" and the like. And in fact Stalin was disposed to cooperate. Cosmetic solutions were devised several times. Thus, Roosevelt and most of his advisers thought they had achieved their goal at the Yalta Conference in February 1945. But their optimism was quickly shaken by new difficulties with the Russians over interpretation of the Yalta agreements regarding Poland. Within a few months of becoming president, Truman patched up this disagreement, but once the war with Japan was over, distrust of Soviet intentions mounted in Congress and among the public. Russian behavior in Eastern Europe was increasingly perceived as a harbinger of more ambitious expansionist aims, and it became difficult to arrest the drift toward the Cold War.

After this became a reality, many people felt that Roosevelt had been naive or foolish in believing that the Soviets would cooperate in the kind of international system he had desired. It is true that the exigencies and pressures of the wartime situation—the need to get along with the Russians in order to ensure the defeat of the enemy powers—had encouraged the president and others to develop a benign, optimistic image of the Soviet Union. But the naiveté that Roosevelt has been charged with was much more apparent after the failure of his hopes for postwar cooperation with the Russians than before. During the war itself, and even for some time after Roosevelt's death, many specialists on the Soviet Union (Charles Bohlen, for one) and other foreign policy experts were by no means sure that his policy would fail. Many of the beliefs, hopes, and expectations regarding the Soviets that appeared to support the president's Great Design enjoyed a considerable measure of plausibility and support; and even skeptics thought that Soviet leaders might cooperate out of self-interest. The generally successful wartime collaboration encouraged such hopes, and they were further reinforced by Roosevelt's assessment of Stalin's postwar intentions and the general endorsement he obtained from Stalin of the concept of a cooperative postwar security system.

It should be noted, further, that despite his generally optimistic personality and outlook, Roosevelt realized that his image of the Soviets might prove to be defective and that his hopes for postwar cooperation might eventually prove to be unfounded. He knew that he was taking a calculated risk, and he remained sensitive to any Soviet actions that threatened the success of his postwar plans. Roosevelt was also quick to undertake remedial measures to bring Stalin back into line whenever necessary.

Dissatisfaction with the way in which Roosevelt's policy was working out emerged quite early, even while he was still alive. At first and for some time, criticism focused not on the objectives of the Great Design for the postwar world but rather on his tactics and to a lesser extent his strategy. Roosevelt's "kid-gloves" treatment of the Russians was criticized as counterproductive by some advisers and officials, among them Averell Harriman, who was to become particularly influential with Truman.

The shift toward a Cold War policy cannot be explained, however, as some early revisionist historians have attempted, by attributing it to the difference between "good guy" Roosevelt and "bad guy" Truman. President Truman was at first genuinely committed to Roosevelt's policy of seeking Soviet collaboration, and he concluded only reluctantly that success was impossible. If it is true that, from an early stage, Truman decided to "get tough" with the Soviets, this was at the level of tactics; the "kid gloves" politeness was thought to be a failure, and the president was urged to be more direct and to engage in plain talk. Truman hoped that this change in tactics would improve communication and facilitate cooperation. He did not change the objective, which remained the same as Roosevelt's for some months to come. Indeed, Truman's move into the beliefs and policies of the Cold War was, as will be shown in the next chapter, a gradual process.

Bibliographical Essay

This chapter draws on a previous publication: Alexander L. George, "Domestic Constraints on Regime Change in U.S. Foreign Policy: The Need for

Policy Legitimacy," in *Change in the International System,* ed. O. R. Holsti, R. M. Siverson, and A. L. George (Boulder, Colorado, 1980). The concept of "policy legitimacy" is adapted from the stimulating article by B. Thomas Trout, "Rhetoric Revisited: Political Legitimation and the Cold War," *International Studies Quarterly* 19 (1975), 251–84.

The account of Roosevelt's plans for a postwar security system draws on a large number of secondary analyses, among them John Lewis Gaddis, *The United States and the Origins of the Cold War, 1941–1947* (New York, 1972); Willard Range, *Franklin D. Roosevelt's World Order* (Athens, 1959); Roland N. Stromberg, *Collective Security and American Foreign Policy* (New York, 1963); and Robert A. Divine, *Roosevelt and World War II* (Baltimore, 1969). On spheres of influence, see Daniel Yergin, *Shattered Peace* (Boston, 1977), p. 59.

Roosevelt's "Great Design" for after the war was conveyed by him in considerable detail in background interviews with a journalist, Forrest Davis; see "Roosevelt's World Blueprint," 10 April 1943; "What Really Happened at Teheran-I," 13 May 1944; and "What Really Happened at Teheran-II," 20 May 1944, in the *Saturday Evening Post.*

9
The Cold War
as International System

I

Much more serious than the initial Allied disagreements over Poland and Eastern Europe was the split that developed with the Soviet Union over occupation policies in Germany. In the face of deepening economic chaos in that country and the failure of repeated efforts to win Soviet adherence to joint measures to check it, President Truman felt compelled, in collaboration with the British and French governments, to restore the German economy in the Western occupation zones and eventually to take steps toward setting up a separate West German government. The Soviets reacted strongly to these developments, which they felt marked the beginning of a revival of German militarism. They imposed tighter controls over Eastern European countries occupied by their troops, ruthlessly eliminating potential political opponents and placing reliable Moscow-oriented Communists in power, and in February 1948 they dismantled the democratic government of Czechoslovakia and installed a puppet government of their own. Four months later, in a forcing play designed to disrupt the process of consolidation in West Germany, they imposed a blockade upon West Berlin, cutting off Western ground access to the city. In response, the Truman administration accelerated the efforts to strengthen Western Europe that had begun with the launching of the Marshall Plan for economic assistance in 1947, opened the negotiations that led to the establishment of the NATO alliance in 1949, and began serious discussion of the advisability of rearming the West Germans, whose manpower would be needed if NATO were to achieve a viable military capability.

The events of the period could be traced in much more detail, but enough has been said to illustrate the way in which a vicious cycle of action and reaction occurred in the relations between the West and the Soviet Union. Its effect was to initiate and escalate what came to be called the Cold War. Each side believed that it was behaving in a justifiably defensive manner in response to obstructionist and threatening behavior on the part of the other. The images Soviet and Western leaders held of each other hardened; each side perceived the other increasingly as harboring hostile intentions. This is not to say that the Cold War was caused merely by mutual distrust and misperception—its origins lie deeper than that, as has already been suggested, in the real and important conflicts of interest that existed between the two sides—but there is no doubt that they were seriously exacerbated by the psychological dynamics of conflict escalation.

False perception and psychological phenomena of this kind are, unfortunately, familiar in international relations, as they are in everyday life. Oliver Wendell Holmes once remarked that in any argument between two persons, six persons are involved: the two as they actually are, each of the two as he sees himself, and each of the two as he sees the other. No wonder, Holmes exclaimed, that the two talk past each other and become angry! In international affairs, the same sort of psychological multiplication process is apt to take place, with much the same effects.

At the end of the war, the dominant view of the Soviets held by American leaders was that they were pursuing limited objectives and were not embarked on an expansionist global policy. Soviet actions in Eastern Europe in 1945 and early 1946 were disturbing but not seriously damaging to U.S.–Soviet relations; and President Truman and many others in the United States were inclined to believe that even Russian behavior in Poland was explicable in terms of the Soviet Union's justifiable security needs. This view of Soviet intentions started to change for the worse, however, when the USSR began to bring strong pressure to bear upon the governments of Turkey and Iran and Greece, when Stalin revived the historic Russian demand for guaranteed passage through the Straits of Bosphorus, when he delayed removing his troops from northern Iran, and when Greek Communists, with outside help, engaged the government in civil war. These developments alarmed American officials. Perhaps erroneously, they believed that Stalin was supporting the Greek Communists, and they regarded this and the Soviet pressures on

Ankara and Teheran as efforts to extend control over areas that lay outside the range of legitimate Soviet security needs. Evidence of expansionist aims seemed further confirmed by Soviet obduracy over the German question, which has already been mentioned, and by the Czech coup of 1948 and the Berlin blockade.

The American image of the Soviet Union steadily darkened during the first postwar years, and the American attitude toward Soviet-American relations became increasingly alarmist. As early as February 1946, in a now-famous telegram from the U.S. embassy in Moscow, George F. Kennan attributed to Soviet leaders a compulsion to probe any "soft spot" in neighboring countries in an effort to discover whether they could advance Soviet power and influence at an acceptable risk. He suggested that if their probes met with firm opposition, they would withdraw, that they could in fact be contained by firmness and by a Western effort to reduce potential "soft spots" in strategically important parts of the non-Communist world. This theory and the arguments with which Kennan supported it assumed increasing credibility in the minds of policy makers in Washington, although it was not until 1949 that the concept of containment was fully translated into new foreign policy commitments and specific policies.

Containment was implemented relatively slowly in part because Truman could not easily obtain congressional and public support for replacing Roosevelt's policy with a tougher approach to the Soviets. There was still much friendly feeling toward the Soviet Union, a carryover from the wartime admiration of the Red Army's resistance to the Nazis. Many people had an uneasy feeling that Truman was betraying Roosevelt's ideals and blundering into a dangerous conflict with the Russians that was really avoidable. Henry Wallace, a former vice president under Roosevelt and secretary of commerce under Truman, was so outspoken in his criticism of the drift toward the Cold War that the president finally dismissed him. The Truman administration was, indeed, so hard-pressed to find congressional and public support for its major containment policies that it found it necessary deliberately to exaggerate the Soviet threat. This later led revisionist historians to criticize the president for having initiated the process that led to the anti-Communist hysteria and the phenomenon of McCarthyism in the late forties and early fifties.

In his memoirs, Dean Acheson, Truman's secretary of state, admits that he consciously denigrated Soviet intentions and portrayed Russia as aiming at world domination in order to gain approval for the president's policies. With a touch of sarcasm toward those who criticized him for oversimplification, Acheson argues that this is sometimes necessary in order to conduct foreign policy effectively in a democracy. "The task of a public officer seeking to explain and gain support for a major policy is not that of a writer of a doctoral thesis. . . . If we made our points clearer than truth, we did not differ from most other educators and could hardly do otherwise."

II

Cold War is a descriptive term that was generally adopted in the late forties to characterize the hostile relationship that developed between the West and the Soviet Union. While loosely employed, the term had an exceedingly important connotation: it called attention to the fact that, however acute their rivalry and conflict, the two sides were pursuing it by means short of another war and that, it was hoped, they would continue to do so. As some commentators noted, however bad the Cold War was, it was better than a hot one, and few would deny that the Cold War was an acceptable substitute for a thermonuclear war with the Russians, if that indeed were the only alternative.

For our purposes we need to go beyond the meaning and significance of the term to consider whether and in what sense this prolonged period of acute and dangerous hostility between the West and the Soviet Union can be regarded as an "international system." We will argue here that the state of Western-Soviet relations during the period of the Cold War, while certainly not an ideal international system, did indeed constitute a primitive one in which certain restraints and norms were present and adhered to. This can be seen if we recall the three prerequisites of an effective international system discussed in the introduction—agreed aims, appropriate structure, and commonly accepted modalities—and if we employ them to analyze the state of Western-Soviet relations during the Cold War.

The Western powers and the Soviet Union had only one major objective in common: the prevention of World War III. Although the Cold War was an extremely conflict-laden type of international system, this single common objective provided an effective counterweight to the many differences and rivalry between the two sides. The desire to avoid a thermonuclear war exerted so powerful an effect on Soviet-American relations because it was coupled with mutual fears that *any* shooting war between American and Soviet forces, no matter at how modest a level initially, could escalate. As a result, both sides gave highest priority to managing effectively the confrontations and crises that developed during the period.

For the reasons indicated, cooperation in "crisis management" quickly became one of the most important means by which the international system achieved its aim and thereby maintained itself. The other important means, employed by each side against its opponent, was deterrence. Some efforts were made to develop other means for regulating rivalry and promoting some cooperation, but they were far less effective so long as the Cold War persisted in its acute form up to, and including, the Cuban missile crisis. These less effective means included efforts to develop arms control; crisis prevention (as against crisis management); accommodation (that is, use of negotiation to arrive at agreements to settle or moderate certain conflicts of interest); and economic cooperation.

As relations between the Western powers and the Soviet Union deteriorated in the late forties a bipolar structuring of the international arena emerged. Each of the two superpowers moved quickly to organize and dominate a worldwide alliance system. There were not enough major powers of relatively equal strength to make possible the reemergence of a multipolar balance-of-power system. (Besides, as noted in the preceding chapter, Roosevelt and others thought that such a system would be neither feasible nor desirable.) Each superpower dominated its weaker allies and attempted to keep its alliances under tight control. There was very little flexibility in making alliances or, for the weaker states, in switching them. The United States and the Soviet Union viewed any possible loss of an ally, even a small one, with great apprehension for fear of its effects on the rest of their alliances. Not all states, it is true, were absorbed into one of the two systems; there were some neutrals, buffer states, and neutralized countries. But it is no exaggeration to say that two powerful hegemonic alliance systems emerged, giving a bipolar structure to the international system that went well beyond that which had characterized the two-alliance variant of the European balance-of-power system at the turn of the century.

III

American foreign policy under successive administrations, beginning with Truman's, pursued two basic objectives: first, to prevent the further spread of international communism (and, if possible, to roll it back); second, to avoid World War III. High priority was attached to both of these objectives, but there was a built-in conflict between them that emerged sharply in certain situations. On these occasions, U.S. policy makers experienced a serious dilemma and the necessity to choose a preferred objective.

Thus, for the United States to adopt assertive policies to stop the spread of communism or roll it back in certain situations was perceived as increasing the risk of a thermonuclear war. On the other hand, there were situations in which, if the United States gave priority to avoiding the risk of war, it might well have to accept the possibility of further spread of communism or its consolidation. During the Cold War, American policy makers, in Democratic and Republican administrations alike, attempted to cope with this dilemmna by considering whether in a given situation the *balance of power* between the Soviet bloc and the free world alliance was at stake. If a Communist success in a certain area was regarded as something that would critically weaken the ability of the non-Communist world to contain the further spread of communism, then the balance of power was threatened. American policy makers then felt inclined to do what they could—always, though, without triggering World War III—to prevent that particular Communist success, even though to do so meant accepting some danger of war. This was the case, for example, in the Berlin crises of 1948, 1958–1959, and 1961.

If, however, a Russian success in a given area would not seriously undermine the ability of the Western alliance to contain the future spread of communism, then American policy makers were generally inclined not to react in ways that would risk World War III. This alternative way of dealing with the policy dilemma is illustrated by Eisenhower's unwillingness to intervene when East Germans rebelled against the Communist regime in 1953. Eisenhower stood aloof once again, despite all the talk from his administration of "liberation" of Eastern Europe, during the Hungarian revolution in 1956 when the new Nagy government took itself out of the Warsaw Pact and called for help from the West. Far from attempting to deter Soviet military intervention in Hungary, Eisenhower was concerned lest Khrushchev, if kept uncertain about U.S. intentions, might become rattled and somehow trigger a general war. Accordingly, Eisenhower told Dulles to find a way of assuring Khrushchev that while the United States did not approve of the Soviet intervention, it would not interfere.

It may be noted that this use of the balance-of-power criterion in making critical foreign policy decisions during the Cold War was similar to its employment by the major powers during the old European balance-of-power system. One difference, however, was that the fear of a thermonuclear holocaust, which had no counterpart in the old system, discouraged both the United States and the Soviet Union from resorting to war as a way of preventing an undesired change in the existing balance of power if to do so would result in a direct clash between American and Russian forces.

IV

There were nevertheless moments of extreme danger when the balance between the antagonists threatened to collapse. This possibility was very real from 1955 to 1963, when Nikita Khrushchev was secretary of the Communist party, for during his tenure of office the requirements of the balance between the superpowers and the unity of the Communist bloc came into conflict.

A new and aggressive spirit became apparent in Soviet policy as soon as Khrushchev's authority was consolidated. This was not the result of temperament, but basically a reaction to the uncertainty and lack of direction that affected all aspects of policy in the two years following the death of Josef Stalin in March 1953. The change in attitude was almost made necessary by new factors at work in the world of communism that appeared to threaten Soviet ascendancy. One of these was growing restiveness on the part of the satellite states of Eastern Europe. Dissatisfaction became so serious in East Germany in June 1953 that Soviet tanks had to be sent in to restore order, and it was reflected in growing discontent in Poland and Hungary. A second was the challenge of the People's Republic of China, whose leaders remained true to Stalinist principles at a time when Soviet leaders seemed to be turning away from them, and who criticized the Soviet Politburo for not being aggressive enough in its relations with the West. Moscow was worried by this disaffection, and when Khrushchev emerged as the strongest force in Soviet politics in 1955, he seems to have concluded that a hard line might calm the criticism in Peking and contain the trouble in the satellite capitals.

Khrushchev inaugurated his policy with energy and a variety of techniques that testified to Soviet versatility and aroused some trepidation in the West. He rapidly built up the strength of the Warsaw Pact, the Soviet counterpart to NATO, while simultaneously making much of the recent acquisition of the hydrogen bomb and publicizing new Soviet jet planes as the best in the world. Throughout 1955 and 1956, the air was blue with Soviet boasting about their superiority in conventional forces, nuclear weapons, and delivery systems. At the same time, Khrushchev began a massive program of economic aid and technical assistance to countries like Egypt, Iran, Afghanistan, Cambodia, Laos, North Vietnam, and Burma—a "ruble diplomacy," as a Princeton economist dubbed it, that made many people in the West believe that by winning the Third World, communism might well succeed in burying the West, as Khrushchev in his cheerful manner said it was going to do.

In launching his policy, the Soviet leader was greatly aided by the misguided Anglo-French-Israeli attack upon the Suez Canal in 1956. The provocation suffered by the British and French at the hands of the Egyptian leader Nasser had doubtless been great, but this could not disguise the fact that the operation both violated the principles of the United Nations and was characterized by deliberate deceit toward their American ally. It was also marked by a degree of military bungling on the French and English side that made a quick success impossible. The result was a fiasco, which Khrushchev exploited with great skill. The Suez crisis diverted the attention of the West from Poland, where there were clashes between the workers and the police, and from the open revolt against the satellite government in Hungary that erupted in October. Khrushchev was able to contain the Polish troubles by means of economic and political concessions and to suppress the fighting in Budapest brutally without having to worry about Western intervention. More important, the crisis shook NATO to its foundations and gave enemies of the West the pleasure of seeing the United States collaborating with the Soviet Union in haling its own allies before the bench of justice in the UN.

Khrushchev seems to have believed that the Western alliance was dissolving and that a few doses of what came to be called atomic blackmail would complete the process. He was doubtless encouraged by the panicky Western reaction to the launching of the first Soviet intercontinental missiles and particularly of the space satellites, an event that led many Western opinion makers to talk as if the Soviets were on the point of winning scientific and hence military mastery of the world. In any event, he now began to make covert threats to NATO members like the one delivered to the British government in December 1957, complaining about the stationing of American bombers with nuclear weapons in

Britain and expressing surprise that a country so vulnerable by its geographical position and so defenseless "against modern weapons" should permit this. Six months later, in July 1958, when NATO troops landed in Lebanon to shore up a disintegrating situation there, he sent an official warning to the American and British governments, reminding them of the atomic strength of the Soviet Union; and he was reported to have said privately that, if American forces made a move toward Iraq, where a pro-Western government had just been overthrown, he would see that the United States Sixth Fleet was reduced to a mass of molten steel.

All of this was designed to weaken the will and unity of the West. The real offensive was opened on 27 November 1958, when the Soviet Union sent a note to the Western powers reopening the German question. At inordinate length but with considerable vehemence, it pointed out that although thirteen years had passed since the end of the war, the German situation was still unregulated. It was now time for the West to recognize that two German states had come into existence and also to end the anomalous position of West Berlin, an enclave in the territory of East Germany still occupied by Western troops. The Soviet Union was willing to allow West Berlin to exist as a free demilitarized city, but not in its present condition. It proposed, for the next six months, to make no changes in Western access to the city; but if no agreement was reached in that period, it would sign a separate treaty with the German Democratic Republic (DDR) and relinquish its occupation rights and powers. The Western powers would then have to negotiate with the DDR over their rights of access, and the DDR, as a sovereign state, would have the right to make whatever conditions it desired.

This note came to be called the Berlin ultimatum, although it was very long for an ultimatum and although time was to show that it wasn't as ultimative as it sounded. It appears to have been motivated in part by the desire to eliminate the escape hatch that West Berlin provided for people in the DDR, who were fleeing to the West in ever-larger numbers, and in part by the fear that the United States might decide to supply the new German army with nuclear weapons (the note suggested that a nuclear-free and neutralized Germany might be considered as a possible solution to the German question). It is possible that Soviet-Chinese relations provided another motive. The Chinese were becoming increasingly independent of Soviet control and were now well on their way to acquiring nuclear weapons. Khrushchev may have hoped that a spectacular victory in the German question would enable him to persuade Peking to

122

recognize his leadership and to give up nuclear weapons as too expensive.

Success, however, depended on a Western cave-in, and this did not materialize. The United States government was aware that Khrushchev was hoping to celebrate his expected triumph at a summit conference. It showed no signs of being interested in such a meeting and, indeed, made clear in its reply to the Soviet note that "the United States could not embark on discussions with the Soviet Union . . . under menace or ultimatum." This put the ball fairly in Khrushchev's court, and he was obviously uncertain of his next step. When the British government suggested that some preliminary meetings of the foreign ministers might lay the basis for a summit meeting, he angrily agreed and, in doing so, tacitly dropped the six-month limit set by his original note. In fact, the whole momentum of the Soviet offensive slowed down. Foreign ministers' meetings and Chinese distractions took up a good part of 1959, and the Soviet leader became increasingly frustrated and at the same time increasingly anxious for a summit meeting that would give him some kind of a success. But when he finally secured President Eisenhower's assent to such a meeting and a date in May 1960 was set, an American U-2 observation plane was shot down deep inside Soviet territory, and the president immediately assumed responsibility for it. Khrushchev was forced to abort the summit.

He did not, however, as some feared at the time, carry out the threats made in the note of November 1958. It was not until May 1961, when a new president was in office and American policy was in disarray as a result of the fiasco at the Bay of Pigs, that Khrushchev felt the time propitious for a new drive toward his German objective. In his meeting with President Kennedy in Vienna, he delivered a new ultimatum. Unless a viable treaty could be negotiated by December, the Soviet Union would sign a separate treaty with the DDR. West Berlin could continue as a free city, but if Western troops were stationed there the Soviets would have to have the same privilege, and access rights would have to be negotiated with the DDR. This time Khrushchev was not seeking to appease the Chinese, who had by now gone their own way, or to persuade the West to agree to a neutral Germany. His eyes were concentrated on Berlin alone, where the number of refugees had reached flood proportions (thirty thousand fugitives from East Germany were to pass through West Berlin in July) and was bringing East Germany to the verge of collapse. Hence Khrushchev's new urgency and the menacing tone of his conversation with the president.

Kennedy was shaken but not cowed. He left Khrushchev with the words "It will be a cold winter" and, instead of bolting into negotiations, he returned home to push the armaments program that had started in February. Some classes of reservists were called up, an earnest of American intentions that elicited floods of new threats from Moscow and a military response of the same nature.

The crunch came in August 1961, and it took an unexpected turn, for on the thirteenth of that month the East German government began the construction of a wall along the boundary between the two halves of Berlin, cutting off mutual access. While this action did not come as a complete surprise to Western authorities, it was not President Kennedy's policy to oppose such a development, and nothing was done to prevent the construction of the wall. This in itself was a success for Khrushchev. He had stopped the drain on the energies of East Germany, he had forced the West to condone a violation of the Potsdam Agreement, and he had greatly increased the number of people in the West who felt that West Berlin could not be protected.

It may be that Khrushchev believed this too, for he kept up the pressure after 13 August. Two weeks after the wall went up, he invited C. L. Sulzberger of the *New York Times* to come to Moscow for an interview, and there asked him to take a private message to President Kennedy stating that he "would not be loath to establishing some sort of contact with him to find a means, without damaging the prestige of the United States, to reach a settlement. But on the basis of a peace treaty . . . and a free city of Berlin." He added that if it came to a showdown, Britain, France, and Italy, which he described as "figuratively speaking, hostages of us," could not be expected to support the United States. When Sulzberger repeated the substance of this conversation to U.S. Ambassador Llewellyn Thompson, Thompson said, "This means war! All of us are going to be dead!" The president's reaction, when Sulzberger saw him at the beginning of October, was almost equally gloomy.

Why Khrushchev did not make good on his threat is by no means clear. It may be that an incident in Berlin at the end of October had a sobering effect upon him. On 25 October, when two American officers in civilian clothes were denied access to East Berlin because they refused to show their papers to East German guards, General Lucius D. Clay, whom Kennedy had sent to Berlin to hearten the shaken population, decided on a show of force to dramatize Allied rights in all parts of the city and sent an armored contingent to Checkpoint Charlie on the wall. The Soviet commander in East Berlin responded in kind (thus proving that the Soviets were *not* ready to relinquish their rights in the city to the East Germans). It was a frightening confrontation, for behind the tanks stood all the nuclear force in the world, and it may have persuaded Khrushchev to change his strategy.

For that is what he did. Instead of making a dead set at Berlin, he chose the indirect approach. He decided to try something in Cuba, hoping apparently to win Berlin as a byproduct of an American humiliation in the Caribbean. That was a grave miscalculation, and it not only put an end to Khrushchev's German hopes but, very soon after the liquidation of the Cuban missile crisis, to his political career as well.

V

Khrushchev's secret deployment of some forty-two medium- and between twenty-four and thirty-two intermediate-range ballistic missiles in Cuba during the late summer and early fall of 1962 brought the superpowers to the brink of thermonuclear war. Unforeseen and unwanted by either side, the tense confrontation was resolved through careful crisis management by both Washington and Moscow. Foregoing an immediate air strike against the missile sites but threatening to make one if necessary, Kennedy undertook a naval blockade of Cuba instead. In the end, the president's use of the strategy of coercive diplomacy to persuade Khrushchev to remove the missiles proved effective. The crisis ended with a hastily arranged quid pro quo in which Khrushchev agreed to take out his missiles in return for a conditional pledge by Kennedy not to invade Cuba in the future.

The crisis was the culmination of the long-standing practice of employing strategic nuclear threats as an instrument of Cold War policy. It does not require much imagination to understand the frustration Kremlin leaders must have felt during the years of American strategic superiority when Washington relied implicitly or explicitly on the threat of "massive retaliation" or to appreciate Moscow's determination to neutralize this American advantage and, if possible, to turn the practice of strategic threats against its makers. We have already noted Khrushchev's efforts to do so in the 1950s as the Soviet Union acquired medium-range nuclear missiles that targeted Western Europe.

Americans were uncertain of the pace at which the Soviets were acquiring long-range strategic nuclear missiles that could reach the United States. Their anxiety provided Khrushchev with an all-too tempting opportunity to neutralize and reverse the Cold War advantage such capabilities had given the United States. The Soviet leader increasingly played on American and Western fears that the Soviets were outdistancing the United States in nuclear rocket capabilities and creating a "missile gap" in their favor. From 1957 to 1962, the Soviet government engaged in a deliberate, systematic, and sustained campaign of deception, issuing grossly exaggerated claims regarding the production and deployment of ICBMs. Khrushchev put these claims to use to invigorate his assertive foreign policy; this was, as we have seen, nowhere more evident and threatening than in the Berlin crises.

Finally, when Khrushchev continued pressure against Berlin after erecting the Berlin Wall, Kennedy publicly disclosed in the early autumn of 1962 that new intelligence conclusively laid to rest the missile gap fear and thoroughly discredited the Soviet leader's bombastic strategic claims. The fact of the matter was that the Soviets had deployed very few ICBMs and that the United States would retain a clear strategic advantage for at least several more years. Kennedy's disclosure did, indeed, quickly defuse the Berlin crisis and put an end to Khrushchev's claims and threats. But it also left the Soviet leader in a difficult position. Not only did he suffer the embarrassment of having his deception unmasked, but he was forced to abandon temporarily the vigorous thrust of his foreign policy until he developed a real strategic capability. There is also reason to believe that his relations with the Chinese Communist leaders were further strained by the affair.

Under considerable psychological and political pressure to recoup this situation and to reinvigorate his foreign policy, Khrushchev succumbed to the temptation to secure a "quick fix" of the strategic imbalance by deploying medium- and intermediate-range missiles, of which he had plenty, in Cuba. The story of the belated discovery of the missile sites in Cuba and the deliberations of Kennedy's Executive Committee, which led to a decision to seek the removal of the missiles by means of a naval blockade coupled with coercive diplomacy, is well-known and need not be repeated here. Instead, let us turn to a discussion of the impact of this brush with thermonuclear war on the Cold War policies of the two superpowers.

VI

The Cuban missile crisis may well be regarded as one of the turning points of recent history, for it facilitated a transition from the era of the acute Cold War to a search for a less dangerous and more viable international system. Thus, one may speak of the missile crisis as having had a "catalytic" effect. That international crisis can have positive results in improving relations between previously antagonistic states is often overlooked in our natural preoccupation with and concern over the danger of war created by tense diplomatic confrontations. But crises often offer statesmen opportunities for constructive change. It is interesting to recall in this connection that the Chinese character for "crisis" has two meanings: the first is the same as the standard meaning of the word in English—that is, threat or danger to important values. The second connotation, however, is something quite different—not "threat" but "opportunity." There is something quite profound in the double meaning which, in the context of international relations, suggests that a crisis can loosen things up; it can lead policy makers to question and to revise if not totally discard some of the old beliefs and policies that led to the impasse; it can make them willing to strike out in new directions.

The Cuban missile crisis had precisely this kind of effect on Khrushchev and Kennedy. Samuel Johnson once remarked to Boswell that nothing concentrates the mind so well as the prospect of being hanged in a fortnight. It is not an exaggeration to say that the horror of the missile crisis was a kind of shock therapy for both leaders. It brought to a head long-standing dissatisfactions with the Cold War on both sides and strengthened their determination to move away from its worst aspects toward a better alternative.

As had happened more than once in history when two countries stepped back from the brink of a war that neither wanted, Kennedy and Khrushchev moved quickly once the crisis was over to bring about a détente in their relations. More important than that, they realized that henceforth they would have to cooperate more effectively to prevent their disagreements from again leading to tense confrontations in which only skill in crisis management could prevent a thermonuclear holocaust. They realized that their two countries would have to go beyond a mere relaxation of tensions to try to reach genuine accommodations and resolution of at least some of their disagreements.

This new spirit and determination led within nine months to the signing of the limited test ban treaty—the first major arms control agreement between the two nuclear superpowers. Even more significant perhaps was the fact that the American image of the Soviet opponent began to undergo significant modification. Kennedy and other American leaders began to view the Soviet Union as a *limited adversary* rather than as a total enemy, as they had during the height of the Cold War. This change

127

was conveyed dramatically by Kennedy in a moving speech at the American University in Washington, D.C., on 10 June 1963, in which he called upon the American people to reexamine their views on the Cold War. He warned his listeners not to take "a distorted and desperate view of the other side, not to see conflicts as inevitable," and not to regard "accommodation as impossible and communication as nothing more than an exchange of threats." He went on to say about the Soviet Union that "no government or social system is so evil that its people must be considered as lacking in virtue."

The containment policy had rested on a particular image of Soviet expansionist behavior, one that attributed malevolence as well as ruthless efficiency to Soviet rulers in their tendency to seize every opportunity to advance their control in the world arena. This devil image gradually gave way as experience showed the Soviet Union was not only often quite cautious in trying to expand its influence but also often unsuccessful. Moreover, it became clear to American policy makers and informed opinion that the rulers and peoples of many new countries—in Africa, Asia, the Middle East—were no pushovers when it came to dealing with the Soviet Union. Time and again, they demonstrated that they were quite capable of accepting Russian (or Chinese) economic, military, and diplomatic support without losing in the process either their desire or ability to remain independent. As evidence of this accumulated, many American leaders began gradually to modify another of the fundamental premises on which Cold War policy had rested, namely, the belief that the different parts of the world were tightly coupled, that the international system was highly unstable, and that the United States had to prevent a setback in any area—no matter how remote or unimportant in and of itself—for fear of its effects elsewhere.

Similarly, another basic Cold War belief was also slowly modified, namely, the belief that the threat of Communist aggression and the instability of the international system required the United States to organize and control the countries comprising the free world. Instead, Americans—and the Russians too—have become gradually more willing to accept the fact that the bipolar structure of the world is once again giving way to a looser, multipolar system.

VII

The changing U.S. image of the Soviet Union associated with the era of détente that replaced the acute Cold War has had important implications for American foreign policy. As we have seen, both Kennedy and Khrushchev emerged from the Cuban missile crisis determined to try to deal with at least some of the conflicts of interest and unsettled issues that had divided the two countries since the end of World War II. Their new attitude and new approach to these problems took three forms; in fact, there was a rather clear tacit agreement as to how to proceed.

First, and most important, Kennedy and Khrushchev in effect agreed that they would try to *decouple,* that is, separate as much as possible, the various issues on which the two countries disagreed. Instead of attempting to resolve *all* of their many disagreements at one time—a task which they knew would be impossible—Kennedy and Khrushchev (and their successors as well) agreed to try to deal with the easier issues first and one by one. (In addition to the partial test ban treaty, there were a variety of other agreements thereafter, such as the "hot line," the non-nuclear proliferation agreement, and the Antarctic Treaty.)

Second, they also agreed to a kind of truce in the Cold War. They agreed to stop arguing about, and thereby exacerbating, their long-standing conflicts over important problems in Central Europe and Eastern Europe, the arms control inspection issue, Cuba, or the issue of U.S. overseas bases near the Soviet Union. Since such issues were evidently too difficult for early solution, Kennedy and Khrushchev in effect agreed to continue to disagree on these matters but—and this is the important thing—without engaging, as they had in the Cold War, in extreme vituperation and political warfare against each other. The two leaders hoped that these more difficult problems might be dealt with later on. With the passage of time, circumstances might change for the better; their mutual suspicions might gradually give way to greater trust and a better working relationship; and then it would be easier to deal with the remaining conflicts.

Third, both sides also agreed to try to strengthen and improve their relationship by cooperating in cultural, technical, and scientific areas and to give more attention to efforts at arms control.

As a result, the Cuban missile crisis led to an important modification of the Cold War. The importance of the shift away from the Cold War image of the Soviet Union for American foreign policy in the détente era that followed can be traced very succinctly (see Figure 5).

Unfortunately, the Cold War persisted in acute form with Communist China for the rest of the 1960s and contributed to the embroilment of the United States in Vietnam. But when a breakthrough to détente with Peking occurred early in Nixon's administration, the rigidity of Ameri-

U.S. Cold War Beliefs	U.S. Beliefs in Post–Cold War Era
1. S.U. an implacably hostile enemy; U.S.–S.U. conflict is zero-sum →	S.U. a limited adversary; U.S.–S.U. conflict is non-zero-sum
2. International system is highly polarized around U.S. and S.U. (bipolar system) →	International system is moving toward multipolarity
3. International system is highly unstable; its different parts are tightly coupled so that a setback for U.S. in one area will have destabilizing effects elsewhere (i.e., "row of dominoes" danger) →	System has gained somewhat increased stability; therefore greater possibility of localizing conflict and delimiting consequences of local setbacks

Consequences of These Cold War Beliefs for U.S. Foreign Policy	*Consequences of These Post–Cold War Beliefs for U.S. Foreign Policy*
1. Exaggerated value placed on importance of distant peripheral areas for overall U.S. security; proliferation of U.S. commitments throughout the world →	Greater differentiation among U.S. commitments; some are more important than others
2. Tendency to believe that all U.S. commitments are equally important and interdependent (failure to honor any one commitment will reduce credibility of all other commitments) →	Greater flexibility in U.S. policies toward third countries
3. Heavy reliance on deterrence strategy; postpone negotiations on outstanding issues with Soviets until U.S. develops "positions of strength"; avoid making concessions (danger of appeasement) →	Greater reliance on negotiation and conciliation to forestall (if not also to resolve) conflicts of interests from erupting into dangerous confrontations
4. Conflicts of interest with S.U. are indivisible (everything is connected with everything else) →	Willingness to decouple the various outstanding issues; i.e., seek agreement on single issues on which an accord with S.U. is possible while setting aside other issues on which agreement is not yet possible

Figure 5

can containment policy toward China softened and was replaced by a mutual if also cautious desire on the part of both countries to search for accommodation, to emphasize areas of agreement and cooperation, and of course to defer issues such as the future of Taiwan, which could not be solved immediately.

Bibliographical Essay

The development of the Cold War generated a great deal of political controversy that quickly spilled over into scholarly studies and has not yet run its course. Herbert Feis provided an early "orthodox" interpretation of the origins and development of the Cold War. Among the many important criticisms of the orthodox viewpoint are the "revisionist" interpretations provided by William A. Williams, Walter LaFeber, Gabriel and Joyce Kolko, Barton J. Bernstein, Lloyd C. Gardner, and Thomas G. Paterson. The present chapter views the origins and development of the Cold War in analytical terms rather than with any intention to attribute responsibility to either of the superpowers.

There are many useful histories of the Cold War, written mostly from the standpoint of American policy. See, for example, Walter LaFeber, *America, Russia, and the Cold War, 1945–1967,* 4th ed. (New York, 1980); Seyom Brown, *The Faces of Power: Constancy and Change in United States Foreign Policy from Truman to Johnson* (New York, 1968); John Spanier, *American Foreign Policy Since World War II,* 7th ed. (New York, 1977); Daniel Yergin, *Shattered Peace* (Boston, 1977); Stephen E. Ambrose, *Rise to Globalism* (New York, 1976); and Thomas G. Paterson, *On Every Front: The Making of the Cold War* (New York, 1979). To his earlier study, *The United States and the Origins of the Cold War, 1941–1947* (New York, 1972), John Lewis Gaddis has recently added a detailed analysis of the different versions of the U.S. containment policy in the years since 1946, *Strategies of Containment* (New York, 1982). The emphasis placed on deterrence strategy in American Cold War policy is examined in detail in Alexander L. George and Richard Smoke, *Deterrence in American Foreign Policy: Theory and Practice* (New York, 1974), which also includes twelve detailed case studies of Cold War crises.

10
Détente and Its Problems

I

To use the term *détente* to describe the far-reaching objectives Nixon and Kissinger set for themselves in their policy toward the Soviet Union is to stretch it beyond its original sense. The word *détente* has a very limited meaning in traditional diplomacy. It refers merely to a "relaxation of tensions." But as indicated in the preceding chapter, in the period that followed the Cuban missile crisis, Kennedy and Khrushchev quickly moved beyond a relaxation of tensions to seek accommodation on at least some of the issues that had divided the two countries. President Nixon and his chief adviser, Henry Kissinger, were even more ambitious in their objectives. They wanted to build the foundation—or at least an important part of the foundation—for *a new international system*. This was to be based upon a more constructive relationship with the Soviet Union that would replace the acutely hostile relationship of the Cold War. Nixon and Kissinger wanted to introduce a new set of norms, rules of behavior, and procedures that both superpowers would adopt and follow in regulating their future rivalry. Therefore, to apply the term *détente* to Nixon's policy toward the Soviet Union is to include in it three developments in international relations which were usually distinguished in traditional diplomacy: relaxation of tensions; accommodation; and the creation of a new international system.

The development of a new international system, of course, could only be a long-range objective. The relatively tight bipolar structure of the Cold War era was giving way to a looser multipolar arrangement. Nixon and Kissinger hoped to influence this development in order to create a new multipolar balance of power of some kind. They were intrigued by the possibility of recreating some features of the old classical balance-of-power system, but they recognized that some of its essential conditions were not present. A more realistic and immediate possibility that appealed to them was the development of a special tripolar relationship involving the United States, the Soviet Union, and the People's Republic of China (PRC). Such a tripolar structure could not be easily transformed into a classical five-power balance-of-power system by adding Japan and Western Europe. Although Japan was a major industrial state, its emergence as a military power could not be viewed as either desirable or feasible. On the other hand, Western Europe already possessed considerable military capabilities, but these were for the most part tied to those of the United States through NATO. Furthermore, Western European political integration would have to proceed much further before the region could play the role of a single international actor in a balance-of-power system.

Under the circumstances, Nixon and Kissinger moved in another direction. The United States would establish a measure of friendly relations with both of the arch rivals, the Soviet Union and the PRC, thereby obtaining some leverage with each that could be advantageous to American foreign policy. The threat posed to the world position of the United States by the policies of either of these two Communist powers would be moderated by engaging each of them in a process of détente and accommodation. In addition, the United States could hope to reduce further the potential threat to its interests emanating from either and to induce their cooperation with American policy by using its unique middle position in the triangular relationship to tilt or threaten to tilt in favor of one or the other.

This is not to say that Nixon and Kissinger viewed the Soviet Union in the same terms as they did the PRC. The major potential threat to American security and worldwide interests was perceived to emerge from the growing power of the Soviet Union. China was not, and would not for many years become, a superpower on a par with the United States and Russia. And so the major reason behind Nixon's opening to China was to obtain leverage for developing a more satisfactory relationship with the Soviet Union. The threat of positive U.S. relations with China was to be part of the "stick" which, coupled with various inducements held out to the Soviet Union, would draw it into a more constructive relationship in which the Soviets would restrain themselves from employing their growing power to make advances at the expense of U.S. interests and those of its allies.

II

What, then, was the strategy that Nixon and Kissinger employed to achieve this new kind of constructive relationship with the Soviet Union? It had four major components, including an element of "appeasement," a term that they carefully avoided.

The first of these called for acknowledging that the Soviet Union was entitled to the same status as a superpower that the United States enjoyed. The Soviets had long wanted to achieve equality of status with the United States; and President Nixon now recognized this, rhetorically and in various symbolic ways, for example, in summit meetings with them. But while such recognition granted the Russians the position and the prestige that they desired, it left undefined what the new status was to mean in practice. The Soviet leaders proceeded to interpret political equality with the United States as meaning that they were justified in pursuing a more assertive foreign policy; American leaders and public opinion in the United States came to view this as a violation of the basis of the détente.

A second element in the Nixon strategy was a conditional willingness to legitimize the present division of Europe in a formal diplomatic manner. A cardinal objective of Soviet policy since 1945, such legitimation was bound to be difficult for American public opinion to accept, and for a long time it had been rejected by American policy makers. The sticking point for the United States was West Germany, where the United States had found it expedient during the Eisenhower administration to insist that reunification was inevitable and desirable and to support the so-called Hallstein Doctrine maintained by the Adenauer government. This doctrine, in the name of reunification, denied any legitimacy to the German Democratic Republic, and under it the West Germans refused to have dealings with any state that extended recognition to the East German regime. There was always an element of disingenuousness about American support of reunification (and to the lip service paid by the Soviet Union to the same principle). In reality, neither the United States nor the Soviet Union would have tolerated a fusion of the two Germanies unless it was sure that the new united nation would end up on its side in the Cold War struggle. But neither said this openly for fear of arousing German nationalist feeling, and the United States avoided any statements that might be taken to suggest that the present division of Europe was acceptable.

By the end of the sixties, however, the situation was different than it had been in the days of Eisenhower and Adenauer, and in Germany the Hallstein Doctrine had lost most of its credibility. When the Social Democratic party came to power in the Federal Republic in 1969, the new chancellor, Willy Brandt, initiated a policy aimed at closer relations with all the states of Eastern Europe (which led in 1970–1971 to new treaties between the Federal Republic and the Soviet Union and Po- land) and an accommodation with the East German regime or, as Brandt put it, an agreement about "practical questions . . . that could alleviate the life of people in divided Germany." The United States government was not at first enthusiastic about Brandt's *Ostpolitik,* but it placed no obstacles in his way, while at the same time insisting that any new treaty between the two Germanies should be preceded by a new Four Power Agreement which guaranteed the rights of the Western powers in West Berlin. Such a treaty was negotiated and signed in August 1971 and was followed, in December 1972, by a new Basic Treaty between the two German states.

Brandt's policy created an atmosphere that encouraged détente and removed a barrier that had inhibited Soviet-American discussions of the division of Europe. President Nixon could now, in pursuance of his own détente goals, agree in principle to discuss the long-standing Soviet desire for a formal document, signed by all European countries as well as the United States, that would recognize existing borders and thereby confirm the Soviets' dominant influence in Eastern Europe and the German Democratic Republic. The discussion was eventually to lead to the Hel- sinki Agreement, signed at the 1975 Conference on Security and Co- operation in Europe, which, as we shall see in a later chapter, obliged the signatories to refrain from using force in order to change frontiers, to facilitate greater movement of peoples and ideas between the two parts of Europe, and to observe and promote the human rights of popu- lations (although the clauses dealing with this last subject were suffi- ciently abstract as to cause much later controversy).

The third element in Nixon's détente strategy called for the United States to enter into a variety of formal agreements with the Soviet Union that would further mutual cooperation and make available economic and technical assistance. The rationale was that the Soviets would acquire from the agreements a strong stake in maintaining a constructive relationship with the West. These agreements and the prospect of additional ones were supposed to create a "web of incentives" that would motivate Soviet leaders to behave with restraint and to moderate their tendency to "probe the soft spots" and seek gains in third areas at the expense of the United States. It was hoped that concessions to the Soviets in the economic and commercial sphere would "spill over" to improve Soviet-American political relations. With this in mind, the two countries concluded a major grain deal in July 1972 and a trade agreement in October.

This was merely the beginning of an impressive record of successful negotiation between America and Russia. It is interesting to note that of the 105 treaties and other agreements that the United States has made with the Soviet Union since 1933, when President Roosevelt extended diplomatic recognition to the USSR, 58, or over half the number, were concluded between 1969 and 1974; and 41 of those were signed between May 1972 and May 1974.

The fourth element of the strategy was especially important to Nixon and Kissinger, for in a sense it was the long-range payoff that they hoped would follow from the other three. This was the development of a set of new norms and rules for the competition between the two superpowers. The détente policy placed great emphasis upon working out strategic arms control limitations and other types of agreements to reduce the danger of a new world war. Two agreements in particular illustrate the nature of the Nixon-Kissinger effort to develop norms for sustaining a new constructive relationship with the Soviets. At the summit meeting in Moscow in May 1972, Nixon and Brezhnev signed an agreement called "Basic Principles of Relations," which Kissinger, in a press conference immediately after the summit, described as defining new rules of conduct for both sides. In this document, the two powers agreed to prevent the development of situations that might dangerously exacerbate their relations; they were to do their utmost to avoid military confrontations and the outbreak of nuclear war; and they further agreed that henceforth they would "exercise mutual restraint in their relations and [would] be prepared to negotiate and settle differences by peaceful means." Negotiations on outstanding issues were to be conducted in a spirit of reciprocity, mutual accommodation, and mutual benefit—that is, neither side would seek one-sided advantages but work to achieve compromises.

A second agreement emerged one year later, in June 1973, at the summit meeting in Washington between Nixon and Brezhnev. On that occasion, they signed an "Agreement on the Prevention of Nuclear War," the content of which repeated some of the provisions of the earlier agreement, emphasizing the need to consult on an urgent basis in situations raising the threat of nuclear war.

The détente policy progressed reasonably well until late 1973, but the expectation that the Soviets would act with greater restraint in their foreign policy was not fully realized. In particular, it was the failure of the Soviet Union to prevent its client states, Egypt and Syria, from initiating war against Israel in October 1973, and the ample military supplies it provided them to conduct that war, that seemed inconsistent with these agreements. In part, the trouble was that the agreements of 1972 and 1973 defining rules of conduct were highly general and inevitably vague. But perhaps the problem was a more fundamental one. The Russians defined détente (or "peaceful coexistence," as they often preferred to call it) differently than did the Americans. To them, détente did not require that they cease support for "progressive" and "liberation" movements in the Third World.

For these and other reasons, the momentum of the détente process slowed down. American support for it declined after the Arab-Israeli war of October 1973, and even more after Soviet assistance to Cuban military intervention in Angola in 1975. As for the Russians, they resented the efforts of Senator Henry Jackson and others to make the Senate's approval of increased U.S. trade with the Soviet Union contingent on its willingness to allow an increase in the emigration of Jews.

After Gerald Ford became president, he was not able to do much to rejuvenate détente, although he did try to move toward a SALT-II agreement by entering into the interim Vladivostok agreement with Secretary Brezhnev. The president also tried for a time to defend détente against the increasingly vocal domestic criticism. During the contest for the Republican presidential nomination in 1976, however, Governor Ronald Reagan made détente the focus of his effective attack upon the Ford administration. Ford eventually thought it prudent to announce that he was dropping the term from his political vocabulary and that henceforth his policy would be called "Peace through strength."

The questions raised about détente in the United States were varied and insistent. Had there been a basic modification of Soviet ambitions and intentions? Was the Soviet Union using détente merely to gain an advantage over the United States? Were the Soviets winning more concrete benefits from the policy than the United States? Were the agreements that had been concluded, or were pending, lopsided? Should the United States put pressure upon the Soviet Union in order to force a liberalization of its policies at home and in Eastern Europe in return for any benefits it derived from détente? Was the Soviet Union taking advantage of détente and the SALT negotiations to surpass the United States in strategic capabilities and to increase its influence in the Third World at its expense and that of its allies?

The necessity of securing legitimacy for long-range foreign policy had, as we have seen, preoccupied Franklin Delano Roosevelt as he made plans for his postwar security system. The problem was well-known to Kissinger and had been touched on in his incisive analysis of the eventual failure of the policies of Castlereagh and Metternich in the post-Napoleonic years. "The acid test of a policy," he had written there, "is its ability to obtain domestic support. This has two aspects: the problem of legitimizing a policy within the government apparatus . . . ; and that of harmonizing it with the national experience." Ironically, Kissinger's détente policy was to encounter, and fail to pass, the same acid test.

Why was the Nixon-Kissinger policy so difficult to legitimize, and why did such legitimacy as it acquired erode so badly? The fact is that the Nixon administration succeeded in creating neither normative nor cognitive legitimacy for its policy. The former it sought to achieve by arguing that détente was necessary in order to prevent a third world war; but although everyone agreed with this objective, few persons thought that the danger was so imminent as to require the United States to bestow important concessions and benefits on the Soviet Union. The cognitive legitimacy of the détente policy was somewhat stronger but, as we shall note, it rested on premises that were increasingly questioned by important elements of the public.

It was more difficult to win public legitimacy for détente than it was for the Cold War, a fact that becomes understandable if one compares the objectives and strategy of the latter with those of the former. During the Cold War, the American objective was simply to contain the Soviet Union until the force of Soviet ideology had spent itself; and to achieve that goal, the United States had relied almost exclusively on deterrent strategy. The détente policy, on the other hand, was more ambitious and more complicated. It aimed at persuading the Russians to mend their ways and to enter into a new constructive relationship with the United

States. To this end, Nixon and Kissinger made use of conciliation and accommodation as well as deterrence—employing, in other words, the carrot-and-stick approach.

The Cold War was also easier to legitimize than détente because it rested upon a simple negative stereotype, the devil image of the Soviet leaders. The détente policy imposed on the government the more difficult task of getting people to view the Soviets as a limited adversary, neither friend nor foe but something in between. The nature of that something was not easy for many people to understand.

The idea of bestowing benefits on the Soviet Union in order to create a web of incentives may have been a good strategy in principle. But in practice, as implemented by Nixon and Kissinger, it aroused increasing concern in the United States. Critics of détente argued that Nixon and Kissinger were giving Moscow many tangible benefits in return for vague promises of good behavior and pious hopes that the Soviets would be induced to limit their ambitions and meddling in third areas. To be fair, this criticism overlooked the fact that the policy did not rely solely on rewards and bribes. Nixon and Kissinger stood ready whenever necessary to reinforce the incentives with measures of the kind associated with traditional containment policy and deterrence strategy. There were a number of occasions when the Nixon-Ford administration reacted firmly, as in response to the Syrian tank invasion of Jordan in September 1970, in the Indian-Pakistani conflict in December 1971, in the case of the possible Soviet submarine base being built in Cuba in late 1970, in the Arab-Israeli War of 1973, and in Angola in 1975.

At first glance, the strategy of rewards and punishments employed by Nixon and Kissinger bears a striking resemblance to what psychologists call "behavior modification." Several questions can be raised about the validity of the carrot-and-stick approach which the Nixon administration used to induce Soviet leaders to modify certain of their foreign policy behaviors and to resocialize them into patterns more consistent with the objectives and modalities of a new regime in American-Soviet relations. In the first place, the effort to resocialize Russian leaders appears to have violated two basic principles of behavior modification. This technique works best when the therapist singles out specific items of behavior that are to be replaced. Nixon and Kissinger, however, described the behavior to be eliminated from Soviet foreign policy in general terms and also used generalities to identify the hoped-for changes (as in the general principles contained in the Agreement on Basic Principles). Second, the timing of the reward to the subject may be critical in influencing him to modify a particular behavior in the desired direction. In behavior modification, a reward is supposed to come after the subject behaves as desired; the function of the reward is to reinforce the new behavior. But Kissinger often gave benefits to the Soviets beforehand, as a bribe.

In any case, whether or not Kissinger applied behavior modification principles correctly in his strategy, he was trying to accomplish something very ambitious, and this raises another question regarding the feasibility of the strategy. Some critics of détente contend that Kissinger overestimated the leverage available to him for accomplishing so difficult an objective. Perhaps it was overly optimistic to believe—and dangerous to encourage the American public to believe—that the web of incentives and penalties available to the Nixon administration would suffice to create a stake in détente so valuable to Soviet leaders that they would give up opportunities to extend their influence in the world. Interestingly, this was among the aspects of détente policy that was most sharply challenged by critics who charged that Kissinger had "oversold" détente.

The legitimacy of détente strategy also suffered because its implementation confused the public. It was perhaps predictable that many members of Congress and the public would fail to grasp the subtleties of a strategy that combined threats and penalties with efforts at conciliation and bestowal of benefits. If the Soviets behaved so badly on some occasions as to warrant threats or penalties, why then reward them in other respects? Should there not be more explicit quid pro quos whereby the Soviets would give up something concrete for each benefit they received? Criticism of this kind not only eroded the legitimacy of détente policy; it brought increasing pressure to bear on the administration to abandon, or at least make significant changes in, the strategy employed. The domestic politics of détente within the United States, magnified by Reagan's unexpectedly strong challenge in the Republican presidential primaries of 1976, forced the Ford administration to drive harder bargains with Moscow and to apply more exacting standards for acceptable agreements. And this constraint applied equally to President Carter's approach to the Soviets.

But perhaps the worst consequence of the way in which Kissinger applied the complex strategy of conciliation and deterrence was that it tended over time to polarize American public opinion. Both the anti-Soviet hawks and the antiwar doves became dissatisfied with the détente policy for different reasons, and with the passage of time they attracted growing public and congressional support. Thus, when Kissinger bestowed benefits on the Soviets, the hawks protested. And whenever Kissinger confronted the Soviets—as in the Arab-Israeli War of 1973 and over Angola—the doves sounded the alarm that the administration was about to start down the slippery slope into another Vietnam.

As a result, Kissinger found himself caught in an increasingly severe whiplash between hawk and dove critics of his policy. Those members of Congress and the public who did understand and sympathize with the intricate logic and rationale of the dual strategy, and who made up the centrist constituency whose support Kissinger so badly needed to maintain the momentum of the détente process, were gradually neutralized by the growing strength and louder voices of the others.

Kissinger's difficulties with his hawkish critics were compounded by other adverse developments which he was unable to control and to which he sometimes inadvertently contributed. These developments included the Soviet leaders' repeated insistence—in part no doubt to quiet the opposition to détente from their own hawks—that détente did not mean that they were betraying their Communist ideology and would forgo support for "national liberation" movements. American hawks interpreted such Soviet statements as exposing the fallacy of the premises underlying Kissinger's hopes for a new constructive relationship with the Soviets. Soviet insistence on defining détente in terms of their own concept of "peaceful coexistence" also revived concern over their intentions. And this concern over the premises of détente policy was much strengthened by the continuing buildup of Soviet strategic and other military capabilities coupled with the failure of the SALT negotiations to limit the arms race. Thus, the question of Soviet intentions, which has periodically agitated American foreign policy experts and public opinion since the end of World War II, emerged once again as a highly salient and controversial issue.

For all of these reasons, the legitimacy of the détente policy eroded badly, a development which enormously strengthened the various domestic constraints associated with democratic control of foreign policy. As a result, Kissinger's ability to conduct a coherent, effective policy on behalf of the laudable objectives of détente was shattered well before the end of the Ford administration. With the deterioration of the stable domestic consensus on détente, Kissinger could no longer count on minimal public acceptance of the variety of actions that implementation of his strategy required. Not only was he no longer given the benefit of the doubt, but some of his activities engendered suspicion that they were designed to serve his personal interests or the political fortunes of his administration. His secretive approach to decision-making and his diplomatic style did much, of course, to enhance the distrust.

No doubt Kissinger believed that his détente policy fell victim to the public's impatience for quick results and its unreasonable demands for frequent concrete indications that the policy was succeeding. It is certainly true that given the ambitious character of the détente objective, which required resocialization of Soviet leaders and their acceptance of the norms of a new regime in U.S.–Soviet relations, it was only reasonable to assume that considerable time and repeated efforts would be needed to accomplish that goal, and that, before Kissinger's behavior modification therapy took full effect, the Soviets would occasionally misbehave. But if so, how could one evaluate whether the strategy was succeeding? Kissinger's critics pointed to instances of Soviet meddling in third areas as evidence of the failure and unsound character of the strategy. Kissinger himself could only retort that Soviet behavior would have been perhaps even more aggressive and the confrontations more dangerous had it not been for détente. Neither side could prove its case, but the critics may have pronounced the strategy of inducing self-restraint in Soviet foreign policy a failure prematurely.

In his own defense, Kissinger quite properly complained that Congress had weakened both the carrot and the stick available to him for influencing the Soviets. First, it had undermined the possibility of increased trade and credits which the Nixon administration had held out to the Russians, and then, in response to Vietnam, it had gradually hamstrung the president's ability to generate credible threats of force to cope with Soviet-backed encroachments in third areas. Furthermore, Watergate and the ensuing downfall of Nixon crippled the energies of the United States in many ways, ruining the domestic credibility of the government, destroying its authority with other governments, and paralyzing key instrumentalities of foreign affairs. The generalized antigovernment feeling aroused in the United States militated against an effective foreign policy. The American people seemed tired of diplomacy in the grand manner, weary of the acrobatics of balance-of-power maneuvers, and eager for a simpler style that would accord with recognizably American values. This kind of policy—Wilsonian rather than Hamiltonian, let alone Bismarckian or Metternichian—Jimmy Carter promised to give them.

IV

The major challenges facing the Carter administration were to reinvigorate public support for a liberal internationalist foreign policy, to overcome national self-doubts as to whether the United States still had a constructive role to play in world affairs, and to counter the drift toward neoisolationism. This Carter attempted to do by downgrading the priority Nixon and Ford had given to nourishing the connection with the Soviet Union and by giving greater priority to developing relations with other countries and to "world order" objectives. To be sure, Carter did not eschew reconstructing détente on a more realistic and sober basis, but he and his advisers gave little evidence of having any well-developed, coherent design or consistent strategy for doing so. The linchpin of Carter's policy toward the Soviet Union—indeed its only clear and consistent objective—was the conclusion of SALT-II. But whereas the Ford administration had brought negotiations for a new SALT agreement close to completion, Carter and his secretary of state, Cyrus Vance, immediately set back the SALT process by launching a new proposal for reduction of strategic weapons in such a manner as to shock and dismay Soviet leaders. To the distrust and hostility already aroused in the Kremlin by Carter's earlier proclamation of a "human rights" campaign, which Russian leaders understandably perceived as the initiation of political warfare against their system, was now added the grim possibility that the new administration would complicate, if not prevent, the achievement of a second SALT agreement, to which the Soviets attached great importance.

The search for a way of reviving and reorienting the détente relationship never recovered from these initial blows. Negotiation of the SALT-II treaty was finally completed and the document signed by the president and Secretary Brezhnev at a summit meeting in mid-1979. But by then public and congressional support had seriously weakened, and Senate ratification was probably dealt a fatal blow by the unexpected discovery of a Soviet combat brigade in Cuba. President Carter's attempt to take a strong line and demand the removal of the brigade or a change in its status was ineffectual, and the Soviet rejection of his demands caused a further waning of public confidence in the administration's competence and a hardening of opposition to the ratification of SALT-II. A few months later, when the Soviets sent troops into Afghanistan, the fate of the treaty was sealed.

Even before Afghanistan, the president had been shifting to a harder stance toward the Soviet Union, partly in an effort to save the arms control agreement, partly to strengthen his chances of reelection. His prospects of the latter were not improved by his denunciation of, and reprisals against, the Soviets for their Afghan action and were seriously damaged by his failure to secure the release of United States embassy personnel who were taken hostage by Iranian militants and by the increasingly unsatisfactory state of the economy.

Ronald Reagan's campaign for the presidency struck sensitive chords with the electorate's dissatisfaction with Carter's foreign and domestic policies. During the four years of the Carter administration, the public had become increasingly concerned over the continued Soviet military buildup and apprehensive that the United States was slipping into a position of dangerous military inferiority vis-à-vis the Soviet Union. Reagan called for a substantial increase in U.S. military capabilities and a stronger diplomatic posture toward the Soviets and, upon being elected, he moved quickly in this direction. While few observers expected that U.S.–Soviet relations would regress to the acute hostility of the Cold War of the late forties and fifties, the possibility of dangerous new confrontations could not be excluded. Whether, when, and in what form the process of détente would be resumed could not be easily or confidently foreseen during the first year of Reagan's administration.

Bibliographical Essay

This chapter draws on a previous publication: Alexander L. George, "Domestic Constraints on Regime Change in U.S. Foreign Policy: The Need for Policy Legitimacy," in *Change in the International System,* ed. O. R. Holsti, R. M. Siverson, and A. L. George (Boulder, Colorado, 1980). In addition to numerous contemporary statements by President Richard Nixon and Henry Kissinger articulating and defending their détente policy, valuable retrospective materials are provided in their memoirs. Kissinger's *White House Years* (Boston, 1979) and *Years of Upheaval* (Boston, 1982) are particularly valuable; see also R. M. Nixon, *RN: The Memoirs of Richard Nixon* (New York, 1978).

A useful collection of documents, addresses, and other official statements on the détente policy is provided by Robert J. Pranger, ed., *Détente and Defense* (Washington, D.C., 1976). Among the many published commentaries and critical appraisals of the détente policy, the most useful for present purposes is Stanley Hoffmann, *Primacy or World Order* (New York, 1978), pp. 33–100, which contains observations regarding the difficulty of gaining legitimacy for the détente policy similar to those offered in the present chapter. Important data and analyses are presented in Dan Caldwell, *American-Soviet Relations from 1947 to the Nixon-Kissinger Grand Design* (Westport, Conn., 1981). See also Stephen A. Garrett, "Nixonian Foreign Policy: A New Balance of Power—or a Revived Concert?" *Polity*, 8 (1976), 389–421; Robert Osgood, ed., *America and the World*, II, *Retreat from Empire? The First Nixon Administration* (Baltimore, 1973).

Analyses and appraisals of President Carter's policy toward the Soviet Union are to be found in contemporary journals such as *Foreign Affairs, Foreign Policy,* and *Orbis.*

Secretary of State Kissinger attempted to deal with the questions posed about détente in the United States in a major statement before the Senate Foreign Relations Committee on 19 September 1974. See "Detente with the Soviet Union: The Reality of Competition and the Imperative of Cooperation," repr. in Henry A. Kissinger, *American Foreign Policy*, 3rd ed. (New York, 1977), pp. 141–76.

11

The Evolving International System

It is perhaps appropriate at this time to ask how one is to describe the present condition of the international system. Certainly there is very little resemblance between today's constellation of world forces and the eighteenth- and nineteenth-century systems that have been described above, and the new variants of older models that attracted fleeting attention in the seventies have come to nothing. There was a time when the staff of *Le Monde* wrote learned articles about the new principle of tripolarity, but not much of that is heard any longer, and President Nixon's belief that we would all be better off if, as seemed entirely possible, we had "a strong healthy United States, Europe, Soviet Union, China, Japan, each balancing the other, not playing one against the other, an even balance," can be seen in retrospect as nothing more than an example of that postsummit euphoria which, in more realistic moments, he deplored.

Anyone who remembers the factors that contributed to the defeat of the Nixon-Kissinger détente policy and who is attentive to the rhetoric coming out of Washington in the first year of the Reagan administration would be inclined to regard the present state of affairs as a return to the early conditions of the Cold War era, a reversion to an essentially bipolar system characterized by the rivalry and antagonism of the two superpowers and their respective blocs of allies. Yet it is not the practice of history to repeat itself; the effect of change is generally stronger than that of continuity; and alliance solidarity is by no means what it was thirty years ago. In Europe, which despite the intermittently troubling

146

crises in the Third World remains strategically the most important arena of confrontation between the superpowers, there are indications that the two alliance systems are in the first stages of dissolution; if this continues, the effects upon the whole system of international relations could be profound.

I

To understand what is happening in Europe, we must start with the fact that while the détente process of the seventies did not live up to the expectations of the Soviet Union and was eventually abandoned by the American public as a dangerous mistake, it appeared to Europeans to have been, with all of its limitations, successful. It had brought a decided alleviation of restrictions upon travel between East and West; it had provided new opportunities for economic collaboration and cultural exchange; and, above all, it had greatly reduced the number of dangerous crises on the approaches to Berlin and other frontiers and had allayed the always-present fear that a major East-West conflict, in which Europe would be the battlefield, would erupt. The resultant relaxation—or as it was called in Germany, *Entspannung,* a word that conveys the feeling of being relieved of a burden—made Europeans on both sides of the Iron Curtain feel that at long last, life was perhaps returning to what it once had been and should be.

This mood was shattered by the Soviet occupation of Afghanistan in 1980 and by the intemperate and ill-considered reaction of the United States government, which led to an abrupt termination of normal communication between the superpowers. The impact upon their European allies was immediate and totally at variance with earlier behavior. In his interesting book *Das Ende des ideologischen Zeitalters,* Peter Bender has written:

> The crisis that erupted as a result of Afghanistan was different from all comparable cases earlier: it was the first East-West conflict that did not strengthen the alliances but divided them. Since the origins of NATO and the Warsaw Pact, nothing united each of the alliances so quickly and effectively as a conflict with the other "camp." . . . For the first time . . . this mechanism failed to function, and on both sides. Over the Soviet occupation of Afghanistan only the Americans and Russians came into conflict: the Europeans from the Bug to the Atlantic distanced themselves from their super-powers. . . . It is true that they assured them of their

147

indestructible "solidarity," but their political energy was concentrated on keeping the crisis far from their own continent. At times, Washington, and perhaps Moscow too, seemed to have no less trouble with its allies than with its antagonist.

In German politics, an anomaly became apparent: at a time when the Soviet-American relationship was more troubled than it had been in a long time, the relationship between the Federal and Democratic republics was closer than it had been since the founding of the two states.

In the months that followed, this new tendency became increasingly evident. In Western Europe, criticism of American policy assumed a sharper edge in Carter's last months and the opening stages of the Reagan administration. There had never, of course, been a dearth of carping: throughout the period of his presidency, Charles de Gaulle had endeavored to persuade the European governments that the United States could not be relied upon as a serious partner, and in 1975, Henry Kissinger had complained about European hostility. But what had earlier been a fretfulness on the part of governments over American failures to consult with them or the American tendency to treat them as secondary powers was now reinforced by a strong popular unease about the direction of American policy. This was particularly so after the new U.S. administration indicated that it intended to place strong emphasis upon rearmament in order to correct imputed Soviet superiorities and began to press its NATO allies on the question of stationing new nuclear weapons (cruise missiles and middle-range Pershing 2 rockets) in Europe. President Reagan's actions and the tone of his speeches—his call for a national crusade to restore the greatness of America and his immoderate accusations of Soviet perfidy—aroused the liveliest kind of alarm among the European allies. Commentators abroad were bitterly critical of the new belligerence, pointing out that American dismissal of détente as a kind of moral flabbiness was an expression of inability to understand the working of international politics or to remember that most wars were caused not by appeasement but by heedlessness and lack of reflection, coupled with the fear of losing prestige. They cited with approval the words of the chancellor of the Federal Republic of Germany, Helmuth Schmidt: "We can afford no gestures of strength and no doughty demonstrations of steadfastness. We've had a noseful of that sort of thing!"

More significant was the sudden marked growth of the antinuclear movement in Europe. This coalition of left-wing socialists, militant Christians, pacifists, environmental protectionists, members of alternative and extraparliamentary groups, and indiscriminate activists had greater popular resonance than anything since the unilateral nuclear disarmament movement in Britain and the antirearmament agitations in West Germany in the fifties. In May 1980, there was a massive demonstration in Bremen on the occasion of a Grand Tattoo celebrating the swearing in of Bundeswehr recruits and the twenty-fifth anniversary of NATO, and before it was over 257 policemen and 50 demonstrators had been injured in bloody clashes. In April 1981, 25,000 demonstrators gathered in Bonn during the annual meeting of NATO ministers, and in May 40,000 gathered there to protest the stationing of new Pershing missiles in West Germany. Similar agitations took place in Belgium, Denmark, and Norway; and in Holland elections in May made antinuclear forces the strongest faction in the Dutch parliament. NATO strategists considered this the greatest blow to the alliance since France withdrew its forces in 1966. It was feared that the "Dutch sickness" might spread, forcing the rescinding of the decision to emplace the new rockets and eventually leading to the paralysis, if not the dismantling, of the treaty organization.

All of this might have been a source of satisfaction to the Soviet government if it had not had troubles of its own to contend with. The time had long gone by when ideology was enough to give solidarity to the Eastern European bloc. Although there had not, in the intervening years, been a defection as spectacular as that of Yugoslavia in 1948, there had been many signs of restiveness under Soviet control and sporadic outbursts of more determined and violent protest like those in East Germany in 1953, Hungary in 1956, and Czechoslovakia in 1968. The onset of new economic troubles in Poland in 1979 soon led, not for the first time, to a major challenge to Soviet overlordship. Russia was obviously reluctant to use the kind of repression that it had resorted to in the fifties and sixties, since it was becoming apparent that even in the German Democratic Republic, generally regarded as the most reliable of the satellites, there was a strong current of resentment against what a secret manifesto published in the West in January 1978 called "the red popes of the Kremlin."

The new Polish crisis, indeed, signified a crisis of the Communist system. As Bender has written, it was one more sign that "the political East had lost what formerly distinguished it from the rest of the world, its ideology. This motivated no longer; it merely legitimized. The faith of the revolutionaries had rigidified into the dogma of the functionaries," who all too often were characterized only by heavy-handedness, indifference to local conditions, and stupidity. During the period of détente, the states of the Eastern bloc had made rapid progress toward becoming normal states, and they began to want to have regular relations with other states, regardless of ideological labels. They had learned that such relations would bring them advantages that were denied to them when they lived in ideological isolation. And, like their Western neighbors, they feared the consequences of the power politics of the Soviet Union and its adventurism in the Third World.

The new bipolarity that followed the failure of the Soviet-American experiment with détente was not, therefore, as monolithic as the superpowers would have desired. Both NATO and the Warsaw Pact were threatened by a lack of enthusiasm for their goals and their very existence, and on the popular level this was reflected in strong resentment against continued subordination to the United States and the Soviet Union. Among intellectuals, there was a welling of up interest in the "Europeanization of Europe." The possibility of a neutralized Europe, or at least a nuclear-free zone comprising the two Germanies and perhaps immediately adjoining states, became the subject of lively discussion, as did the idea of a European defense community to protect détente, in which the ties between the members would become stronger than their connections with the superpowers, and there would be no need of NATO and the Warsaw Pact. There were many ideas, and most of them, in the context of contemporary realities, were doubtless impractical. But common to them all was the desire to free Europeans from their vulnerability to the requirements of the new and dangerous rivalry between the Soviet Union and the United States. In the last months of 1981, that sentiment was becoming stronger rather than weaker, and there was little doubt that if it continued, it could not help but affect the nature of the international system, and not necessarily for the worse.

II

Related to these developments and reinforcing them is another trend that may have a substantial impact upon the future direction of European, Third World, and other members of the international community. This is the phenomenon of "complex interdependence" between states and peoples, particularly in the economic sphere, but extending increasingly also into life-essential ecological and biospheric systems. The growth of interdependence provides incentives for cooperation among states and, at least potentially, imposes constraints on some of the traditional forms of competition and rivalry.

The growth of complex interdependence and the changes associated with it are causing important modifications of traditional "realist" premises regarding the essential characteristics of international systems and politics. Thus, the long-standing assumption that states are the dominant actors in world politics has been challenged by the growth in numbers and strength of nongovernmental actors such as multinational firms engaging in international transactions more or less independently of governments. The related "realist" assumption that states act as coherent units in international relations is also being substantially modified in view of the fact that subunits of different national governments tend increasingly to interact directly with each other on specific matters engaging their specialized responsibilities, sometimes with little direction or control by their own governmental leaders. This has been true, for example, of aspects of the development of relations between the two Germanies since the early seventies.

Another traditional realist assumption called into question is the long-standing belief that the "high politics" of military security dominates the "low politics" of economic and social concerns. Nonmilitary issues—for, example, international monetary policies, problems of trade, and commodity prices—have assumed greater importance in interstate relations to the point that the hierarchy of issues for a country's foreign policy is not always dominated by questions of national security defined in military terms.

The traditional realist assumption that force is a usable and effective instrument of foreign policy also needs considerable qualification, especially as regards the major powers. There is increasing evidence of the declining efficiency of military power and threats of force as means for settling conflicts between superpowers, and not merely because nuclear weapons have limited use for everyday diplomacy. The superpowers, in turn, may feel new constraints against the use of force as an instrument of policy against lesser powers. Middle-rank and "weak" states, however, obtaining increasing access to conventional weapons, continue to make considerable—some would say growing—use of military force in efforts to achieve their foreign policy objectives.

As the relevance and utility of force as a means of settling conflicts of interest declines, the distribution of nonmilitary forms of power and influence among states within specific issue areas becomes important. In other words, military power is less fungible across different issues than

151

it used to be. Attempts by strong states to employ their military superiority as leverage to obtain better outcomes in specialized nonmilitary issue areas such as fisheries and prices for oil or coffee are becoming less effective and are less often resorted to.

III

All this will doubtless influence the future structure of the international system and will encourage the creation of modalities to manage the overlapping interests of its members. One notes that progress in structuring and managing relations among states often proceeds in an ad-hoc, issue-specific way. Some problems of mutual interest have been dealt with by setting up formal international organizations, for example, the World Health Organization, the International Postal Union, and, more recently, the International Atomic Agency. In addition, states directly interested in a particular problem adopt a variety of looser, less formalized arrangements. Such arrangements or *regimes,* as they are often called, typically include a set of procedures and substantive rules worked out by the interested parties to regulate their relationship in a given issue area. Since World War II, specific regimes have been developed to guide states and nongovernmental actors in a wide variety of issue areas including aid to underdeveloped countries, environmental protection, fisheries conservation, regulation of multinational corporations, international meteorological coordination, and food, shipping, telecommunications, and monetary policy, and, of course, regulation of trade. Regimes vary in the formality, comprehensiveness, scope, and effectiveness of the arrangements made.

The increasing use by states of regimes to structure and order their relations is one of the most interesting and hopeful developments in contemporary world politics. While the creation of a viable world government continues to be infeasible, regimes can provide some of the functions of world government. In creating a regime, the interested parties in effect are exercising a *legislative* function. Regime formation and operation is a partial substitute for a central world government which, were it to exist, would be expected to legislate and administer such arrangements for dealing with specific problems.

One can hope that with the proliferation of regimes and a continuation of the trend toward complex interdependence, we can move to a more comprehensive structure that will cut across the major groupings of states and subsystems and eventually provide some kind of more closely knit international community. We can also hope that if such a development gathers momentum, the network of constructive relationships into which states are drawn and the mutual benefits they derive from their participation will dampen the potential for conflict in those of their competitive relationships that remain inadequately managed.

While this encouraging prospect has some basis in identifiable trends and untapped opportunities present in the world today, further progress in this direction will be at best slow and uncertain. The development of building blocs for a more viable, stable, and peaceful world order is certain to progress quite unevenly within and among the various regional groupings of developed and underdeveloped states, for conflicts of interest not only run across regional lines, in the form, for example, of "North-South" disputes over financial and material resources or contests between the oil-producing lands of the Middle East and their Western customers, but also affect intraregional relations, causing differences between Common Market members on agricultural policy, dividing Arab states with respect to their attitude toward Israel, and causing rivalries and clashes between African states or those of South and Southeast Asia. The world system will continue to be plagued by dangerous crises, by war and threats of war. This reality has important implications for the study and conduct of international relations, and some of these will claim our attention in the second part of this book.

Bibliographical Essay

A useful discussion of emerging patterns in contemporary world politics is provided in Seyom Brown, *New Forces in World Politics* (Washington, D.C., 1974). For developments in political-economic relations in the various subsystems, see Joan Edelman Spero, *The Politics of International Economic Relations* (New York, 1977). On recent developments in Europe, see Peter Becker, *Das Ende des ideologischen Zeitalters: Die Europäisierung Europas* (Berlin, 1981); on the secret manifesto from the German Democratic Republic, "Das Manifest der ersten organisierten Opposition in der DDR," *Der Spiegel,* 1 (1978), 21–24 and 2 (1978), 26–30; and on the European antinuclear movement, "Pazifismus '81: 'Selig sind die Friedfertigen,' " *Der Spiegel,* 25 (1981). The emergent phenomenon of complex interdependence and its implications are analyzed in Robert O. Keohane and Joseph S. Nye, *Power and Interdependence: World Politics in Transition* (Boston, 1977).

II
Maintaining the System:
Problems of Force and Diplomacy

12

Negotiation

During the course of the last several centuries, both the international and domestic contexts of diplomacy have, in ways described in earlier chapters, changed dramatically, and technological advances in communications and transportation have altered its modalities. Even so, its chief instrument, negotiation, has essentially remained much the same. Indeed, by focusing on the fundamental characteristics of negotiation, we can identify the elements of both continuity and change in the efforts that states have made throughout the modern period to deal with conflicting interests and to promote their mutual interests.

Prerequisites for Negotiation

Fred C. Iklé has written that whatever the context or the substantive issue, "two elements must normally be present for negotiation to take place: there must be both common interests and issues of conflict. Without common interests there is nothing to negotiate for; without conflict there is nothing to negotiate about." This observation poses useful questions to ask in studying efforts to initiate negotiation, for it throws a sharp light upon a basic reason for success or failure. Even so, it should be noted that because of other considerations, governments sometimes enter into negotiations even when they are aware that there is no shared basis of interest. For example, a refusal to enter into negotiations sometimes may be politically damaging at home or present an image of inflexibility abroad that may harm relations with allies and neutrals. Then, too, even though the interested parties do not expect or want an agreement, they may nonetheless begin talks with the goal of gaining propaganda advantages at the expense of the opponent. Negotiations undertaken exclusively or largely for side effects of this kind have become more frequent with the rise of public opinion and mass media during the course of the diplomatic revolution. Finally, one or both sides may invite diplomatic exchanges simply in order to size up the opponent, to acquire information, to mislead and deceive him, or to "maintain contact" and use talk as a substitute for the possibility of violent action. Such reasons for negotiations, even when there is no expectation or desire for an agreement, may also be more common in the modern era than during the nineteenth century.

As these observations suggest, the objectives and goals of negotiation are by no means limited to seeking an agreement. Upon closer examination, therefore, the two prerequisites for negotiation emphasized by Iklé should be understood to apply to the initiation of serious negotiations aimed at achieving an agreement of some kind. It should also be noted that the two sides may not share the same view regarding the prospects of a negotiated agreement. Sometimes, and again perhaps this is more common in the modern era, when one side is more eager than the other to commence negotiations, its adversary may attempt to exact concessions as a payment for entering into negotiations.

Types of Agreements

Governments may seek different types of agreements via negotiations. Four kinds of agreements may be usefully distinguished since they reflect different ways in which states act to regulate their relations.

1. *Extension agreements* provide a formal ratification and continuation of existing arrangements. Examples are extensions of tariff agreements and renewal of overseas base rights.
2. *Normalization agreements* terminate an abnormal situation in relations between two or more parties. Diplomatic relations may be reestablished, trade wars ended, or a cease-fire put in effect.
3. *Redistribution agreements* benefit one side at the expense of the other. Examples are changes in territorial boundaries, in share of markets, in degree of political influence in third areas, and in financial contributions to bilateral or multilateral organizations.

158

4. *Innovation agreements* set up new arrangements or undertakings that benefit both parties (though not necessarily equally). They include the treaties that established the European Common Market and the International Atomic Energy Agency; the Austrian State Treaty of 1955 that established an independent but neutral state in place of the four-power occupation; and the General Agreement on Tariffs and Trade (GATT) in 1947 that paved the way for tariff reductions and elimination of other barriers to trade.

The characteristics as well as the contexts of the negotiating process may differ depending on which type of agreement is being sought. When the parties are dealing with a number of outstanding issues, they may negotiate for several different types of agreements simultaneously.

Negotiation is essentially a process of communication and interaction that entails a number of tasks and purposes. These tasks are interrelated in practice but will be singled out for separate discussion here.

Procedural Arrangements and Agenda-Setting

Before substantive negotiations begin, and sometimes even before the sides commit themselves to enter into them, the actors must agree on a time, place, agenda, and other modalities such as conference arrangements and the diplomatic level (that is, foreign ministers, ambassadors, or lesser diplomatic officials) at which the discussions will be held. Any of these procedural matters may itself generate disagreement. Indeed, procedural wrangling may be an ominous sign of how far apart the two sides are on the substantive issues or reflect hostility and lack of trust. One side may also deliberately use procedural disagreements for tactical purposes—to achieve side effects such as propaganda advantages, to demonstrate toughness and resolve, to extract concessions, or to gain negotiating advantages. Procedural disagreement at the very outset of negotiations seems to have become much more common in the modern era. Certainly the tenacity with which one side or the other argues over seemingly minor procedural matters has taken on new dimensions in an age when passionate ideological and other differences have displaced the cultural homogeneity that facilitated diplomatic processes in the European system. In the Korean truce negotiations of 1951, the Vietnam peace talks, and the Geneva conference following the Arab-Israeli War of October 1973, agenda-setting and conference arrangements with respect to such trivial matters as the shape of the table and placement of the participants were the subject of prolonged and bitter wrangling. They were regarded as reflections of status and thus were of symbolic importance. With respect to the agenda itself, the two sides may disagree not only on what items and issues are to be discussed, but also on how these items are to be worded and in what order they will be taken up.

Acquisition and Exchange of Information

In the opening stages of a negotiation, or in "exploratory discussions," the two sides often seek to clarify the precise nature of their conflicting interests and the common concerns that have brought them to the negotiating table. The object at this stage may be to verify or correct initial beliefs regarding the prospects of an agreement. Is the common interest in reaching an agreement really strong enough, and are the conflicting interests not so intractable that there is a genuine possibility of working out a solution satisfactory to both sides?

In attempting to answer this question, each negotiator seeks from the other side a clear, authoritative, and reasonably specific statement of its demands. It is expected that, while each side will state its maximum terms for an agreement at the outset, at least some of these initial demands will be subject to modification during the course of persuasion and bargaining. At some point, one side may ask the other to give a general assurance that under certain conditions it will be prepared to moderate some of its demands.

Often, one side may seek to determine whether the other will negotiate in good faith, whether it is serious in attempting to explore the possibility of a mutually acceptable agreement, whether a relationship of trust can be established between the negotiators, and whether they can proceed to enter into serious and delicate negotiations on the basis of mutual confidence and what Iklé has called the "rules of accommodation." The answer to these questions is often elusive, and it may require considerable time and patience before both parties have satisfied themselves that it is prudent and timely to proceed to the next stages.

Ascertaining the Opponent's Resistance Point
and Determining Whether There Exists a Settlement Range

Having ascertained the other side's maximum demands, each negotiator presses to find out its minimum objectives, that is, the least it is willing to settle for. Because this is presumably each side's irreducible goal in the negotiations, it is sometimes referred to as the *resistance point*.

Information about an opponent's resistance point is not always easily, quickly, or reliably obtained. Understandably, a negotiator may be reluctant to reveal his minimal demands prematurely. Since this constitutes valuable information to the other side, each would like to be assured that the opponent too is going to disclose his minimal demands. Very often neither side will move from its maximum demands to a complete disclosure of its minimum demands without satisfying itself that its opponent is ready to do the same. This emphasizes once again the importance of patience in negotiations until trust and a spirit of reciprocity can be established. Even so, negotiators may continue to conceal their true minimal demands, even while moderating their maximum demands. One must distinguish, therefore, between "declared" as against "real" resistance points. In any case, at some stage one or both sides may conclude that it is fruitless to probe further in order to find out the opponent's real resistance point.

At this stage, having established what appear to be each other's resistance points, the two sides can identify how far apart they are from an agreement and assess the significance of the gap between their declared minimum demands. It is important here for each actor to judge whether somewhere between the two resistance points there is a settlement range, or one or more possible settlements which both sides might prefer to no agreement. This stage in the negotiations is depicted in Figure 6.

If the actors feel that the gap between the resistance points is too great and see no conceivable settlement, they may begin to feel it is useless to continue the negotiations. A stalemate develops in which further efforts may be made to clarify and alter each other's resistance points. As a result, the gap may be narrowed somewhat. If the possibility of a settlement through further negotiation is still not considered likely, the stalemate may continue. One or both sides may now utilize the negotiations

Figure 6

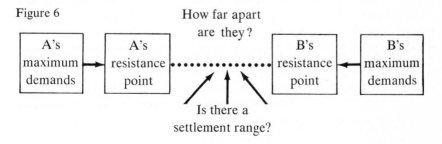

How far apart
are they?

Is there a
settlement range?

for propaganda purposes or other side effects. Or they may agree to report back to their governments and ask for new instructions. Finally, they may agree to call off the negotiations temporarily or permanently; or one side may do so unilaterally. Sometimes one side (or both) will make minor concessions simply in order to keep the negotiations going or to get them started again.

Analyzing the Opponent's Resistance Point

Once a preliminary settlement range has emerged, each side seeks to find out more about the other side's resistance point. What set of interests, concerns, and attitudes lies behind the opponent's present resistance point? Information bearing on this question will help each actor find out whether there are ways of satisfying the opponent's essential demands without jeopardizing its own interests. Or such information may enable one to find ways of weakening or changing the other's minimal demands. At this stage in the negotiations, each side also wants to know how eager its opponent is for an agreement. Is the other side under some time constraint or domestic pressure to achieve resolution of the current issues? Information that permits shrewd guesses or a better understanding of what lies behind the adversary's ostensible resistance point helps each side determine its combination of persuasion and bargaining.

Searching for a Referent or General Principle
That May Facilitate Agreement

When the issues in a dispute are complex, the parties to the negotiation may seek to bridge the gap between their resistance points in stages. One approach is to identify a referent or general principle that will provide a standard or framework that will assist in working out the specific details of a settlement. It may be difficult to choose the general principle, since one side may regard the proposed principle or referent as biasing the type of agreement that can be reached. Referents and principles that have proven useful in the past include the concepts of "power" and "balance of power" in determining territorial settlements and spheres of influence during the European era, "secure frontiers" in seeking political/territorial settlements at the end of many wars, and "parity" or "strategic equality" in SALT negotiations.

162

Persuasion and Bargaining

If the parties believe there is a potential agreement somewhere within the settlement range, they engage in persuasion and bargaining to move each other toward an agreement. "Persuasion" is usefully distinguished from "bargaining." In the former, efforts are made to get the other side to understand why your demands are so important to you and why you think theirs are excessive and difficult to accept. In arguing the merits of the case, one may appeal to reason and to emotion.

"Bargaining," on the other hand, is characterized by concessions, conditional offers, threats, and inducements. It may also include proposals for compromises, trades, and quid pro quos. Bargaining is generally facilitated if the two sides subscribe to similar rules of accommodation.

Agreement will be facilitated, too, if either side can strengthen the other's perception of their broader common interests, thus causing it to modify its minimum demands. This is sometimes attempted via the strategy of *linkage,* in which one side encourages the other to be more conciliatory by persuading it that, depending on how the current dispute is resolved, it stands to benefit or suffer in other issue areas.

Search for Creative Solutions

Negotiations that have reached a stalemate after the possibilities of persuasion and bargaining appear exhausted are sometimes unexpectedly successful because one side or a third party thinks of a quite novel way of resolving the disagreement. It may be possible for the parties to break the stalemate by enlarging the range and scope of issues brought into the negotiations. This may, at the extreme, extend to a review of their entire relationship. The actors may gain a new perspective on the matter under negotiation by undertaking a clarification or reorientation of their overall relations.

Bargaining Strategies

The parties to a negotiation in the modern era have often brought quite different diplomatic styles to bear. There was much less variance in the diplomatic styles and bargaining strategies employed by major powers in the European balance-of-power system. Diplomats in the classical era agreed upon and generally adhered to reasonably well-defined rules of accommodation. The diplomatic revolution has played havoc with the cultural homogeneity and consensus that facilitated negotiation in the nineteenth century and, in the modern era, the actors sometimes have different conceptions of negotiation. As noted below, diplomats representing totalitarian states often regard negotiation as another form of combat rather than as a vehicle for resolving or moderating conflicts of interest.

Two bargaining strategies may be identified: the *accommodative* and the *optimizing* approaches. Negotiators socialized in commercially oriented societies often pursue an accommodative approach to bargaining; that is, they do not ask for much more in a negotiation than they think is reasonable and likely to be acceptable. In contrast, negotiators socialized in revolutionary or totalitarian cultures often pursue an optimizing strategy, trying to achieve as much as possible in negotiation, not fearing to be unreasonable, combative, and abusive. Negotiators employing optimizing bargaining tactics are less likely to disclose their real resistance point and feel no obligation to reciprocate concessions.

Enforcement and Verification of Agreements

The question whether an agreement, if reached, will be honored by one's opponent is often of concern during the negotiations and may influence attitudes toward the shape of the agreement. That is, certain ways of resolving the issues may be perceived as less attractive, or even as unacceptable, because confidence is lacking in their enforceability. There are several dimensions to this problem that may be addressed during the course of the negotiations. First, the question often arises whether a contemplated agreement is "self-enforcing" or whether implementation will depend on the good faith of each side. Self-enforcing agreements are generally preferred (though not by states that do not want to be tied down to an unsatisfactory agreement); but it is often not possible to devise them. Particularly invidious are agreements that are asymmetrical in this respect, that is, when one side makes concessions that are irreversible, whereas its opponent's reciprocating concessions are such that it can take them back later on. A related question that plagues certain types of negotiations is whether violations of the agreement can be detected in a timely and unambiguous way. If this possibility is present, then one or both sides will attempt to contrive workable provisions for

164

identifying and dealing with violations. Such provisions may be incorporated into the agreement. Agreement on enforcement provisions is less of a problem when the parties have unilateral means of monitoring them.

Multilateral Negotiations

The simple two-actor model presented thus far is much complicated, of course, when more than two parties engage in negotiations. Multilateral negotiations did occur frequently in the European system; witness the many conferences of the five great powers comprising the concert of Europe. Multilateral negotiations of this kind were more complex and difficult than most bilateral negotiations, to be sure, but the challenge posed to diplomats was more manageable because the system was a relatively well-ordered one and because of the cultural homogeneity of the European statesmen. The absence of these conditions in the international system of the post-European era and other changes brought about by the diplomatic revolution have significantly altered the nature and difficulties of multilateral diplomacy in the modern era. This is strikingly evident in any number of post–World War I international conferences, beginning with the Paris Peace Conference that came at the end of that conflict. In contrast to their predecessors at Vienna, the leaders of the victorious powers came to Paris with quite different conceptions of the kind of international system that should be created, and the process of peacemaking was one of continual adaptation to these different objectives and priorities. They also discovered, as had their predecessors at Vienna, that their intention of making all the important decisions themselves was bitterly resented by the lesser powers and that concessions, in the form of a limited share in decision-making, had to be made to them in order to alleviate that feeling. Finally, unlike the peacemakers at Vienna, they were continually subjected to the pressures of public opinion and domestic politics in their own countries. All of these constraints complicated their work and contributed to the unsatisfactory nature of the peace settlement of 1919.

These forces affected other large conferences in the interwar period—the disarmament conference of 1932 is a case in point—and they were present once more at the largest of the postwar meetings, the Conference on Security and Cooperation in Europe, which was held between 1973 and 1975.

The Conference on Security and Cooperation in Europe

No formal peace conference was held at the end of World War II as had been done in 1814–1815 and 1919. The closest approximation was the Conference on Security and Cooperation in Europe (CSCE).* By 1973, when it opened, considerable dissatisfaction had accumulated on all sides concerning the continued division of Europe and the dangerous tensions that had arisen during the course of the Cold War. Many of the representatives of the thirty-five states who gathered at Geneva in July 1973 wished to effect a change for the better, although there was no common agreement concerning what form that change should take.

Repeatedly during the Cold War, the Soviet Union had requested a European conference on security. Its early offers to participate in such a conference must certainly have been calculated merely to test Western solidarity. The demand that attendance be exclusively European and the timing of Soviet military and political offensives guaranteed that its requests would be rejected. In retrospect, however, it is evident that subsequent Soviet proposals became increasingly legitimate. By 1971, Willy Brandt, always interested in the opportunity for small steps toward more normalized East-West relations, was willing to cosponsor the CSCE. The addition of this valuable spokesman in the West and increasing superpower interest in détente improved the prospects for the conference considerably. Unrealistic demands were dropped, agendas were proposed, and the initiation of CSCE was linked to progress in other talks on other issues. Gradually, opposition to CSCE gave way, and delegations were able to gather in Geneva to open negotiations. A serious handicap was the limited importance attached to the conference by the United States and the limited benefits American leadership expected from it. Pressure applied by European allies eventually achieved U.S. attendance, but American skepticism remained.

At Geneva, thirty-five states negotiated on the basis of multinational consultation and consensus. The conference adopted the remarkable rule, unthinkable at the time of the Congress of Vienna, that decisions would ultimately require unanimous approval of all states, large and small. And in contrast to the Paris Peace Conference, *all* of the thirty-five states participated in the actual negotiations. Various texts were

* The case study on the Conference on Security and Cooperation in Europe that appears below was prepared in its original form by Captain Alan Carver, U.S. Army.

submitted to small working committees in an effort to narrow differences. But texts continued to circulate to all participants until bracketed phrases were resolved to the satisfaction of all. This extraordinarily difficult and lengthy process was not confined to the conference alone. In the West, members of the European Economic Community occasionally discussed common positions and appointed spokesmen under their arrangements for political cooperation. Likewise, the members of NATO at the conference met periodically to prepare positions and select specific members to introduce proposals. The conference was also included on the agenda of the NATO council and was discussed at meetings attended by both the U.S. president and the secretary of state. The essentially solid front maintained by the members of the Warsaw Pact also suggests prior consultation. Nevertheless, neither the West nor the East was able to stifle all indication of disaffection and dissatisfaction with the positions adopted by the superpowers.

The negotiating positions of individual states were also subjected to diverse domestic influences and were not prepared by a single individual or governmental agency. All delegations with one exception arrived headed by diplomats of ambassadorial rank. The American delegation was initially headed by a senior foreign service officer, but in order to conform to the composition of the other missions, the State Department eventually replaced him with the U.S. ambassador to Czechoslovakia. He did not play a central role, however, in the formulation of the U.S. position, nor was the U.S. position prepared in Geneva by the delegation at all. Military confidence-building measures, an important agenda item, were discussed in Washington by representatives of the National Security Council staff, the Defense Department, and the State Department. Economic issues were discussed by representatives of the State Department, the Treasury, the Commerce Department, and Special Trade representatives. All other issues were generally dealt with by an interoffice committee within the State Department. Major positions were presented to the secretary of state for approval. Members of the delegation were occasionally replaced over the two-year period of general negotiations, and experts were frequently added to advise on specific issues. Congressmen and the undersecretary of state for European affairs made several visits to Geneva to attend conference deliberations. By 1975, the CSCE was being examined by several congressional subcommittees as well. The bureaucratic influences evident in the American CSCE process were remarkable for a nation that expressed little real interest or pur-

pose at the conference, but they reveal the important changes in negotiations produced by technological advances and the increased complexity in international affairs and domestic politics.

Beyond vague notions of improved security and a desire for the continued progress of détente, the larger Western powers failed to bring a
clear set of objectives to the conference. The Soviets, on the other hand,
perceived the opportunity to achieve very specific and desirable ends in
their interest. The conference offered them an opportunity to gain formal recognition of Eastern European borders and the acceptance of
principles of sovereignty and nonintervention that would confirm Soviet
influence in Eastern Europe and provide de facto recognition of the status quo. Many of these issues involved areas of dispute that had existed
since the conclusion of World War II. The importance of these objectives led Brezhnev to stake his personal prestige on a rapid and favorable outcome. And, indeed, when the conference convened, it appeared
that the Soviets were well-prepared to exercise an optimizing strategy
and in an excellent position to deliver a diplomatic coup.

Several factors combined to rob the Soviets of a clearcut victory. The
smaller countries attending the conference were able to gain much greater
attention for human-rights issues than either of the two superpowers was
willing to grant, the Soviet Union because of the potential for embarrassment and the United States because of the nebulous nature of the issue
and the likelihood that it would jeopardize détente and prevent meaningful negotiations at Geneva. The tenacity of the human-rights advocates
and the broad participation afforded all of the thirty-five delegations in
attendance assured the inclusion of the human-rights issue on an equal
basis with the other issues under negotiation. A second factor complicating the negotiations for the Soviets was the limited public interest in
the conference in the West. In the United States, little attention was paid
to CSCE by the media, the public, or Congress until 1975, after the negotiations were largely completed. Secretary of State Kissinger himself
was skeptical of the potential benefits to be derived from the conference
and preferred bilateral talks between the superpowers to the more difficult
multilateral format of CSCE. Public opinion in Europe showed only
slightly greater interest. The Soviet government had come to Geneva intent on concluding the process in time for a victory announcement at the
Twenty-fifth Congress of the Communist party of the Soviet Union, and
Brezhnev's prestige would suffer if a favorable conclusion was not
brought about in time. Originally expected to be a short and uncompli-
cated conference dealing with security and economic issues, the CSCE

proved to be a complex and difficult process. The important role of the smaller Western states and the elevation of the human-rights issue coupled with the self-imposed Soviet deadline ultimately worked to the advantage of the Western nations. However, the handicap of poor preparation and vague objectives played a large part in minimizing Western ability to make the most of their fortunate position.

CSCE was finally thrust into the limelight in the United States when plans were announced for a possible summit-level meeting in Helsinki for signing the accords. The press, Congress, and the public were caught by surprise at the new importance attached to the negotiations. A great deal of controversy was generated by belated efforts to discover the impact and scope of CSCE, and the Ford administration sought to counter this by immoderate enthusiasm for what had been accomplished at Geneva. A spokesman for the White House said that the meeting would "codify East-West détente" and pointed out proudly that "the sheer size of the contemplated summit" would outstrip the Congress of Vienna and the Paris Peace Conference. "Maybe the pope himself would go to Helsinki," he said, adding that the meeting would be "a landmark event culminating nine years of East-West exchanges."

When the results of the security conference became clear, many Americans found these dithyrambs hard to justify. William Safire wrote in the *New York Times* before the end of the Helsinki meeting, "In case you hadn't heard, World War II will soon be coming to its official end. The Russians won." Former Undersecretary of State George Ball reviewed the terms of the agreement in *Newsweek* in an article entitled "Capitulation at Helsinki." Both writers, and many others, pointed out that the one clear and unambiguous result of CSCE was that the West explicitly accepted the new frontiers that the Russians had drawn all over Eastern Europe at the end of the war and thus implicitly accepted the ideological division of Europe. Article III of the agreement stated clearly that all signatory powers regarded each other's existing frontiers as inviolable. This gave the Soviets the formal recognition of their eastern gains that they had been seeking since 1945.

It was true that they did not get everything their own way. They had to accept the idea that, at least in theory, frontiers could be changed by peaceful agreement, which left the door open for German reunification. They had to agree that there would be no intervention in other countries' internal affairs, which would make it more difficult for them to act again as they had in Czechoslovakia in 1968. And they were forced, when Western delegations argued that Europe could never be normal unless people could travel where they wanted to, to accept some provisions, in the so-called Basket III clauses, about the movement of people and ideas, about family visits from East to West, marriages between citizens of different countries, and human rights in general. But these commitments, which represented the great victory of the smaller powers and the neutrals at Helsinki, were loosely drafted and in such general terms as—in Ball's words—"to portend only minuscule holes in the Iron Curtain." To Americans in particular, these Soviet concessions seemed an inadequate exchange for the gains they had registered.

The final act of CSCE was attacked also for the lack of adequate measures for enforcement. The conference had agreed upon periodic meetings of experts to consider alleged violations, but this arrangement—perhaps inevitably, considering the ambiguities and residual disagreements buried in the agreements—did not prove to be very satisfactory. The first review meeting, in Belgrade in 1977, resulted in a stalemate when the Soviet Union resisted an inquiry into its conformity with the standards of human rights required by the agreement. Similar difficulties developed at the second review meeting in Madrid in 1980–1981. This was disappointing, although it probably had a favorable spinoff effect for the West, inclining the neutral states, who have a strong commitment to the Helsinki Agreement and to human rights in general, to view Soviet professions more realistically than they have always done.

As the story of CSCE indicates, one consequence of the expanded membership of the diplomatic community has been a tendency on the part of the lesser states to demand not only representation but active participation and a voice in the settlement of international issues. The reliance by the superpowers on arsenals of sophisticated nuclear weapons that cannot rationally be employed to advance national interests has generally enhanced the relative importance of small nonnuclear nations whose power is derived from their inherent flexibility and combined capacity to influence the nature of superpower confrontation. Likewise, the increased influence of public opinion, bureaucratic practices, and domestic politics has made diplomacy more complex a process and less an art to be practiced by the individual statesman of great talent and personal influence.

Several implications can be drawn from the changing character of negotiation. There is little prospect that the broadening trend in representation will recede. Bilateral negotiations will increasingly require ratification by the wider community of states if their effects on security are to be broadened and confirmed. Reliance on multinational consensual solutions will make the negotiation process difficult and results less definitive and binding. Coalitions will be less cohesive and less subject to superpower manipulation. These tendencies necessitate governing principles of restraint, mutual respect, and accommodation. When disaster can result as competing parties battle for mutually exclusive ends without restraint, each with moral justification, principles must operate to make resolution possible. Certainly, the resolution of the diverse interests brought about by the increased heterogeneity and expansion of the international community is the challenge of the diplomatic revolution of our time.

Bibliographical Essay

On negotiation in general, see the classic works of Wicquefort and Callières and the modern study by Harold Nicolson, all cited after chapter 1. The discussion above of the simple two-actor model of negotiation draws on a number of sources, in particular Fred C. Iklé, *How Nations Negotiate* (New York, 1964). Among political scientists who have written extensively on negotiation is I. William Zartman; see, for example, *The 50% Solution* (New York, 1976), especially chapter 1, "The Analysis of Negotiation"; and, with respect to "referents" in negotiation, "Negotiation: Theory and Reality," in *Journal of International Affairs,* 29 (1975), 69–77. Important contributions to a general theory of negotiation, one not confined to diplomacy, have been made by many other writers including those who have analyzed labor-management negotiations. See, for example, Richard E. Walton and Robert B. McKersie, *A Behavioral Theory of Labor Negotiations* (New York, 1965).

The Conference on Security and Cooperation in Europe, having taken place so recently, has not as yet generated many detailed scholarly accounts. See particularly William I. Bacchus, "Multilateral Foreign Policy Making: The Conference on Security and Cooperation in Europe," in *The Politics of Policy Making in America,* ed. David A. Caputo (San Francisco, 1977), pp. 132–65. Besides contemporary reports in journals like the *Economist* and editorial analysis in periodicals dealing with international relations, little else can be found without a fair amount of effort. A good starting point is H. Molineu, "Human Rights and Détente: The Case of CSCE," an unpublished report prepared at Ohio University in March 1977. An analysis of the text of the CSCE agreement was written by H. S. Russell in the *American Journal of International Law,* 70 (1976), 242–72, entitled "The Helsinki Declaration." Extremely useful materials are to be found in "Conference on Security and Cooperation in Europe," Hearings before the Subcommittee on International Political and Military Affairs of the Committee on International Relations, 94th Congress, 1st Session, May 6, 1975.

13
Deterrence

Deterrence consists essentially of an effort by one actor to persuade an opponent not to take action of some kind against his interests by convincing the opponent that the costs and risks of doing so will outweigh what he hopes to gain thereby. In this simple and quite limited sense, deterrence rests upon the assumption of a "rational" opponent, that is, one who can be expected to calculate the utility of his alternative courses of action on the basis of available information. Logically speaking, the first step in formulating a deterrence policy is to weigh the *interests* of one's country that are engaged in the area that may be threatened by hostile action and to assess how important they are. The next step is to formulate and convey to the opponent a *commitment* to defend those interests. The deterring power backs its commitments by *threats* to respond if the opponent acts. Such threats must be both *credible* and *sufficiently potent* in the eyes of the opponent—that is, pose a level of costs and risks that he regards as of sufficient magnitude to overcome his motivation to challenge the defending power's position.

There are two interdependent dimensions of credibility. First, the deterring power must convey to the opponent that it has the *will and resolution* to defend the interests in question; second, it must possess *capabilities* for doing so that it regards—and persuades the opponent to regard—as appropriate and usable for the defense of those interests. The former will have no persuasive force unless the deterring power has the ability to deal, by effective and appropriate measures, with the kinds of action that its opponent may take. American experience with the doctrine of massive retaliation is relevant here. In an effort to extend the threat of American strategic nuclear power, the Eisenhower administration in the early 1950s ominously warned it would "retaliate massively," not only against Soviet initiation of an all-out war, but also in a variety of possible lesser encroachments against free world countries. The credibility of massive retaliation for deterring Soviet or Chinese Communist initiation of lower-level conflicts declined, however, as the Soviets developed strategic nuclear capabilities of their own. Accordingly, the Kennedy administration and its successors moved to develop stronger conventional military capabilities that would be more appropriate and usable in limited encroachments of various kinds and hence would be more credible in deterring them. Threats will lack credibility, of course, when a defending power lacks the capabilities needed for protecting an outpost. In these circumstances, the defending power can threaten to punish the aggressor in other ways, by broadening the arena of conflict or by engaging in retaliation or reprisal.

The study and practice of deterrence as a discrete foreign policy strategy did not become prominent until after World War II. Since then, the advent of nuclear weapons has elevated the role of deterrence strategy to a preeminent position in the study of international relations. It should not be assumed, however, that the concept of deterrence has forever languished in obscurity. Throughout history, city-states, kingdoms, empires, and nation-states have all sought to prevent or deter the actions of rivals which they found inimical to their best interests. Many of these past practitioners of deterrence understood quite clearly the requirements for a successful policy, and a study of their actions can reveal much about the nature of deterrence and its usefulness in the international arena.

The historical cases chosen for analysis in this chapter offer three interesting and different views of deterrence in action.* In the first case, England was reasonably successful in its attempt to prevent a dangerous expansion of the terms of the Quadruple Alliance by the other European powers, while in the second, the Western Allies could not prevent Hitler from invading Poland. In the last case, the question of success or failure regarding the United State's commitment to Israel is not so easily answered, for the results are certainly mixed. There can be no doubt, however, that in each of the three cases, the international community

* The case studies in this chapter were prepared in their original form by Captain Richard J. Hoffman, U.S. Army.

173

lay poised on the brink of a major conflict which only a successful application of deterrence could avoid.

A number of factors complicate the use of deterrence strategy as an instrument of foreign policy. This was always the case, but the diplomatic revolution introduced new complications, which will be evident as we move from our oldest case study to the most recent one.

France and the Congress System, 1816–1822

The peace of Europe in the post-Napoleonic period was to be secured by an alliance of the four victorious powers, Britain, Austria, Russia, and Prussia, in which each party pledged to act in concert with the others to prevent France from again seeking hegemony in Europe. This coalition, first formalized in the Treaty of Chaumont in March 1814, was confirmed as the Quadruple Alliance on 20 November 1815, after Napoleon's Waterloo campaign had reminded the Congress of Vienna members of the pressing need for a collective security agreement. As with the Chaumont agreement, the Quadruple Alliance was primarily aimed at restraining French aggression, but a provision was made for periodic meetings among the great powers "for the maintenance of the Peace of Europe."

The Quadruple Alliance was not the only accord concluded in Vienna in 1815. Another federation, called the Holy Alliance by its chief proponent, Alexander I of Russia, came into being as well. In this pact, the signatories agreed that the principles of Christianity should guide the conduct of nations in their international and domestic affairs. The exact purpose of the alliance never became clear, but its obscure wording later offered Austria's foreign minister, Prince Metternich, the possibility of constructing a conservative bulwark against any future revolutionary tide that might sweep through Europe, endangering its crowned heads. The British foreign secretary, Viscount Castlereagh, wisely refused to sign the document, and the Congress of Vienna concluded its work with the Second Peace of Paris, which established the shape of Europe in the years to come.

The next European congress convened at Aix-la-Chapelle in September 1818, and the principle topic on the agenda was the readmittance of France as the fifth great European power. This was readily accomplished, but Czar Alexander submitted a memorandum in which he proposed that the great European powers should confirm their adherence to the territorial settlement of Vienna and guarantee all legitimate regimes existing at that moment. Alexander's memorandum began a long series of confrontations between the czar and Castlereagh, in which the British foreign secretary strove successfully to prevent him from widening the specific principles of the Quadruple Alliance into a reactionary agreement on the order of the Holy Alliance. The confrontation culminated on 5 May 1820, on which date Castlereagh issued a famous memorandum to the powers of Europe stating Britain's unalterable opposition to any agreement involving the intervention of one state in another's internal affairs.

Unfortunately, Alexander found support for his cause growing as a wave of revolution swept Europe in 1820. The revolt of the Spanish army in January and the granting of a liberal constitution was followed by the assassination of the French king's nephew in February, an uprising in Naples in July, and another revolt in Portugal in August. As concern over these actions mounted, the powers, with the exception of Britain, met in Troppau in October and endorsed the principle of conservative intervention in the so-called Troppau Protocol. Later Russia, Prussia, and Austria met at Laibach to authorize Austria to intervene in Naples and restore the Bourbon dynasty, a task that was quickly accomplished. The next congress of Europe met at Vienna in October 1822 to consider the French government's proposal that it be allowed to intervene in Spain and restore the Bourbon monarchy there. The British, led after Castlereagh's death by George Canning, strongly opposed French intervention in Spanish affairs. Nevertheless, all of Canning's efforts, including numerous diplomatic notes and the withdrawal of his representative, the Duke of Wellington, were insufficient to deter the other powers from authorizing France to intervene. By April 1823, French armies were on the march for the first time since 1815, and within six months Ferdinand VII was back on the Spanish throne.

At this point, another issue arose to occupy the attention of the great powers. Spain's American colonies had taken the opportunity provided them by the revolt to declare their independence from the mother country. With his throne now restored, Ferdinand set about seeking assistance in recovering Spanish colonial possessions. He received support from a France interested in securing a share of the Latin American trade and a Russia anxious to partake in any action that might weaken Britain's position and strengthen its own. Canning, however, was fiercely determined to preserve Britain's newly developed economic ties with the former colonies and prevent any further expansion of the Holy Alliance. In a series of strongly worded memoranda, he exploited French indecision by affirming Spain's right to seek by its own efforts to recover its former colonies, but asserted that the British government would view with grave alarm the attempt of any other power to intervene in Latin America. He followed up these memoranda by a series of frank discussions in October 1823 with the French ambassador, Polignac, which won him a French promise of nonintervention in return for a vague statement of British interest in a conference on Spain's American problems. This was followed in December by the promulgation of the Monroe Doctrine, in which the United States, backed by the British Royal Navy, asserted its protectorate over the Western Hemisphere, thus effectively eliminating the threat of Spanish intervention. The combined effect of these two diplomatic maneuvers showed Europe that the power of the Holy Alliance stopped at the water's edge, and the crisis ended.

The Western Allies' Attempts to Deter
the Attack on Poland, 1938–1939

The attempts of the Allies, Britain and France, to deter the German attack on Poland really began in March 1939 when, after German troops had occupied Prague in violation of the Munich Agreement, British prime minister Chamberlain realized that Hitler was not to be trusted and had to be opposed by threats of force. He was joined in this conviction by the French government, which after the Sudeten crisis was reduced to following Britain's lead in its foreign policy. Chamberlain wasted no time in attempting to build a new bulwark against German aggression in Central Europe. A mutual assistance pact was concluded with Turkey, and promises of support and protection were extended to Greece and Rumania. By far the most important action taken was the pledge of support given Poland by Britain and France on 31 March 1939.

The question was now whether this would suffice to prevent Hitler from attacking Poland. Given the uncertain state of the Allied armed forces, and the difficulty they would have in rendering Poland timely military support regardless of their state of readiness, it became obvious that the Allies would require the support of the Soviet Union if they were to have any chance of preventing further aggression.

This idea proved to be easier to articulate than implement. To begin with, the Allies and the Soviet Union, although in general agreement that the course of German expansion must be contained, were of two minds when it came to implementation. The Allies, led by Chamberlain, were deeply suspicious of Russian motives, and only belatedly did they approach the Soviet Union in mid-April to inquire if the Soviet government might wish to extend a unilateral guarantee to the western frontiers of Poland and Rumania. The Soviets declined the Allied offer, but inquired in turn about the possibility of a comprehensive alliance between themselves and the Western powers. In the Soviet view, a necessary requirement for the success of such an alliance would be their ability to station troops in Poland and Rumania to defend these countries in case of aggression. The Poles and the Rumanians, being understandably wary of the Russians, would have nothing to do with this idea, and the matter stagnated until August 1939.

The Germans, however, had been far from quiet. On 28 April 1939, Hitler denounced the Nazi-Polish Nonaggression Pact of 1934 and the Anglo-German Naval Agreement of 1935. Later, in May 1939, Germany and Italy announced the signing of the Pact of Steel, a formal military alliance that seemingly indicated the commencement of hostilities in the near future. In point of fact, Hitler had decided to go to war over Poland, and he began urgently to seek a rapprochement with the Soviet Union in order to avoid a two-front war.

For their part, the Soviets, discouraged by the lack of success with the Allies, had initiated conversations with the Germans in the spring of 1939. By way of warning to the Western powers, the Soviets replaced the pro–collective security foreign affairs commissar, Litvinow, with the staunch nationalist Molotow. Even as the Allies were seeking to respond to these moves, the Soviets agreed to open negotiations on a new economic pact with Germany, while at the same time inviting the Allies to send a military mission to Moscow to discuss the possibilities of defending Poland and the Baltic states. Having pitted the two opponents against each other in a race for Soviet favor, the Russians now waited for the outcome.

If they were in a race, the Allies were unaware of the necessity for speed. Their military mission, traveling by ship, took until 11 August to arrive in Moscow and, when informed by Marshal Voroshilow that the time had come for a military convention, the head of the British mission revealed that he had no power to conclude agreements. This performance contrasted unfavorably with that of the Germans, who were working at top speed to reach an accommodation. On 14 August, German foreign minister Ribbentrop proposed by wire that he fly to Moscow "to lay the foundation for a final settlement of German-Russian relations." The Russians accepted the next day, and when Ribbentrop arrived in Moscow, the two parties concluded a nonaggression pact that provided for the partition of Poland and the absorption by the USSR of Finland, Estonia, Latvia, and Bessarabia. The Germans got Lithuania and avoided the specter of a two-front war. The new partners announced the signing of the pact to a stunned world on 21 August 1939, the same day the British mission finally received its credentials.

With the signing of the Nazi-Soviet Pact, Hitler resolved to crush Poland without delay. Perhaps he felt that Britain and France would renege on their promise to Poland as they had to Czechoslovakia; but having prepared Germany for war, he had by now determined to continue his string of conquests by force of arms. Thus, even the resumption of peacetime conscription by Britain on 28 August failed to change his mind. On 1 September 1939, the German army, in response to a contrived border incident, commenced its well-planned invasion of Poland. Britain immediately informed the German government that it intended to honor its pledge to Poland unless the invasion was halted at once. Receiving no reply, the British government informed the Germans on 3 September that unless it was assured by 11 A.M. that all action would cease immediately and that the German forces would withdraw from Poland, a state of war would exist between Germany and Britain.

U.S. Deterrence Policy in the Middle East

The evolution of the United States security commitment to the state of Israel has been a slow, and some might say precarious, process since the United States supported the 1949 United Nations partition of Palestine and subsequently recognized the newly proclaimed state in May 1949. This action, taken by President Truman against the counsel of some of his closest advisers, was the beginning of what was later to become a "moral" commitment by the United States to Israel's continued existence. The process was extensively aided by Zionist organizations within the United States and abroad. The government of the United States, however, was not blind to its very real strategic and economic interests in the Middle East among the Arab states. On the contrary, the "Arabists" of the State Department, led by Secretary Marshall, pursued a determinedly even-handed policy in the Middle East despite strong Israeli pleas for economic and military assistance. This situation continued until the Suez crisis in 1956.

Egypt's President Nasser precipitated the crisis by nationalizing the Suez Canal in July 1956. The British, French, and Israeli governments, brought together in an alliance of convenience, resolved to rectify their common grievances against Egypt by force of arms. While the Israelis cleared the Sinai, a combined Anglo-French force attempted to seize the canal zone. Unfortunately for the allies, the United States, now led by President Eisenhower and Secretary Dulles, felt that their actions violated the 1947 UN mandate and joined with a majority of the United Nations in calling for an immediate withdrawal of all foreign forces from Egypt. Britain and France complied, but Israel, led by Prime Minister Ben Gurion, refused to withdraw Israeli forces unless guaranteed that Israel would have free passage through the Straits of Tiran and be free of terrorist attacks from the Gaza Strip. At this point, the United States stepped in to guarantee the placement of a UN force in the Gaza Strip and the Israeli right of passage in the straits. This guarantee constituted the first significant commitment by America to Israel and was "operationalized" on 20 February 1957 when President Eisenhower pledged in a public address that the United States recognized the concept of free right of passage in the Gulf of Aqaba and was prepared to exercise this right itself and with other nations.

After the Suez crisis, the United States attempted to return to an even-handed policy in the Middle East, but the growing belligerency of the Arab states and the increasing involvement of the Soviet Union in the region made this policy hard to maintain. The next test for the U.S. Mideast policy came in 1967 when Nasser, acting under pressure from the Arab League, took steps to test the credibility of the U.S. commitment and to demonstrate Egypt's support for the Palestinian cause.

On 14 May 1967, Nasser ordered the Egyptian army to occupy the Sinai Peninsula. When this move was unopposed by a U.S. administration deeply involved in Vietnam, Nasser was emboldened on 16 May to request that the UN security force be removed. To the surprise of everyone, including Nasser, Secretary General U Thant complied. At this point, President Johnson, who for political and personal reasons stemming from the U.S. experience in Vietnam was strongly opposed to any unilateral American action in the Mideast, urged Premier Eshkol of Israel and President Nasser to act with restraint. The United States then attempted to resolve the crisis in the UN, but Nasser took matters into his own hands on 22 May and closed the Straits of Tiran to Israeli shipping.

Johnson recognized that this last act was a true test of the commitment Eisenhower had made in 1957, but he was unable and unwilling to generate congressional support for unilateral action. Instead, it was decided that the situation could best be resolved through multilateral action by the UN Security Council. A proposal was made for a UN fleet to break the blockade, and Johnson asked the Israelis for time to put this proposal into effect. The Israelis at first agreed to wait two weeks before taking action but later felt compelled to launch a preemptive attack on Egypt, Jordan, and Syria on 5 June 1967. This initiated the so-called Six Day War in which the Israelis utterly defeated the Arab forces and occupied the Golan Heights, the West Bank of the Jordan River, and the Sinai.

Once hostilities commenced, U.S. policy shifted to attempting to obtain a UN–directed cease-fire. Significantly, however, Johnson extended the level of the U.S. commitment to Israel by intervening on its behalf to prevent the Soviet Union from coming to the aid of the Arabs. In this way, a U.S. strategic umbrella was raised over Israel, and America became actively committed to the principle of preventing gross Soviet interference in the Mideast. Interestingly enough, the Johnson administration further modified its Mideast position by not calling for an immediate withdrawal of Israeli forces from the occupied territories and by stepping up arms shipments to Israel.

This policy continued through the immediate postwar period, which saw the United States committed to maintaining Israeli military strength while at the same time supporting UN Resolution 242, which called for the eventual return of the occupied territories. The U.S.–Israeli bond was drawn even tighter by the Jordanian crisis of 1970, when the United States, now led by President Nixon and his adviser Henry Kissinger, used Israel as a proxy in deterring the Syrians from overthrowing King Hussein of Jordan. In American eyes, it now seemed that the best deterrent to another Mideast war was to maintain an Israel militarily strong enough to deter attack while the United States sought to establish a meaningful peace in the region and enlisted the aid of the Soviet Union in restraining its Arab clients.

This grand design, however, was to have unhappy consequences. The "no war–no peace" situation that followed the 1967 war proved to be incompatible with Arab pride and national interest. Following the inconclusive War of Attrition in 1969–1970 and the so-called "year of decision" in 1971, Egypt's new President Sadat and Syria's Assad were anxious to break the deadlock. Both countries had been extensively resupplied with Soviet arms, and on 6 October 1973, Egypt and Syria attacked Israel on the Sinai and Golan fronts respectively. The attack caught the Israelis unprepared, as a result both of U.S. pressure not to preempt as in 1967 and of the Israeli government's independent decision to avoid a costly early mobilization. In the ensuing fighting, the Israelis again prevailed, but not before they had suffered heavy casualties. More important, the United States found itself once more intervening on Israel's behalf in order to prevent unilateral Soviet intervention and eventually had to undertake a major commitment to both Egypt and Israel in the hope of resolving the Arab-Israeli problem.

Analysis

Inherent in the calculus of deterrence lies the assumption of a rational opponent, one who can be deterred from a given course of action if the costs of pursuing it clearly outweigh the benefits to be gained thereby. While it is not the purpose here to explore all the ramifications of this assumption, it can be said that in making it, a grave and often fatal error may be committed. Not all opponents are rational and, even if they are, their circumstances may be such as to prevent them from adhering to conventional "rational" analysis. The efforts of the Quadruple Alliance and the congress system were both almost brought to grief by the seemingly irrational desire of Czar Alexander II to suppress "liberal" regimes anywhere they might appear. Chamberlain's policy of appeasement floundered for the most part on the rocks of Hitler's insatiable and irrational demands. Even in 1967 and 1973, the Egyptian leaders Nasser and Sadat were forced to take risky, and by their opponents' calculations irrational, steps against Israel by pressures generated both domestically and in the Arab world at large. Thus to assume that the opponent will act in a rational manner may be the first and often greatest mistake.

Setting aside the rational-opponent assumption, the deterring power must consider the question of its own and its opponent's national interests in order to calculate the utility of the various policy options. It is often difficult to determine one's own national interests let alone those of an opponent; but a failure to do so can result in the disintegration

181

of even the best deterrence strategy. This can be readily seen in the way in which the congress system sufficed to deter French aggression after 1815, both as a result of the solidarity of the Quadruple Alliance powers and the desire of France itself to renounce its hegemonic efforts, but started to show signs of strain as the divergent interests of the great powers began to manifest themselves on the continent and in the New World. Likewise, the Allied desire to deter the German attack on Poland was hampered by the divergent interests of obtaining Russia's participation in the security agreement while limiting its penetration of Eastern Europe. Lastly, the United States has had great difficulty establishing the priority of its own interests in the Middle East among such conflicting goals as preserving the state of Israel, preventing Soviet penetration of the Arab World, and assuring itself and its allies of adequate supplies of Arab oil, all of which it seeks to accomplish in conjunction with or opposition to Arab, Israeli, and Soviet interests in the region.

Having successfully assessed its own and the other party's interests, the deterring power must now make an explicit or implicit commitment to defend the ally, territory, or interest it perceives as being threatened. This, too, is often not as simple a task as it might first appear. In the first case, the commitment of the members of the Quadruple Alliance to prevent further French military action outside of France was clearly articulated from the start both in the terms of the alliance treaty and in the pledging of a specific quantity of troops in the event of a French violation. The commitment to prevent the intrusion of the Holy Alliance into South America was clearly stated both by Canning's actions and those of the United States government, for example, by the promulgation of the Monroe Doctrine.

By way of contrast, Canning's first attempts at preventing French intervention in Spain, and Chamberlain's attempt to pledge Allied support for Poland, although clearly articulated, suffered from other deficiencies which will be discussed later. The U.S. commitment to Israel, in contrast to both previous examples, evolved slowly between 1948 and 1973 in a series of ad-hoc operationalizations in which the United States sought to maintain its policy flexibility in the Middle East while the Israelis sought to obtain an iron-clad guarantee of their security. The resulting ambiguous commitment did little to provide stability to the region or to relieve Israeli anxieties. As can be seen from the three cases studied, the articulation of a clear commitment is neither a simple nor sufficient means of implementing a deterrence policy.

As discussed earlier in this chapter, the deterring power must back up its commitment with threats that are both credible and sufficiently potent in the eyes of the aggressor to prevent him from attempting the undesired course of action. The credibility of a threat is broken into two components, the first of which is the will and resolution of the deterring power to defend the interests in question. In the successful examples of deterrence among the case studies, it is evident that there exists a strong correlation between the demonstration of firm resolve and the success of the policy. When the Allied powers faced France in 1815, they were firmly opposed to allowing France to involve Europe in another set of wars, and they manifested this opposition in their use of occupying troops to enforce the terms of the peace. Likewise, Castelreagh and Canning both relied on European respect for British will and resolve in attempting to combat the pernicious actions of the czar. Both presidents Johnson and Nixon clearly showed their determination in 1967 and 1973 to prevent any possibility of Soviet troop involvement in the Mideast, and they backed up their threats with visible force.

In contrast, the will and resolve of the Allied powers was in considerable doubt in 1939 as a result of the policy of appeasement that they had followed since 1937 and the lack of strong indication of Allied determination. Similarly, the lack of resolve on the part of both American administrations prior to the 1967 and 1973 wars reflected the deep internal divisions brought on by Vietnam and Watergate respectively.

But will and resolve are not sufficient to guarantee success. The deterring power must possess the other component of credibility, namely, the capability for inflicting damage on the opponent. In this regard, the members of the Quadruple Alliance were demonstrably capable of defeating France in the years after 1815 if they acted in concert. In the same vein, Britain was capable, by virtue of its naval superiority, of preventing any extension of the Holy Alliance to the New World. The United States also possessed sufficient capability vis-à-vis the Soviet Union to prevent unilateral Soviet involvement in the 1967 and 1973 wars.

Where capability fails, however, is in those instances where the force the deterring power possesses is either not appropriate or usable in the given situation. All Britain's vaunted sea power could not prevent France from occupying Spain if the other great land powers approved of France's action. In the case of Poland in 1939, the Western Allies were, without the support of the Soviet Union, in no position to inflict unacceptable losses on Germany in the short run or to render timely assistance to their ally, Poland. Because of the distaste for foreign ground combat engendered by U.S. involvement in Vietnam, President Johnson found himself unable or unwilling to honor Eisenhower's 1956 commitment in reference to the Straits of Tiran; and President Nixon and Secretary Kissinger found that, much to their surprise, supplying arms to Israel was not a sufficient means of preventing an Arab attack. Thus, the question of a deterring power's capability can be seen as a key point in the development of a successful strategy.

In considering the second aspect of the threat, we must ask, Is it sufficiently potent to overcome the opponent's motivation to change the status quo? Here the level of opponent's motivation is the key. The newly restored Bourbon monarchy in France was in no way inclined to start another series of disastrous wars in Europe after 1815, and thus it submitted willingly to the restrictions placed on it by the Quadruple Alliance in that year, and by Britain alone in 1823. By the same token, the Soviet Union was not inclined to risk a nuclear confrontation with the United States as long as the existence of its client states in the Mideast was preserved and it was allowed an equal role in determining the outcome of any conflict.

On the other hand, it can be safely stated that Hitler had decided in 1939 to seek further solutions to his foreign policy problems by force of arms; as a result, the Allied threats were doomed to insufficiency without either Soviet assistance or a vastly expanded military establishment, which they did not possess. In 1967 and 1973, the costs of a war with a militarily powerful Israel and the enmity of the United States, were insufficient to overcome pressures within the Arab camp on both Nasser and Sadat to take some drastic action to change the status quo. It can be seen, then, that a sufficiently potent deterring force must exist not only in reality, but more important, in the mind of the potential aggressor as well.

Having examined these three historical cases within the general framework of deterrence theory, it is now desirable to turn to some of the specific components of that theory which have not yet been mentioned.

The first proposition that deterrence theory stresses is that *deterrence is not simply a matter of announcing a commitment and backing it with threats.* The validity of a given commitment is directly related to its possessing a demonstrable or reasonable relationship to the maker's real national interests. This can be seen quite clearly in each of the three cases studied. Before the French invasion of Spain in April 1823, it was obvious to the other European powers that Britain opposed any action to suppress the Spanish revolt; but they were also aware that Britain's real interests lay elsewhere, in its international trade and in the maintenance of its naval supremacy. Thus, while the other powers sanctioned the invasion of Spain, they were unwilling to proceed from there with the reconquest of Portugal and the Spanish colonies, and thus risk almost certain war with Britain. The Allied guarantee to Poland in 1939 suffered from a similar confusion of commitment and national interest. Hitler rationalized that Poland was of little value to the Allies and that, like Czechoslovakia, in the end they would abandon it in the interest of encouraging German expansion eastward rather than westward against themselves. The same sort of problem occurred in 1973 when Sadat correctly deduced that the U.S. commitment to Israel did not extend to territory captured by the Israelis in the 1967 war and thus attempted to recover Arab morale and the Suez Canal by force of arms. Initially willing to leave the Israelis to their own resources, the United States was finally forced to act when the flow of Russian arms in Arab hands threatened to decide the issue in a manner extremely adverse to U.S. Mideast policy. Thus, it can be seen that a commitment must be validated by its relationship to an appropriate national interest.

The second observation to be made about deterrence is that *it is heavily context-dependent*. That is to say, as a deterrence situation changes, so does the calculus of the commitment-threat calculation. This phenomenon was present in both sides of the situation in 1939. As the Allies saw their appeasement plans shattered and their safeguards destroyed one after another by German actions after 1936, their level of commitment increased until, after Prague in 1939, it became apparent that Hitler would have to be stopped in Poland. Unfortunately, Hitler perceived the situation in exactly the opposite manner. He reasoned that Allied resolve had been steadily waning since his reoccupation of the Rhineland and had collapsed at Munich in 1938. He therefore felt that Poland was his for the taking with only a small risk of a major war if he was quickly successful. In 1967, Johnson was painfully unable, because of Vietnam, to honor the commitment to Israel made by the Eisenhower administration in 1956–1957. The conditions of a possible U.S. unilateral action had been so drastically altered since that time that Israel was forced to resolve the situation itself and hope that the United States would support it ex post facto.

The very nature of this second characteristic of deterrence leads directly to the third point emphasized in deterrence theory. Since deterrence is heavily context-dependent, *it is often difficult to design a strategy that will deter all options available to the dissatisfied power.* When the Quadruple Alliance was formalized in 1815, it was intended to prevent a revolutionary France from upsetting the European status quo. Little did the signatories guess that by 1823 France would have become one of the most reactionary powers in Europe, and desirous of invading Spain to suppress a liberal revolt. It is no wonder that the Quadruple Alliance had difficulty deciding on the proper course of action. Likewise, the Allied attempts to deter Germany from attacking Poland were based on the assumptions that Hitler did not want a general European war with the possibility of a hostile Soviet Union at his rear, and that if war did come, Poland would be able to resist long enough for the French army to make itself felt. Hitler circumvented these problems by signing a previously inconceivable nonaggression pact with the Russians, and by overrunning Poland in a matter of weeks, not months. Despite all its diplomatic efforts, the United States was unable to guarantee Israel's security from a variety of Arab threats ranging from economic blockade to terrorist attacks to full-scale offensives by conventional forces. It can thus be seen that in each of the three cases studied, the deterring powers found themselves forced to reevaluate their commitments as the dissatisfied powers altered their strategies in accordance with perceived weaknesses in these commitments.

Still another point emphasized by the theory is that *deterrence often fails in stages* rather than all at once. Each of the three cases illustrates this point. The difference of interests among the members of the Quadruple Alliance manifested itself slowly in the series of European conferences conducted after 1815. In 1939, the Allies had several clear warnings of the impending collapse of their position in Poland; namely, the change in Nazi rhetoric, the Pact of Steel between Germany and Italy, and the dismissal of Litvinow by the Russians. Nasser's step-by-step occupation of the Sinai in 1967 represents an almost classic example of a commitment failing in stages. At each stage, the United States proved powerless to honor its commitments, and Nasser became bolder with each success. Even in 1973, the evacuation of Russian noncombatants forty-eight hours prior to the Egyptian attack provided Israel and U.S. intelligence with a warning (though it was not recognized as such) of the invasion to follow. The usual deterrence commitment, then, does not collapse all at once like a house of cards, but rather weakens slowly like a dike being worn away by the sea. The key question is whether or not the deterring power has the perception, the will, or the capability to shore up its commitment before it is too late.

The three cases as well as many others that have been studied illustrate the final proposition emphasized in modern deterrence theory—that *deterrence is often at best a time-buying strategy,* and as such it is only one instrument of foreign policy and not a substitute for a creative approach that also relies on other means. The Allied powers in 1815 clearly recognized this fact when, at the Congress of Vienna, they allowed for the rapid rehabilitation of France in the international system and established their deterrence commitments accordingly. By reintegrating France and establishing the concert of Europe, the members of the Vienna Congress laid the groundwork for a system that prevented a major war in Europe until 1854. This was truly a successful application of the strategy of deterrence in conjunction with other diplomatic means.

The same cannot be said for the Versailles Conference that met after the First World War. In their efforts to deter Germany from further aggression and to isolate the Soviet Union in order to prevent the spread of communism, the Allied powers created two "pariah" nations that would later combine to thwart the deterrent provisions of the Versailles Treaty and eventually conclude the 1939 Nazi-Soviet Pact which would make the Second War virtually inevitable.

In the Mideast, the United States has finally, as a result of two Arab-Israeli wars which led to superpower confrontations, realized the necessity of doing more in the region than supplying arms to Israel and countering Soviet actions with threats. The peace treaty between Egypt and Israel concluded under U.S. auspices at Camp David in 1978 marks a significant step toward a resolution of the Arab-Israeli conflict which, it is hoped, will obviate the need for further U.S. deterrence commitments to Israel. It is not by rigid preservation of the status quo that the future may best be preserved, but rather by vigorous and intelligent attempts to resolve the causes of conflict at their roots.

Bibliographical Essay

The general theory of deterrence on which this chapter draws is to be found in Alexander L. George and Richard Smoke, *Deterrence in American Foreign Policy: Theory and Practice* (New York, 1974). Some of the most useful discussions are Bernard Brodie, *Strategy in the Missile Age* (Princeton, 1959), chapter 9; Karl W. Deutsch, *The Analysis of International Relations,* 2nd ed. (Englewood Cliffs, N.J., 1978), pp. 154–61; Robert Jervis, "Deterrence Theory Revisited," *World Politics,* 31 (1979), 289–324; Stephen Maxwell, "Rationality in Deterrence," Adelphi Paper No. 50 (London: Institute for Strategic Studies, August 1968); Patrick M. Morgan, *Deterrence: A Conceptual Analysis* (Beverly Hills, Calif., 1977); John Raser, "Theories of Deterrence," special issue, *Peace Research Reviews,* 3 (1969); and Thomas C. Schelling, *The Strategy of Conflict* (Cambridge, 1960); see especially chapters 2, 3, 5, and 8.

14

Coercive Diplomacy

The strategy of coercive diplomacy (or *compellance,* as some prefer to call it) employs threats or limited force to persuade an opponent to call off or undo an encroachment—for example, to halt an invasion or give up territory that has been occupied. Coercive diplomacy therefore differs from the strategy of deterrence, discussed in the preceding chapter, which employs threats to dissuade an opponent from undertaking an action that he has not yet initiated.

Coercive diplomacy needs to be distinguished from pure coercion. It seeks to *persuade* the opponent to cease his aggression rather than bludgeon him into stopping. In contrast to the crude use of force to repel the opponent, coercive diplomacy emphasizes the use of threats and the exemplary use of limited force to persuade him to back down. The strategy of coercive diplomacy calls for using just enough force to demonstrate resolution to protect one's interests and to emphasize the credibility of one's determination to use more force if necessary. In coercive diplomacy, one gives the opponent an opportunity to stop or back off before employing force or escalating its use, as the British did in the early stages of the Falklands dispute in 1982. To this end, the employment of threats and of initially limited force is closely coordinated with appropriate communications to the opponent. All-important signaling, bargaining, and negotiating dimensions, therefore, are built into the strategy of coercive diplomacy.

Coercive diplomacy offers the possibility of achieving one's objective economically, with little bloodshed, fewer political and psychological costs, and often with much less risk of escalation than does traditional military strategy. For this reason, it is often a beguiling strategy. Leaders of militarily powerful countries—like Lyndon Johnson, for example, in his unsuccessful use of air power against Hanoi in 1965—are tempted to believe that they can, with little risk to themselves, intimidate weaker opponents to give up their gains and objectives. If the opponent refuses to be threatened and, in effect, calls the bluff of the coercing power, the latter must then decide whether to back off himself or to escalate the use of force.

It is important to identify the conditions necessary for successful employment of this strategy, since in their absence even a superpower can fail to intimidate a weak opponent and find itself drawn into a costly, prolonged conflict. Comparison of cases of successful coercive diplomacy (for example, the Cuban missile crisis) and unsuccessful ones (for example, the U.S. effort to coerce Japan prior to its attack on Pearl Harbor) has enabled researchers to identify a number of such conditions. Three in particular appear to be of critical importance: the coercing power must create in the opponent's mind a sense of urgency for compliance with its demand, a belief that the coercing power is more highly motivated to achieve its stated demand than the opponent is to oppose it, and a fear of unacceptable escalation if the demand is not accepted. We must recognize that what one demands of the opponent can affect the balance of motivation. If one demands a great deal, the opponent's motivation not to comply will likely be strengthened. But if the coercing power can carefully limit its demands to what is essential to itself without thereby engaging important interests of the opponent, then it is more likely to create an asymmetry of motivation that favors the success of the strategy.

The essentials and drawbacks of the strategy of coercive diplomacy have long been known, although its use in the European balance-of-power era was evidently not systematically articulated. Rather, it was part of the conventional wisdom of those who engaged in statecraft and diplomacy. Properly analyzed, however, older historical cases of coercive diplomacy can contribute to a more refined understanding of the uses and limitations of this strategy as an instrument of foreign policy.

Coercive diplomacy bears a close resemblance to the ultimata that were often employed in the conduct of European diplomacy. A full-blown ultimatum has three components: a specific, clear demand on the opponent; a time limit for compliance; and a threat of punishment for noncompliance which is both credible and sufficiently potent to impress upon the opponent that compliance is preferable. These three components are not always fully present in efforts at coercive diplomacy. The demand on the opponent, for example, may lack clarity or specificity. It may not be accompanied by a specific time limit for compliance, and the coercing power may fail to convey a sense of urgency. The threat of punishment for noncompliance may be ambiguous, of insufficient magnitude, or lacking in credibility. Generally speaking, dilution of any of these three components in the ultimatum may weaken its impact on the other actor's calculations and behavior.

There are several variants of coercive diplomacy. In addition to the full-ultimatum version of the strategy already mentioned, there is what has been called the "try-and-see" approach. In this variant of the strategy, only the first element of an ultimatum, a specific and clear demand, is conveyed, and the coercing power does not announce a time limit or attempt to create a strong sense of urgency for compliance. The try-and-see form is not uncommon; a coercing power often shies away from employing the ultimatum form for one reason or another. Instead, it takes one limited action, as the United States did in attempting to pressure Japan for several years before Pearl Harbor, and waits to see whether it will suffice to persuade the opponent before threatening or taking the next step. There are several variants of the try-and-see strategy. In some circumstances, as in two of the historical cases we shall examine later in this chapter, a gradual "turning of the screw" may be more appropriate than the ultimatum form.

Systematic study of cases of coercive diplomacy has shown that this strategy, perhaps even more so than deterrence strategy, is highly context-dependent. This means that the strategy must be tailored in a rather exacting way to fit the unique configuration of each situation. But the special configuration of a crisis in which coercive diplomacy may be employed is seldom clearly visible to the policy maker and, as a result, the strategy can easily fail. For this and other reasons, as our historical studies will suggest, efforts to engage in coercive diplomacy rest heavily upon skill at improvisation. The actor employing coercive diplomacy must continually evaluate the risks of what he is doing. He must slow the momentum of events as necessary in order to give the opponent time to digest the signals sent him. He has to choose and time his actions carefully to make them compatible with the opponent's ability to appraise the evolving situation and to respond appropriately, and he must always leave him with a way out of the crisis. As these remarks suggest, coercive diplomacy includes some of the important requirements of crisis management, a topic that will be taken up in the next chapter.

Generally speaking, the strategy of coercive diplomacy is in fact more difficult and problematical than is often thought to be the case. Leaders who consider using the strategy against opponents enroaching on their country's interests often erroneously assume that prevailing conditions favor its successful use, that the communication of their demands and threats will be clear and credible to the opponent, and that they are more highly motivated by what is at stake than the opponent. Practitioners of coercive diplomacy also often mistakenly rely solely on threats of punishment for noncompliance with their demands instead of offering incentives for compliance as well. They fail to recognize as clearly as President Kennedy did in the Cuban missile crisis that the objectives on behalf of which coercive diplomacy is exercised can sometimes be achieved only if one makes genuine, even substantial concessions. It will be recalled that Kennedy and Khrushchev did negotiate and agree upon a quid pro quo which ended the missile crisis, Khrushchev agreeing to remove the missiles and bombers in return for Kennedy's pledge not to invade Cuba. Coercive diplomacy, then, is best conceived as a flexible strategy in which what the stick cannot always achieve by itself one can possibly obtain by adding a carrot. Thus, as already noted, in contrast to pure coercion, coercive diplomacy typically requires negotiation, bargaining, and compromise.

To demonstrate coercive diplomacy in practice, three case studies will be briefly outlined and the causes of its successful or unsuccessful application evaluated.* The first case, the Egyptian crisis of 1838–1841, occurred during the period of the classical balance of power in Europe. While not as well-known as our other two cases, this case is chosen because it indicates that even before the impact of the diplomatic revolution had made itself felt, problems of misperception and communication could hamper the effective use of this strategy against weaker states. The second case, the American effort to coerce Japan between 1938 and 1941, illustrates how an overly ambitious use of the strategy boomeranged and led to the Japanese attack on Pearl Harbor. The third case, Arab oil diplomacy in the early 1970s, demonstrates that coercive diplomacy remains today an attractive and, under special conditions, use-

---

* The three case studies presented in this chapter were prepared in their original form by Captain Alan Carver, U.S. Army.

ful instrument of statecraft. As these cases will show, coercive diplomacy strategy is highly context-dependent; careful consideration must always be given to the circumstances, known and unknown to the actors involved, contributing to the course of events in each case. The warning suggested by these case studies is clear. Success in the application of coercive diplomacy is not easily achieved. Disaster is always a single bad decision away.

The Egyptian Crisis (1838–1841)

On 25 May 1838, Mehemet Ali, the Turkish viceroy in Egypt, announced with French encouragement his determination to establish Egypt's independence from the Ottoman (Turkish) Empire. Egyptian military preparations demonstrated that he meant to impose his decision on the Turkish sultan and expand the territories under his rule in the process. This was not Mehemet Ali's first attempt. Some years earlier, the European powers had permitted Russia to intervene, forcing him to back down. In 1838, however, a joint response by the two powers now best able to frustrate Mehemet Ali's designs, England and Russia, was prevented at first by their own competition for influence in Turkey and their disagreement over a proper solution for the Eastern Question. When Czar Nicholas realized that the sultan would not choose to rely on his aid alone, he quickly fashioned several important concessions that finally brought about Anglo-Russian cooperation.

For a time, pressure from England and Russia moderated events and restrained both the sultan and the Egyptian pasha. In April 1839, however, the Turkish army attempted to drive Mehemet Ali and his forces from occupied Syria. He handily defeated them, and the Turkish navy defected to Egypt. With Constantinople on the point of surrender, the five European powers, England, Russia, Austria, Prussia, and France, collectively asked that the sultanate make no concessions without consulting them.

Lord Palmerston, British foreign secretary, proposed in August 1839 that the five powers comprising the concert system unite to secure Mehemet Ali's withdrawal from Syria and the restoration of the integrity and security of the Ottoman Empire. In his proposal, Palmerston stressed that refusal by one power need not prevent the others from acting; this was intended as a warning to the French, whose refusal to agree to any coercive action against the Egyptian pasha persisted, adding a new entanglement to the crisis. The Austrian government, directed in its foreign policy by Prince Metternich, was not convinced that coercion of Mehemet Ali was possible without French cooperation, and it continued to search for a program of action that all five powers could support until June 1840, when insurrection in Syria stimulated the necessary urgency to win Austrian participation. Palmerston, however, did not gain the full support of the British cabinet until 5 July, and this only after he threatened to resign. Once this final hurdle was negotiated, joint action by Austria, Prussia, Russia, and England was possible.

On 9 July, representatives of the four powers met in London, and on 15 July, they jointly accepted the provisions of the Egyptian Convention, an instrument they concocted for the purpose of coercing the pasha. The convention demanded that he return to the Sultan all gains from the war with Turkey, including the Turkish fleet. Turkish laws were to be reimposed in his remaining territories, and Egypt would be reinstated as a Turkish possession. In return, he would receive hereditary rule over Egypt and lifetime control of southern Syria. An ingenious form of ultimatum was contrived to provide incentives for quick compliance. If he failed to agree to the demands within ten days after receipt of the ultimatum, he would lose all claims in Syria. If the demands were not accepted in twenty days, he would lose Egypt as well. Simultaneously, pressure was applied to France, which was still supporting him, to prevent intervention on behalf of Egypt. When Mehemet Ali refused to comply with convention demands, an Anglo-Austrian naval squadron was sent to Beirut. In September, it bombarded the town and assisted in the landing of Turkish forces. The same squadron later entered the port of Alexandria and threatened similar action. By February 1841, Mehemet Ali had retired to Egypt. He had been forced to reopen negotiations and renounce his claim to Syria. In exchange, he was permitted to continue ruling Egypt.

The initial failure of coercive diplomacy with regard to Egypt had several causes. First, the four-power threat was not entirely credible. Mehemet Ali had no reason to expect more than an ineffectual naval blockade. The dispute among the four European powers concerning whether they ought to take action without France was ended only a few weeks before the ultimatum was dispatched. Therefore, joint action, even by four of the European powers, was not entirely certain; besides, it was not clear that the four powers were more highly motivated by what was at stake than was Mehemet Ali. As it turned out, the four powers were obliged to demonstrate their willingness to engage in a cooperative military action in order to convince Mehemet Ali that the price of noncompliance would be severe. In the end, contrary to his lingering hopes, the French proved unwilling to defend the Egyptian position, perhaps as a result of Palmerston's efforts to deter them from doing so. All these developments combined to alter Mehemet Ali's perception of the situation. Only the incremental application of military power convinced him of his adversaries' commitment. After the initial ultimatum was rejected, limited force persuaded him that he would get off cheaply by conceding. When the necessity of imposing the full punishment ended, the European powers were anxious to conclude the crisis without causing him to become desperate and so granted him a generous peace. The continual policy evaluation and adjustment required for success is evident in this example of coercive diplomacy.

U.S. Policy Toward Japan (1938–1941)

Between 1938 and 1940, Japanese expansion into China proceeded in earnest and became increasingly worrisome to the United States. War in China represented a heavy commitment of men, resources, and prestige on the part of the Japanese. Their stated ambition was the creation of a "greater East Asia co-prosperity sphere." Aggressive and militaristic policies demonstrated a fundamental belief in Japanese destiny. U.S. interests in China were minor in comparison and lacked the driving force that characterized Japanese actions. Moreover, the ability of the American government to make strong signals of displeasure and warning to Japan was limited by domestic politics. And, in any case, the strength and credibility of objections to Japanese violations of certain treaties and international laws were severely diluted by American policies of isolationism and "correct" neutrality.

Despite these domestic constraints, the United States eventually responded to Japanese expansion with an embargo on certain military goods and a cancellation of credits in 1939. Later that year, the Japanese-American commercial treaty of 1911 was abrogated. These measures were meant to restrain Japan and moderate its policies in Asia. However, this policy of coercion through economic punishment was not precise and did not make clear to the Japanese what the next step might be. Cordell Hull, the American secretary of state, was reluctant to stop all trade with Japan in order to maintain leverage but would not specify how he expected to use this weapon in the future. Despite these early pressures, clear communication of a firm U.S. commitment to back rhetorical demands on Japan was lacking, and the Japanese leaders were entitled to believe that they were more strongly motivated to resist U.S. demands than U.S. leaders were to enforce them. The stake in the conflict of interests in Asia was clearly greater for Japan than for the United States. Minor efforts were made to avoid flagrant antagonism of the Americans, but the Japanese continued their policy of military expansion so that, by 1940, the Dutch East Indies and French Indochina were threatened.

The United States continued to send conflicting signals, containing elements of both a hard and a moderate line, for some time, reflecting a lack of consensus among policy makers in Washington. Meanwhile, economic sanctions were increased by selective embargo. By mid-1940, moderate voices in the U.S. government were largely silenced by a general dissatisfaction with the evident failure of limited measures. During that summer, more severe embargoes were imposed. Having been presented with few concrete demands, the Japanese were somewhat startled by the avalanche of new economic hardships that now faced them. Rather than make compliance more attractive, however, the new American policy of stepped-up pressures boomeranged, making the Japanese government only more determined to acquire secure and independent sources of raw materials and weakening the moderates within the Japanese cabinet. The new U.S. threat to escalate pressures confirmed Tokyo's worst fears about the future and prompted a faster pace of expansion. It seemed certain in Tokyo that the United States did not want war with Japan and would not easily be driven into one, especially as the war in Europe accelerated and turned against the Allies resisting Hitler. The embargo of needed materials was interpreted as a challenge, not a warning, a challenge that would not be backed up by the United States. The fact that Japan had imposed similar embargoes to protect her own war-making potential was ignored, and hardliners in Tokyo denounced each new American restriction as unwarranted and a sign of bad faith.

On 27 September 1940, Japan joined the Tripartite Pact, allying itself with Germany and Italy and thereby conveying a counterwarning to the United States against further interference in Asia. Japan derived few concrete benefits from the alliance, but in the United States it fostered new anxieties, linking Japan with aggression elsewhere. Nevertheless, the American government was not prepared for direct confrontation with Japan and continued a policy of weak countermeasures and uncompromising demands. Negotiations proved fruitless, each power resolutely demanding total concession. A critical turning point that severely escalated the diplomatic confrontation occurred on 25 July 1941, when the United States imposed a total embargo on oil and froze Japanese assets in American banks. U.S. strength and resolve were on the increase, and the threat of escalation was now clear. In November, Japan was presented with demands that included withdrawal from all occupied territories, repudiation of the Tripartite Pact, and an end to expansion. Faced with visions of economic strangulation, Japan chose the alternative, war with the United States. Pearl Harbor was, in this sense, a rational response to the choice posed by the American ultimatum, for the alternative—acceptance of U.S. demands—was even more unpalatable than war with a stronger opponent, the outcome of which was uncertain.

The Japanese decision was not a hasty one, but evolved as a product of cabinet and domestic politics. By September 1941, plans for war had turned to rehearsals, and October was established as the time for decision. In mid-October, the Konoye cabinet fell, and General Tojo became prime minister. Although the deadline had been reached, the new government elected to continue to seek an alternative to what would certainly be a dangerous war. The tightening restrictions on Japan's oil supply, however, had imposed a time limit for adopting a military option. As supplies diminished, the chances that war could be sustained until independent sources were secured grew smaller. So far, Roosevelt had refused to make a firm commitment to respond to a Japanese attack on British and Dutch possessions in the Pacific, but the risk that such an attack would trigger U.S. military intervention seemed to require a preemptive attack on American means to do so. On 5 November, the new Japanese cabinet resolved to stake everything on their last set of proposals. Cordell Hull was presented with them on 20 November. Two days later, Admiral Yamamoto was directed to rendezvous the Japanese fleet on 3 December. The U.S. ultimatum on 26 November, demanding that Japan surrender its position of power in Asia after years of investing resources and prestige in a policy of expansion, made the outcome certain. On 1 December at 2 P.M. Tokyo time, the imperial council made the decision for war.

The American failure to clarify and, particularly, to limit policy objectives from the beginning enormously strengthened Japanese motivation not to comply. Unable to understand that Japan would not suddenly reverse long-held values and beliefs and agree under pressure to dismantle ten years of expansion, the U.S. government simply reinforced Japanese attitudes about the world. And by initiating a complete embargo of American oil, Washington in effect gave Japan an eighteen-month deadline for the achievement of petroleum self-sufficiency. The few carrots offered by the United States to encourage compliance with its demands—most-favored nation status and a mutual nonaggression treaty—did not affect Japanese motivation or their analysis of costs and benefits. The only Japanese counterproposals, an offer to withdraw from Indochina upon the conclusion of the war with China if the United States would support both a negotiated settlement that favored Japan and the restoration of full Japanese-American relations, were bluntly rejected in Washington, thereby preventing any chance of a compromise. The incorrect image of the Japanese position held by many top American decision makers prevented a more precise and calculated application of coercive diplomacy and doomed U.S. policy to failure. The situation developed its own dynamics beyond the control of either country, and war became inevitable.

Arab Oil Diplomacy (1973–1974)

Perhaps no other event in recent years caused a greater change in the attitudes and actions of the major industrialized countries than the Arab oil embargo of 1973. The international system continues to this day to adapt itself to the new conditions that made themselves apparent at that time. The tactical reaction was swift, but the repercussions persist.

Between 1956 and 1973, the demand for imported oil in Japan and the countries of Western Europe had increased phenomenally. To a lesser extent, this was also true in the United States. At the same time, the Arab states gained a gradual appreciation of the potential of the oil weapon. When it was ultimately used to change Western political attitudes regarding the Arab-Israeli conflict, it represented an almost unique attempt by militarily weak, nonindustrialized states to coerce powerful, industrial nations by economic means alone. In doing so, the Arab states involved set in motion a dramatic realignment of Western positions and beliefs.

OPEC was established in 1960 to protect its member states from reductions in crude oil prices. Because of extensive oil supplies and a lack of solidarity among its membership, its early achievements were minimal. In the late 1960s, a more radical direction developed, corresponding to rising Arab nationalism and fostered by Western support for Israel. As a result, OPEC nations attempted during the Six Day War in 1967 to capitalize on their economic clout, but they failed. The principal cause of the failure was Saudi Arabian reluctance to participate. The United States, almost totally self-sufficient in oil, proved generally immune to the action, and shortfalls elsewhere were minimal, reduced by a quick Western response. After 1967, oil was not regarded in the West as a credible weapon, and few protective measures were taken against a repetition of the attempted embargo.

Between 1970 and 1973, a military stalemate existed in the Middle East, and the West, particularly the United States, expected that the uneasy quasi-peace would continue indefinitely. The Israeli refusal to return the territories captured in 1967, however, produced greater unity among the Arab states and strengthened the desire for a change in the status quo. These conditions were accompanied by a recognizable transformation in the oil market that confirmed greater European and Japanese reliance on Arab oil. Thus, several changes occurred after 1967 that increased both the potency of oil as an economic and political lever and the Arab appreciation of this fact.

On 6 October 1973, Anwar Sadat launched an Egyptian attack into the Sinai with initial success. A coordinated Syrian attack in the north followed. Although achievement of Sadat's war objectives was not expected to be dependent on a simultaneous diplomatic offensive, agreement by Saudi Arabia to participate in an Arab oil embargo, if necessary to exert additional pressure, made the war option more attractive to Sadat. On the twelfth day of the eighteen-day war, the Arab oil ministers met to agree upon a plan for the use of the oil weapon. All conditions seemed right for an embargo, and the war with Israel strengthened the case of its advocates. It was realized from the beginning that pro-Arab countries had to be guaranteed oil to prevent a commonly hostile response. This required careful orchestration with specific target nations and clear objectives. It also required an appropriate trigger to justify use of the oil weapon.

The United States had at first resisted pressures to intervene on behalf of Israel, expecting a repeat of 1967; accordingly, the Arab states were satisfied merely to threaten an embargo in order to deter U.S. military assistance to Israel and, more generally, to encourage American diplomatic pressure on Israel to give up the occupied Arab territories. As events turned more and more against the Israelis, however, the American government changed its policy. On 14 October (Day 8), it began a massive airlift to embattled Israel. Almost immediately, the tide of battle shifted. An Egyptian offensive calculated to relieve pressure on the Syrian front was repulsed and, within days, the Israelis began and completed an encirclement of the Egyptian Third Army. With Egypt and Syria hard-pressed, the oil embargo assumed greater potential importance as a defensive tool aimed at the eventual cease-fire negotiations and as a diplomatic weapon for inducing Western Europe and Japan to adopt more sympathetic attitudes in the Arab-Israeli dispute. In mid-October, six OPEC states announced a 70 percent price hike and an immediate 5-percent production cut. They also threatened that each month Israel occupied territory beyond its pre-1967 borders and Palestinian rights went unrecognized, the production cuts would continue. Shortly after this first announcement, Saudi Arabia reduced production and threatened the United States with an embargo. When a massive aid package for Israel was submitted to Congress by the Nixon administration on 20 October, OPEC imposed an embargo on all states that would not adopt an "even-handed" policy toward the Arab-Israeli conflict.

Several aspects of the embargo are noteworthy. First, the demand to restore Palestinian rights under the 1967 United Nations Resolution 242 was extremely vague, opening the way for interpretation and dispute. Second, not all the Western governments who were victims of the oil embargo could directly affect the outcome of the war or the form of the final settlement. Many could do little more than meet minimal demands by supporting the Arab position in official statements. Because the United States was the principal target, this was not an insurmountable problem as long as an anti-Arab bloc was not allowed to form. To avoid a bloc response, OPEC was forced to provide oil in response to minimal concessions by certain states, although this generally reduced the effectiveness of the embargo.

The central problem was that the United States, in a position to do the most in response to the OPEC demands, was the least affected by the production cuts. The most telling effect of the embargo was its tendency to weaken Western alignments by striking at the United States through its most vulnerable partners, Japan, Great Britain, and West Germany. A direct challenge might not have been the best strategy in any case, since it was important not to force the United States and Israel too far apart. If American-Israeli relations became too strained as a consequence of the embargo pressures, even the American government might not have been able to deliver the desired diplomatic concessions. Unless the Americans preserved their ties with Israel, no advantage, at least in the short term, was possible. The combination of these concerns and Saudi Arabia's continued reluctance to alienate the United States totally required OPEC to adopt a flexible policy that could be delicately balanced over time.

The orchestrated approach of the try-and-see variant of coercive diplomacy was best suited to these circumstances and was appropriately selected by the OPEC states. Adoption of limited, flexible objectives, which were subsequently redefined on the basis of appraisals of what was possible and what was not, and a careful targeting of the embargo on the United States and its allies were all part of the Arabs' ingenious oil diplomacy offensive. They achieved asymmetry of motivation in their favor by indirect pressure. If long-term Arab interests became endangered during the course of the oil embargo, concessions could be made and careful monitoring of developments could enable the Arab leaders to avoid unnecessary escalation of the crisis. Even Western public opinion was courted by advertising campaigns in countries affected by the embargo. Finally, when the United States announced its willingness to adopt a more "even-handed" approach in the Middle East, the embargo was lifted. No further benefit was possible, and moderate but substantial change had been achieved. If not totally successful, the Arab oil embargo demonstrated a remarkable appreciation for the opportunities and limits of coercive diplomacy.

Analysis

In the case of the Egyptian crisis of 1840, coercive diplomacy initially failed because the threat used was less than credible and the opponent's fear of escalation was limited until actual force was employed. The U.S. policy toward Japan in the years before 1941 failed because core values held by the Japanese were nonnegotiable, and American demands merely increased their intransigence. In the case of the Arab oil embargo, a limited, rational strategy was used. It was adapted over time to changing circumstances and abandoned when reasonable success was obtained. Apparent in each case is the potential for error and the importance of circumstances.

Each of the case studies also reflects features of the diplomatic revolution. Bureaucratic decision-making and the influences of domestic politics, for example, stand out in the two later cases. No single official or agency was able to give consistency to the course of events or national responses. The inability of major powers to keep weaker states in check and the impact that nonsuperpower actors can achieve are also features of no little note. OPEC is just one example of the multitude of new agents in international affairs contributing to the complexity that seems an irrevocable characteristic of the diplomatic scene. It is also clear that advance in communications and intelligence-gathering have not appreciably reduced the problems of diplomatic decision-making despite the increased pace of international events and the flood of information now available to statesmen. As a result, misperception remains a severe problem in the application of coercive diplomacy. Time is compressed, the number of influences that must be considered has multiplied, and the military superiority of the superpowers has proven to have limited usefulness and awesome risks. Other forms of power and the influence of smaller states have assumed increased significance as a consequence. Under new circumstances, the requirements and limits of coercive diplomacy deserve more than passing consideration. The theory involved can do little more than identify the necessary conditions for success and warn of inherent dangers. It still remains for governments to determine when its use is appropriate and worth the risk.

Once coercive diplomacy is employed, statesmen must recognize that bargaining has not stopped but may have only just begun. No ultimatum can be so final that concessions cannot be made to slow the momentum of events when necessary. The importance of timing is crucial in coercive diplomacy. An opponent must be permitted the opportunity to digest the situation as presented to him and choose his answer. If adequate time is not provided, his response may well be reckless and ill-considered. The responsibility for the pacing of events, for determining the appropriate sense of urgency, and for clear communications must be assumed by the nation that adopts this strategy. Feedback must be anticipated and incorporated into future actions. Without orchestration, events can easily backfire, producing more harm than good and making victims of all concerned.

It is apparent that coercive diplomacy deals not with absolute power but with relative power under specific circumstances. Assessment of that power relationship is a function of perception and rough calculation. The state that engages in coercive diplomacy cannot have full control over the outcome because so much depends on the image of the situation that the other side develops and on the conclusions that are reached as a result. The fundamental danger of the strategy is related to this fact. What may be seen as an inexpensive policy can easily deteriorate when challenges are accepted and action becomes necessary. Coercive diplomacy is a policy that must be rationally and cautiously implemented with an eye to all the dangers and limits of what may be obtained. It is a sharp tool, at times useful, but difficult to employ when one is faced by a recalcitrant opponent. Although it often assumes an attraction that is difficult to resist, its apparent usefulness must not make it a substitute for more manageable strategies when there are suitable alternatives.

Bibliographical Essay

The general theory of coercive diplomacy on which this chapter draws can be found in Alexander L. George, David K. Hall, and William E. Simons, *The Limits of Coercive Diplomacy* (Boston, 1971). Other useful discussions are available in Paul Gordon Lauren, "Ultimata and Coercive Diplomacy," *International Studies Quarterly*, 16 (1972), 131–65; Lauren, "Theories of Bargaining with Threats of Force: Deterrence and Coercive Diplomacy," in *Diplomacy: New Approaches in History, Theory, and Policy*, ed. Lauren (New York, 1979); Thomas C. Schelling, *Arms and Influence* (New Haven, 1966); Glenn H. Snyder, "Crisis Bargaining," in *International Crises: Insights from Behavioral Research*, ed. Charles F. Hermann (New York, 1972); and Glenn H. Snyder and Paul Diesing, *Conflict Among Nations* (Princeton, 1977).

The Egyptian crisis is addressed in most of the general diplomatic histories available and these are most suitable by way of introduction and for the general reader. The Eastern Question as it concerned the great powers has itself produced a vast amount of literature containing references to this period, since it served as background for later disputes. Both Kenneth Bourne's masterly *Palmerston: The Early Years, 1830–1841* (New York, 1982) and C. K. Webster, *The Foreign Policy of Palmerston, 1830–1841* (London, 1951), however, provide more detailed accounts than the general histories while limiting their descriptions to manageable proportions. They are useful as well in their perceptions of the central characters involved. W. A. Miller, *The Ottoman Empire and Its Successors 1801–1927*, 3rd ed. (London, 1966) and the more recent work by S. J. Shaw, *History of the Ottoman Empire and Modern Turkey* (Cambridge, 1976–1977), are also recommended as background sources and for their bibliographies.

The U.S. policy toward Japan before World War II receives admirable treatment in the well-respected work by Herbert Feis, *The Road to Pearl Harbor: The Coming of the War Between the United States and Japan* (Princeton, 1950). While this book provides an excellent starting point, the serious reader might try *Japan's Decision for War,* ed. Nobutaka Ike (Stanford, 1967), or P. W. Schroeder's *The Axis Alliance and Japanese-American Relations* (Ithaca, N.Y., 1958). For those interested in the Japanese perspectives and bureaucratic decision-making in the prewar years, R. J. C. Butow, *Tojo and the Coming of the War* (Princeton, 1961) is also recommended, although U.S. policy is treated in a more peripheral fashion than in the other works. All of these books can direct the reader to more technical or primary sources on the subject.

The number of articles dealing with the oil embargo of 1973 is enormous and nearly all, particularly the later, more scholarly, retrospective ones, deserve reading. The *Adelphi Papers* published by the International Institute for Strategic Studies have much to recommend them in this vein. Nos. 111 (*The Arab-Israeli War—October 1973: Background and Events*), 114 (*The Middle East and the International System,* Part I—*The Impact of the 1973 War*), 115 (*The Middle East and the International System,* Part II—*Security and the Energy Crisis*), 117 (*Oil and Influence—The Oil Weapon Examined*), 128 (*The Arab-Israeli Dispute—Great Power Behavior*), and 136 (*Oil and Security—Problems and Prospects of Importing Countries*) are all of interest. M. Heikal, *The Road to Ramadan* (New York, 1955) includes a chapter on the oil weapon, but the author clearly considers it a subordinate feature of the 1973 war. Nadav Safran, *Israel, The Embattled Ally* (Cambridge, Mass., 1978) adds the dimension of U.S.–Israeli relations before, during, and since the embargo.

15

Crisis Management

The history of relations among states is studded with innumerable diplomatic confrontations, some that were resolved peacefully and others that ended in war. Crises are generated by conflicts of interests which erupt into war-threatening situations either through the deliberate action of the parties involved or through inadvertence. In the ensuing crisis, policy makers are called upon to make delicate diplomatic and military decisions under the pressure of time and events. Such decisions may result not merely in success or failure for the nations they represent, but in the preservation or destruction of the existing international order.

A familiar phenomenon during the European balance-of-power era, crisis management has taken on a new urgency in the age of thermonuclear weapons. Shortly after the harrowing experience of the Cuban missile crisis, Secretary of Defense Robert McNamara remarked soberly, "Today there is no longer any such thing as military strategy; there is only crisis management." This was, to be sure, an overstatement, but it emphasized the critical role of the managerial aspect of the unprecedented Soviet-American confrontation of 1962.

The necessity and the modalities of effective crisis management did not emerge for the first time during the Cuban crisis. The two superpowers had already acquired considerable experience in controlling and managing tense situations in Berlin. It is nevertheless essentially correct to say that before Cuba, there was little in the way of an explicit theory of crisis management to guide policy makers who wanted to protect the national interest without becoming involved in a war. Robert F. Kennedy has written that shortly before the discovery of the missile sites, his brother had read Barbara Tuchman's book *The Guns of August,* which tells how Europe stumbled into war in 1914. It is possible that this helped alert him to the kinds of mistakes that can be made by statesmen at moments of high crisis. But certainly there was no handbook of management techniques to help the president.

Inspired by the Cuban experience, scholars and policy researchers have now studied the tasks and requirements of crisis management in considerable detail. Both within the government and in research institutes, crises that have occurred since World War II have been examined with an eye to the light they might throw upon problems of information-processing and decision-making under crisis conditions, on the special requirements of command and control, on the means of coordinating diplomatic and military actions, and on the problems of communication with an opponent during crises and the advisable methods of maintaining it.

Not all of this work (some of which remains highly classified) need or can be summarized here. For our purposes, it is enough to identify the general tasks and requirements of crisis management that have been emphasized by those who have studied it. Analysis of a number of crises—some successfully managed, like the Cuban missile crisis, and others not, like the outbreak of World War I and the Chinese intervention into the Korean War in 1950—supports the proposition that it facilitates management of a crisis if one or both sides limit the *objectives* they pursue in the confrontation and/or the *means* they employ in pursuing them. But it must also be noted that limitation of objectives and means will not suffice for managing a crisis without war. These studies indicate that *both* sides must understand the following requirements of crisis management and be willing and able to act in accordance with them:

1. *Maintain top-level civilian control of military options.* Of surpassing importance for crisis management is top-level civilian control over the selection and timing of military actions. This requirement may extend even to control over specific tactical maneuvers and operations that might lead to an undesired clash with the opponent's forces.
2. *Create pauses in the tempo of military actions.* The momentum of military movements may have to be deliberately slowed down in order to provide enough time for the two sides to exchange diplomatic

signals and communications, and to give each side adequate time to assess the situation, make decisions, and respond to proposals.

3. *Coordinate diplomatic and military moves.* Whatever military moves are undertaken must be carefully coordinated with political-diplomatic actions and communications as part of a carefully integrated strategy for terminating the crisis acceptably without war.

4. *Confine military moves to those that constitute clear demonstrations of one's resolve and are appropriate to one's limited crisis objectives.*

5. *Avoid military moves that give the opponent the impression that one is about to resort to large-scale warfare and, therefore, force him to consider preemption.*

6. *Choose diplomatic-military options that signal a desire to negotiate rather than to seek a military solution.*

7. *Select diplomatic-military options that leave the opponent a way out of the crisis that is compatible with his fundamental interests.*

Both Kennedy and Khrushchev displayed a keen awareness of these requirements and regulated their behavior in accordance with them in the Cuban missile crisis. But the principles have not always been well understood by policy makers in other crises. President Truman, for example, failed to observe them when he dealt with the intervention of Chinese Communist forces into the Korean War in November 1950. In any case, mere awareness of the requirements of crisis management by no means assures that they will be effectively implemented. Leaders of one or both sides may have imperfect control over their military forces. Military forces may have been designed and structured in ways that rob them of the flexibility needed in a crisis. Military doctrine governing use of forces may, as in the events leading to the outbreak of World War I, which will be discussed later in this chapter, deprive governments of the kinds of limited mobilization and deployment options required for careful management.

It must be recognized that crisis management requires novel concepts of planning, control, and conduct of military operations and that these requirements may strain the experience, imagination, and patience of military professionals. The seven requirements for crisis management noted above impose stringent constraints on the use of military force and can easily lead to serious tensions between the military and political leaders of a nation. It is not easy to adapt military capabilities to meet these exacting requirements unless weapons systems possess flexible characteristics and unless planners are ingenious in contriving somewhat novel uses of existing forces. Moreover, options that meet these criteria and are therefore considered "usable" by a president who wants to manage the crisis effectively tend to be quickly used up. If the Cuban blockade had failed, there were few remaining options that President Kennedy could have used without triggering war. Efforts by strategists and civilian leaders to transform force into a highly refined, discriminating instrument that will support an assertive foreign policy and also be appropriate for crisis management eventually break down if pushed too far.

In sum, effective adherence to the principles of crisis management requires, among other things, appropriate military capabilities, doctrines, and options, effective command and control from top-level authorities to tactical units, intimate interaction between civilian and military planners in order to design usable options compatible with crisis-management requirements, and skill and flexibility in adapting contingency plans to unexpected developments as a crisis unfolds.

Utilizing the seven requirements of successful crisis management, it is possible to compare the relative performance of policy makers in different crises and to come to a deeper understanding of the impact of the diplomatic revolution on the management of crises in general. The three cases chosen—the Crimean War, World War I, and the 1973 Arab-Israeli War—are particularly significant in that their outcomes reflect directly not only the international community's ability to resolve conflict short of general war, but the more far-reaching question regarding the preservation or dissolution of the then current international system.*

The Crimean War (1854)

The origins of the crisis precipitating the Crimean War lay in the slow disintegration of the Ottoman Empire and the destabilizing effect this process was to have on the concert of Europe system established in 1815. Four of the five European powers—England, France, Russia, and Austria—possessed some vested interest in the affairs of the sultan's domain, while the fifth, Prussia, remained an interested observer. The Russians, led by an active Czar Nicholas, had long-standing concerns in

* The case studies in this chapter were prepared in their original form by Captain Richard J. Hoffman, U.S. Army.

the region that brought them into conflict on religious grounds with the France of Napoleon III, and on economic ones with an England divided politically over the Corn Law issue of 1846. Austria, although always interested in its Balkan frontier, was in the process of recovery from the divisive effects of the 1848 revolution, and its young emperor, Franz Joseph, was reluctant to engage in foreign adventure without a sure guarantee of success.

The same could not be said for the newly proclaimed emperor of the French, Napoleon III. Anxious to improve France's reputation abroad and his own at home, Napoleon in early 1852 pressured the sultan into a series of concessions concerning the rights of Roman Catholic orders in the holy lands. These concessions seemed to conflict with earlier privileges granted Greek Orthodox holy orders in 1740, and the czar, as protecter of the Greek Orthodox faith, felt compelled to act in their defense. His initial action was to dispatch an envoy, Prince Menshikow, to demand, as he did with some arrogance, that Turkey reverse its earlier decision and give formal recognition to Russia's right to protect Orthodox believers in the Ottoman Empire. As a result of Menshikow's blunt negotiations, a decree apportioning religious rights in the holy lands was published on 4 May 1853. Unsatisfied, the czar sent Russian troops to occupy the Danubian Principalities with the intention of holding these Turkish dependencies until his original demands were met.

In doing so, Nicholas acted in the belief that Austria and England would support him. Austria, as a result of indecision in the ruling council, remained neutral. England, ruled by a coalition cabinet, pursued two policies simultaneously. The pro-Russian faction, headed by Prime Minister Aberdeen, sustained Nicholas in his belief. Unfortunately, the anti-Russian faction, led by the popular home secretary, Lord Palmerston, and assisted by an independently minded ambassador to Turkey, Stratford Canning, did its best to stir up opposition to the Russian move both at home and in the court of the sultan.

As the governments of Europe sought a solution to the deepening crisis, a council of ambassadors convened in Vienna in July 1853. The result of these consultations was the "Vienna Note" of 28 July 1853, which held the promise of acceding to Russia's demands while preserving Turkish sovereignty. At this juncture, Ambassador Canning intervened to persuade the Turks to reject the note and assured them that should the situation require it, England would support Turkey with force. The sultan's ministers then demanded that the Russians withdraw from the principalities and, receiving no answer, declared war in October.

The first major action of the Russo-Turkish War was a naval battle at Sinope in the Black Sea on 30 November 1853, in which the Russians destroyed the totally outdated Turkish fleet. At this point, the czar attempted to resume negotiations, but events began to pass beyond his control. At home in England, Palmerston was using the power of a jingoistic press to whip the British public into a war frenzy over the alleged "massacre" at Sinope. Meanwhile, Canning, acting on his own authority, concentrated the British and—with the French now following the British lead—French fleets near the Dardanelles to stiffen the Turks and provide the opportunity for intervention. Despite the efforts of Aberdeen, Palmerston's exertions had the desired effect, and the British cabinet was forced to authorize the deployment of the combined fleets into the Black Sea in January 1854.

Taking this action as a *casus belli,* Nicholas broke relations with Britain and France in February 1854. In return, the two powers demanded evacuation of the principalities. When the czar failed to respond, Britain and France declared hostilities in March, thus opening the Crimean War.

World War I

Like the Crimean War, the origin of the final crisis of 1914 lies in the distintegration of the Ottoman Empire and the repercussions this had on the international situation. The Europe of 1914 was very different, however, from the one of 1854. The European concert of five great powers established in 1815 had been replaced by 1914 by a bipolar arrangement of alliances. The states of Germany, Austro-Hungary, and Italy were committed to the Triple Alliance, while those of Britain, France, and Russia comprised the Triple Entente. These alliance systems had by 1914 divided Europe into two heavily armed camps, in which the actions of any member of an alliance involved, by custom or commitment, the national interests of the other members.

In this tense international situation, the unsettled affairs in the Balkans had remained a festering sore since the Bosnian crisis of 1908. The Austrians remained convinced of the need to crush Serbia at the earliest possible opportunity. For their part, the Serbs fostered dreams of a Serbian-led Slav national state, and the Russians sought to advance their traditional interests at the Straits of the Dardanelles.

When Austrian Crown Prince Ferdinand and his wife were assassinated by Serbian terrorists on 28 June 1914, the policy makers in Vienna decided to use the event as a pretext for a permanent resolution of the Serbian problem. Their next prime concern was to secure German support for the operation in order to counterbalance the threat of Russian intervention. This they received on 5 July 1914 when the German kaiser in effect issued a blank check to the Austrian emperor to resolve the matter as he saw fit, assuring him of Germany's support. The Austrian response was a harsh ultimatum that they issued to the shocked Serbs on 23 July. The terms were such that compliance would deprive Serbia of independence. Under Russian pressure to compromise, the Serbians composed a masterful reply that acceded to most of the Austrian demands save the virtual occupation of Serbia. Unsatisfied, the Austrians commenced their preparations and declared war on Serbia on 28 July 1914.

With the reality of a Balkan war established, the focus of events now shifted to attempts to localize the conflict short of a general European conflagration. Although most of the powers involved recognized a need to accomplish this task, their alliance systems, war plans, and generally inept political leadership balked their efforts. On 29 July, the Russians made the first major attempt at limitation when, in response to the Austrian move, they announced a partial mobilization aimed only at war with Austria, in the hopes of keeping Germany out of the conflict. Their hopes were ill-founded, however, for despite the misgivings of the kaiser and the chancellor, Bethmann Hollweg, Chief of the General Staff Moltke was already contemplating Germany's mobilization against both Russia and her principal continental ally, France. When on the same fateful day Bethmann Hollweg learned from the British foreign secretary, Lord Grey, that Britain would stand by its commitments to France and Belgium if they were attacked, the stage was set for a war of global proportions.

The kaiser and chancellor tried on 30 July to hold off the now escalating crisis, but even as Bethmann Hollweg sought to restrain the Austrians short of war, the Austrian chief of staff, Conrad von Hötzendorf, was receiving a telegram from Moltke urging him to mobilize the Austrian army at once. The Austrian government gave orders to that effect on 31 July, and the Russians, their attempt at partial mobilization a failure, responded with a full callup against Germany and Austria. On 31 July, the German government sent an ultimatum to Russia, demanding that this be halted. When the czar failed to comply, Moltke ordered German mobilization on 1 August, with a formal declaration of war against Russia following on the same day. Dismissing the kaiser's attempt to limit German mobilization to the Russian front as an invitation to disaster, and in any case impossible, Moltke secured the dispatch of an ultimatum to France and a diplomatic note to Belgium demanding free passage for German troops. When these demands were refused, Germany declared war on both countries on 3 August 1914 and began to invade Belgium. The British, honoring their public commitment to preserve Belgian neutrality and their private agreements with France, declared war on Germany on 4 August. Thus, by 4 August 1914, all the major European powers, save Italy, which had declared itself neutral on the grounds that Austria and Germany had initiated the conflict, were locked into what was to be the most devastating war the world had yet seen.

The 1973 Arab-Israeli War

Although the 1967 Arab-Israeli conflict seemed to have resulted in a resounding Israeli victory, its conclusion resulted in bitter antagonisms that were later to burst forth in more violence. By 1973, the Egyptians and Syrians had little to show for their efforts since the self-proclaimed "year of decision" in 1971. Both Arab states had been substantially supplied with up-to-date Russian military equipment and resolved to break the existing stalemate by force of arms.

The other powers involved in this Middle East dispute were, of course, the two superpowers, the United States and the USSR. For its part, Russia at first attempted to restrain the Arab states from overt military action through diplomatic efforts and a slowdown in the delivery of arms; later, the Soviet leaders reluctantly dropped their opposition to Arab use of force. The United States, led by its ubiquitous secretary of state, Henry Kissinger, pursued a policy of "no war—no peace" with the hopes of eventually ejecting the Soviet Union from the Middle East and assuming the role of moderator in the Arab-Israeli conflict.

Nevertheless, the stalemate abruptly ended on 6 October 1973 when the armed forces of Syria and Egypt launched coordinated offensives on the Golan and Sinai fronts respectively. The Israelis, although not taken totally by surprise, were heavily outnumbered as a result of an internal decision not to mobilize until attacked. Consequently, the Arab forces scored tactical successes on both fronts with the Egyptians eventually forcing the abandonment of the Bar-Lev fortified line along the Suez Canal. By 7 October, the Israeli army had stopped the Syrian attack, and by 8 October, it began to counterattack on the Sinai front as well. These attacks were not initially successful, but the pressure generated on the Arab armies was so severe that they appealed to Moscow for aid.

Although the Russians were at first wary of the Arabs' decision to resort to force, the actions of their clients placed them in an unenviable position. To refuse the request for aid would jeopardize their entire position in the Middle East, while to grant it would risk the possible escalation of the conflict. In response to this problem, the Russians began a massive airlift of military supplies on 10 October and dispatched Premier Kosygin to Cairo on 16 October to observe the situation at first hand. By 18 October, it had become apparent that the course of the war was turning against the Egyptians, and Sadat authorized Kosygin to initiate a cease-fire in place on the Sinai front. On 20 October 1973, Secretary Kissinger visited Moscow at Brezhnev's request to negotiate a cease-fire. The result of that trip was UN Resolution 338, enacted on 22 October, calling for a cease-fire in place and the start of negotiations. On his return from Moscow, Kissinger stopped in Tel Aviv to apprise the Israelis of his actions and to ensure compliance with their part in the cease-fire. Dependent on the American airlift, which had begun on 14 October in response to the Soviet effort, the Israelis had little choice but to agree to the conditions of Resolution 338, and on 22 October it seemed that peace had been restored.

But the cease-fire of 22 October was not to last. It is difficult to determine who first violated it, but by 23 October the Russians were reporting Israeli violations as the Israeli army sought to continue its encirclement of the Egyptian Third Army east of Suez and the Egyptians fought to escape. At the superpowers' request, the UN Security Council met that night and passed Resolution 339, which confirmed 338 and authorized the dispatch of UN observers to the battlefield. Unfortunately, a new cease-fire agreed to on 24 October collapsed almost as soon as it was enacted, and Sadat sent a note to Brezhnev and Nixon asking for joint military enforcement of the UN cease-fire. At this point, the crisis passed into its most dangerous stage.

The Russians apparently wished to avoid direct intervention, but they were determined to make the U.S. have its client live up to the 22 October agreement. Accordingly, Russian airborne forces were put on alert for possible movement to the Middle East, and that evening Brezhnev sent Nixon a note suggesting joint intervention and threatening to act unilaterally if necessary.

The American response was swift, and as events were to prove, decisive. Six hours after receiving the Brezhnev note, Nixon dispatched a reply warning against unilateral intervention and stating that such an action would violate the U.S.–Soviet agreement on the prevention of nuclear war. To signal the seriousness of the situation, the president placed American military forces in a precautionary alert status known as DEFCON 3. At the same time, Secretary Kissinger was meeting with the Israeli ambassador and urging in the strongest possible language that Israel abide by the cease-fire of 22 October. Later that day, 25 October, the UN Security Council met to pass Resolution 340, which increased the size of the UN observer force and called for an immediate cease-fire with a return to the 22 October 1973 positions of the combatants. This time, under strong U.S. pressure, Israel complied, and the fighting stopped.

Freed from the need for intervention, the Russians contented themselves with sending seventy observers with the UN force and making public pronouncements about their peacemaking efforts. Satisfied that the UN and Israel had the situation well in hand, and that the USSR no longer seriously contemplated intervention, the United States relaxed its alert on 26 October, and the crisis ended.

Analysis

With the help of the seven requirements mentioned at the beginning of this chapter, we can now make some general comments about these cases and also about the way in which the diplomatic revolution that has been mentioned so frequently in these pages has affected the art of crisis management.

1. With regard to the maintenance of top-level civilian control over military options, there can be no doubt that the modern policymaker enjoys many technological advantages over his predecessor. Improvements in communications and transportation allow him to exert personal control over military forces stationed in practically any area of the globe. One has only to compare the relative inaccessibility of the crisis area in 1854 with Kissinger and Kosygin's ability to fly to the threatened region in a matter of hours to appreciate the handicap that Aber-

deen had in controlling Ambassador Canning and his use of the fleet in the Crimean case. Additionally, rapid worldwide communications enable the top policy makers to be in instant contact with their military forces, even though they may be half a world away.

But the vast growth in the size and diversity of a modern world power's internal bureaucratic organization and the complexity of the international alliance structure have created new problems for the exercise of top-level civilian control. Here the problems experienced by the German chancellor prior to World War I in controlling his own military organization, Foreign Office, and principal ally give notice of the difficulty often experienced in coordinating the affairs of a modern nation state. How much more difficult then the task of the superpowers in 1973, who had to control not only their own forces but those of their client states as well! Indeed, had the two superpowers been able to exert better control, the Egyptians and Syrians might not have started the war, and the Israelis might not have brought about the resulting nuclear confrontation.

2. With regard to the need to slow up the tempo of military action, crisis managers in the modern era are likely to encounter greater difficulties than did statesmen in the nineteenth and early twentieth centuries. With events driven at an ever-faster pace by improvements in communication, transportation, and weapons technology, political leaders are under pressure to make critical decisions in shorter and shorter time intervals. This becomes evident when one compares the duration of the three crises above. The crisis leading up to the Crimean War lasted from 1852 until the outbreak of war in 1854, a period of two years. The crisis leading up to World War I was of little more than one month's duration. The critical period in the 1973 Arab-Israeli War lasted less than a week, with the principal action taking place in the course of forty-eight hours. It is difficult, indeed, to create pauses when the momentum of events is so pressing.

Second, the increasing impact of public opinion upon decision making has complicated the policy maker's task of slowing down or "freezing" the crisis. In 1854, only Britain experienced difficulty in controlling the press of public opinion for immediate resolution of the crisis. By 1914, despite the attempt of professional diplomats to ignore it, and their success in doing so in normal times, public opinion in time of crisis was apt to be whipped up by the sensational press, a phenomenon of significance in several European capitals in the last days before war broke out. So demanding has public sentiment become in the years since then that Secretary Kissinger's ability to restrain the Western press while the United States and the Soviet Union moved to resolve the Arab-Israeli conflict before it caused a general war was a remarkable performance.

3. The requirement for coordinating diplomatic and military moves in a crisis also encounters new difficulties under the impact of the diplomatic revolution. First, decisions that shape the capabilities and doctrines of modern military forces do not always take sufficiently into account the task of managing these forces in crises. Policy makers who possess forces only capable of being utilized in large-scale warfare are severely limited in their ability to coordinate military and diplomatic moves. In the World War I case, for example, the opposing sides possessed mass armies, inflexible plans for mobilization, and intricate war plans which, if employed, necessitated the resort to full-scale military conflict. Thus, the attempts of Germany and Russia at coercive diplomacy became de facto declarations of war once mobilization was instituted. This situation contrasts unfavorably with events in the 1973 war, in which both the United States and the USSR were able to coordinate their diplomatic notes with selective alerts of portions of their armed forces.

The second problem for modern decision makers derives directly from the first. The very flexibility of modern military forces complicates their use. It is extremely difficult to predict how a given military move will be perceived by an opponent. For example, certain Soviet naval maneuvers during the 1973 crisis raised the question whether the Russians had the limited aim of backing up their client Egypt or intended to pose a threat to the U.S. Sixth Fleet in the Mediterranean. Likewise would the deployment of U.S. carriers to the eastern Mediterranean be viewed as a tactical move to support Israel or a strategic one to position them to attack the USSR proper? Problems such as these repeatedly confront modern policy makers when they seek to coordinate diplomatic and military moves in the nuclear age.

Finally, with the substantial increase in the number of individuals and departments that participate in a modern government's foreign policy, special efforts must be made to coordinate diplomatic communications with overall policy and military actions. Ambassador Canning's handling of the Vienna Note is a minor example of the failure to do so when compared to the situation in 1914, when all sorts of people tied up the telegraph lines of Europe until no one knew who spoke for the

German Empire or what its policy actually was. These examples contrast unfavorably with the 1973 crisis, in which communication was confined primarily to the five principals: Nixon, Kissinger, Brezhnev, Meir, and Sadat, with notably successful results.

4. The diplomatic revolution has both complicated and aided the ability of statesmen to confine military moves in a crisis to those that constitute clear demonstrations of their resolve and are appropriate to their limited objectives. As already noted, the scope and complexity of military action has increased greatly from the time of the Crimean War. In 1854, the British cabinet was unable to restrain Ambassador Canning from needlessly provoking the Russians with the British fleet. Prior to the First World War, civilian leaders found it difficult to prevent their military organizations from expanding a conflict through the use of force. The inability of Russia and Germany to force their professional military to modify their existing mobilization schedules and war plans to meet the current diplomatic situation illustrates how militarily expedient moves can have unintended consequences.

Fortunately, policy makers have benefited from technological change as well. During the Crimean War and World War I crises, the policy makers of the involved nations depended on the activities of their legations, intelligence networks, and the international press for information. All of these sources in turn depended upon transmission of the written word, and as such they were continuously subject to misinterpretation. By contrast, modern policy makers have at their disposal all the sophisticated intelligence means of the modern age. The advent of high-level reconnaissance aircraft and satellite photography gives the contemporary decision maker the ability to interpret his opponent's military moves for himself.

5. Advances in military technology have made it vastly more difficult to avoid military moves that give the opponent the impression that large-scale warfare is about to be initiated. The nature of modern warfare has been so altered that in many situations a great premium has been placed on the ability of a belligerent to launch a preventive strike, thus gaining a rapid, decisive victory while limiting its own losses by retaliation. The limited regular forces possessed by the belligerents in 1854 effectively precluded one power from overwhelming another preemptively. By 1914, however, the mass armies of the major powers made the delay of mobilization by even a single day an almost fatal mistake. It is no wonder then that when German Chief of Staff Moltke

pressed the kaiser to order German mobilization in response to a similar Russian action, it was difficult for the kaiser to refuse.

In the contemporary nuclear environment, the situation is even graver. If a policy maker hesitates for even an hour when confronted with a nuclear threat, total destruction of his nation could result. It is thus not surprising that the tense diplomatic exchanges between Nixon and Brezhnev in 1973 were carefully worded to allow time for reflection. Neither Secretary Brezhnev nor President Nixon wanted to place his opponent in a position similar to that of the German kaiser and risk the nuclear exchange that might follow.

6. The very destructiveness of modern weaponry, with its capacity to annihilate not only military forces but civilization as well, has greatly strengthened policy makers' incentives to choose diplomatic-military options that will signal a desire to negotiate rather than to seek a military solution. Since the Second World War, the leaders of every major country have been acutely aware of the possible costs of seeking a military solution in a crisis. Because of this firm belief in the horrors of modern war, the contemporary policy maker is much less likely to indulge in the belligerent nationalism of Palmerston or fatalistically accept the inevitability of war, as civilian leaders did in 1914. The current generation of policy makers in the industrialized world is likely to explore every possible avenue of negotiation rather than resort to force. The problem is whether or not the next generation will hold the same views and, if so, will be able to restrain Third World leaders, like Sadat in 1973, who may feel compelled to utilize force to accomplish their goals.

7. As a result of the increase in the ideological nature of many international disputes, it has become more difficult to select diplomatic-military options that leave an opponent a way out of the crisis compatible with his fundamental interests. The conflict between the interested parties in 1854 was only nominally over the question of the Christian minorities in the Ottoman Empire. The real reasons behind the crisis were those of classical power politics. By 1914, however, nationalism and imperialism had combined forces to add an extra dimension to the international situation. Ideology was notably present in the 1973 crisis, first as a function of the Arab-Israeli rivalry and ultimately as a sort of Islamic jihad against the developed world by means of the oil embargo. Separating the opponent's fundamental interests from his rhetoric is one of the truly difficult tasks facing modern foreign policy makers.

Fortunately, they will be greatly assisted in this task by the vast improvements already made in communications and transportation, which provide policy makers the luxury of face-to-face negotiations, and by improvements in the study of human crisis behavior. The importance of the ability of Secretary Kissinger to fly to Moscow in 1973 cannot be underestimated, but of even greater significance is the sober realization among policy makers in the thermonuclear age of the potential for misinterpretation in a crisis, and the need to eliminate it. Because of this, the disastrous misperceptions of a Palmerston, a Czar Nicholas, or a Bethmann Hollweg may be avoided in the future.

The results of this analysis show that the decision makers' decreasing capability to avoid escalation, coupled with an increasing limitation on their traditional means of control, brought disaster in two of the cases studied: the Crimean War and World War I. The successful example of crisis management in the 1973 Arab-Israeli War (and, earlier, in the Cuban missile crisis) clearly illustrates how decision makers must maximize their capabilities, as Kissinger, Nixon, and Brezhnev did by their personal visits and carefully phrased responses, while minimizing their limitations by controlling the media, their own forces, and those of client states. One thing is clear from everything that has been said: if catastrophe is to be avoided, decision makers in a crisis must be capable of functioning at a very high level. The tragic consequences of carelessness and lack of reflection on the part of single individuals is apparent in all of the cases reviewed.

Bibliographical Essay

For a more detailed discussion of the requirements, modalities, and problems of crisis management, see A. L. George, D. K. Hall, and W. E. Simons, *The Limits of Coercive Diplomacy* (Boston, 1971). Important analyses of the problem of crisis management are found in a number of other sources, including Coral Bell, *The Conventions of Crisis: A Study in Diplomatic Management* (London, 1971); Ole R. Holsti, *Crisis, Escalation, War* (Montreal and London, 1972); Thomas W. Milburn, "The Management of Crises," in *International Crises: Insights from Behavioral Research*, ed. Charles F. Hermann (New York, 1972); Richard Smoke, *War: Controlling Escalation* (Cambridge, Mass., 1977); Phil Williams, *Crisis Management* (New York, 1976); and Oran Young, *Politics of Force* (Princeton, 1968), chapters 8, 9, 10, 13.

16

War Termination

Students of military strategy have not given much systematic attention to the problem of terminating wars, and military planners have also traditionally neglected this problem, concentrating upon how to start wars and fight them successfully rather than upon how to end them if things do not go according to plan. Japanese leaders, for example, developed an ingenious plan for a surprise attack upon Pearl Harbor but had no notion of how the resulting war with the United States might be concluded.

I

In considering this subject, one must distinguish between a mere cessation of hostilities and a peace agreement that attempts to resolve the conflicting aims over which the battle has been waged. Hostilities may end with a cease-fire or armistice that leaves the issues at stake unsettled and defers their consideration to a later peace conference. Indeed, an end to the fighting may be accompanied or followed by a variety of outcomes. The total military defeat of one side, which stands at one extreme, poses much simpler problems for the peacemakers than do conflicts that grind to a military stalemate and can be settled only by negotiations.

Students of war termination have to distinguish also between various types of war, each of which poses somewhat different problems for termination. In total war, each side strives for complete victory, that is, the unconditional surrender of its opponent. Examples of total war include World War I, which did not start out as such but gradually became so, and World War II, which was more nearly a total war from the outset. In such conflicts, negotiation plays a lesser role in war termination than in wars fought for limited objectives with limited means. There are several types of limited war. In some, there is a rough symmetry of objectives, both sides viewing the conflict as limited, while in others the aims and stakes of the two sides are markedly different. Terminating a symmetrical limited war poses problems that differ significantly from those encountered in an asymmetrical conflict in which one side regards the stakes as being limited while its opponent views them as being virtually without limit.

Falling into the latter category are many wars between great and small states: for example, anticolonial and insurgency wars in which those on the weaker side fight for their independence and perceive their very existence to be at stake. In such contests, the leaders of the militarily weaker side can make virtually unlimited demands on their people. By waging a war of attrition against the great power and exacting prolonged and mounting sacrifices, the small state hopes to wear down popular support for the war in the stronger state and eventually to convince its people and leaders that the costs of continuing the war outweigh the objectives for which they have been fighting. A great power has other disadvantages in this type of war, for it has many other interests and commitments to meet which compete for scarce resources with the demands of the war. Although it possesses formidable military capabilities, it may find many of them inappropriate for the kind of warfare imposed on it by its weaker adversary. Also, it often happens that a great power is held by its own people, as well as by world opinion, to a higher standard than its weak adversary if it uses morally repugnant means of warfare. The war in Vietnam, which we will discuss in detail later in this chapter, is a prominent recent example of this type of asymmetrical conflict, but one can recall many other such wars, for example, the Boer War at the turn of the century and the French-Algerian War of the 1960s.

Generally speaking, the war objectives of both sides are more flexible in a symmetrical limited war than in total war, and it is easier for their governments and peoples to envisage compromise settlements. At the same time, however, initially limited low-level conflicts may escalate; both the objectives for which the war is being fought and the value placed on them may increase as the war progresses and, with this, escalation of means employed may follow.

II

Many different variables are capable of prolonging wars or speeding their termination. The number of these variables and the complexity of their interaction has increased as a result of the diplomatic revolution. A state's decision to continue or to terminate a war and its ability to do either may be affected by the personalities of its leaders, its political structure, the role of military leaders and their ability to influence the decision-making process, and the role of public opinion and organized interest groups.

In addition to these domestic factors that influence the willingness and ability of governmental leaders to terminate a military conflict, various aspects of the international system may also play a significant role. Local conflicts often have complex international dimensions that reduce a warring state's freedom of action and create dilemmas for its leaders. For example, a great power, like the United States in Vietnam, may remain in a local war longer than it would otherwise wish to because it feels obliged to maintain the credibility of its commitments elsewhere in the world and its general "reputation for resolve." But at the same time, a great power attempting to fight and win a limited war, like the United States in the Korean War, may be constrained by its other alliance commitments, which compete for its resources.

In many military conflicts, one or both combatants may be dependent on allies for material or diplomatic support, but their willingness to provide it often shifts during the course of the war. Weak states often require a secure sanctuary in a neighboring country in order to maintain a combat capability. The strong power may be reluctant to attack the sanctuary because of the political-diplomatic costs or the fear of a major escalation of the conflict. Considerations of this kind constrained the United States from bombing Manchuria during the Korean War after the Chinese Communists intervened. International organizations like the United Nations or regional organizations like the Organization of African Unity play a variety of roles in influencing war termination. The UN may legitimize one side's war objectives and bring pressure to bear on the other side to moderate its terms. It often brings pressure for a cease-fire on both sides and may attempt to formulate the terms of a compromise settlement.

The international dimension of war termination was of considerable importance, of course, in many conflicts fought in the era of the European balance-of-power system. With the developments associated with the diplomatic revolution, the structure and dynamics of international politics have become more complex. So far as termination of ongoing military contests is concerned, international pressures in the modern era operate in a multiplicity of ways, not always consistent with each other, to facilitate or prevent cessation of hostilities, and sometimes in both ways simultaneously.

Let us consider more systematically factors that hamper war termination. Once governments become involved in a war, they often find it much more difficult to back out of it than they had imagined, even if they keenly regret having entered it. Students of international relations have observed this phenomenon often enough to be able to identify some of the reasons for it. In certain conflicts, as in World War I, the leaders and peoples of the countries at war may continue to pour out blood and treasure because they are determined to achieve a settlement that will provide a more secure and peaceful world than existed before the fighting began. In this fashion, the objectives for which a war is fought—the so-called war aims of the belligerents—may differ from and go well beyond the causes of the war and the reasons for having entered it. The example of Woodrow Wilson comes to mind. Having tried to keep the United States out of World War I but being forced into it by the resumption of German submarine warfare, Wilson then embraced the ambitious objective of making the world "safe for democracy." But even before U.S. entry into the war, European leaders and peoples had set themselves far-reaching war aims. Unwilling to return to the uneasy balance-of-power situation that had existed in 1914, they sought to achieve through military victory a sufficient punishment and weakening of their opponents to make it impossible for them to fight another war in the future, and thereby to ensure a "lasting peace." A similar phenomenon occurred again during World War II.

In the classical European balance-of-power era, an enemy in today's war could become one's ally at some future point. Wars between the major powers were usually limited in their objectives and, if they ended with one side victorious, the loser paid to be sure, but the victor did not usually seek to crush or fatally weaken his opponent. It was not unusual deliberately to limit one's gains from a victorious war, to grant generous terms in the interest of a "peace of reconciliation." As the role of ideology, nationalism, and public opinion increased in international affairs, these factors encouraged a tendency to view the current enemy as the embodiment of evil rather than as a potential ally. Such psychological aspects operate to prolong wars and to hinder attempts at termination.

A related factor that often prolongs war is conveyed in the proposition that "sacrifice creates value." As the costs of the war mount, this fact itself often strengthens, at least initially, the determination of leaders and public alike to achieve the objectives for which the war is being fought. Such escalation of motivation may, in turn, lead to escalation of war objectives and/or the military means employed to gain them. As was true in World War I, leaders of the nation disposed to seek a compromise settlement may be constrained by the public's mood and its demand that the outcome of the war "justify" the enormous sacrifices already made. It may be some time before prolongation of the war and mounting sacrifices reverse the public's mood sufficiently to permit the opposite proposition—that it is time to "cut one's losses" and to "stop throwing good money after bad."

Another factor that prolongs some wars is the stubborn refusal of leaders who involved their country in a war that is proving to be increasingly disastrous to "admit" their mistake by seeking a way out. Their insistence on victory or "peace with honor" for the nation may be buttressed, often unconsciously, by personal and partisan motives. Whatever the explanation for the fact that leaders and governments become locked into a disastrous war, often the move to terminate the conflict can gain momentum only through a change in leadership, whether through orderly constitutional methods or extralegal means.

Entrance into a war usually alters the internal structure of power and influence within a government. As many observers have noted, with the onset of war, a country's military leaders and the governmental departments and industrial sectors most closely associated with the war effort move closer to the center of power. Fred Iklé writes:

> As "diplomacy breaks down" at the beginning of hostilities, the role of foreign ministries in dealing with the enemy is much diminished. Officials in the foreign ministries may still write background papers and plan for possible future peace settlements, but the influence that comes with day-to-day decisions is transformed to military staffs. At the very moment that the diplomats are being expelled from the enemy capitals, the military leaders come to command a vastly increased segment of national resources.

The heightened influence of military leaders during wartime sometimes gets completely out of hand, as in Japan during World War II, when military fanatics took ruthless action against leaders who favored a move toward peace. It would be erroneous to conclude, however, that military leaders are always less disposed to peace than other governmental officials. In many crises, military leaders have been more reluctant to resort to force than civilian leaders, and in some wars military leaders have taken the initiative for terminating hostilities.

The role of the military as it affects war termination, then, should not be oversimplified or distorted. It is misleading to speak of "the military" as if it constitutes a homogeneous actor; actually, there is considerable diversity of opinion and judgment within most military organizations. It stems not only from the differentiation of the armed forces into army, air, and naval services but also from functional roles and specializations held by the heads of the several services in the central governmental establishment and among the general staff or joint chiefs of staff and theater commanders. In the United States, with similar observations no doubt applying to other countries as well, there are three sources of wartime advice given by the military, each a little different from the other. The first comes from the commander of the theater in which the war is being fought. This usually stresses the importance of that particular theater and the need to support the effort there and indicates a belief in eventual success in that theater. It is often overly optimistic. The second comes from the heads of the individual services who are normally located in the nation's capital. These officers tend to focus more on the role of their service in the war and in the postwar world, and they try to increase its budget and power in relation to the other services.

The third is from the senior military advisers to the nation's leadership, often a number of military officers detached from their services to serve in a joint staff for planning purposes. These advisers tend to be closer to the overall political realities of the war and less influenced by parochial considerations. Because of its more objective view, this last group carries great weight in war-termination calculations.

Still another factor that works to prolong a war is the tendency of civilian and military leaders alike to postpone serious efforts to negotiate an end to the war until they have achieved an advantage on the battlefield. The commonsensical logic behind this preference is that a superior military position on the battlefield will yield additional diplomatic leverage at the negotiating table. Hence, the side that suffers a disadvantage in combat often prefers to postpone serious negotiations until it has corrected the military balance. What defeats this logic very often is that *both* sides operate with the same premise. When both sides take this approach to ending the conflict, as in World War I, they take turns escalating the war and seeking a battlefield success that will prove decisive or influential in obtaining a better negotiated settlement. The quest for a politically decisive military advantage often proves elusive, and the conflict is needlessly prolonged. Analysis of the Korean, Algerian, and Vietnam wars shows how efforts to employ additional increments of force as a means to induce the opponent to moderate his position in the negotiations did not succeed.

Wars are also often prolonged as a result of military estimates that prove too optimistic regarding the expected effectiveness of one's own military strategy and unrealistically downgrade the capabilities and will of the opponent.

What factors, then, set into motion and facilitate efforts to terminate a conflict? Generally speaking, a belligerent state will not consider ending the war unless it stands to realize at least the minimum—that is, the most important—goals for which it has been fighting. But it must also have the resources and the will to continue fighting for this minimally acceptable outcome. As the cost of the war increases, so may the disposition to question whether the minimal goal is worth the continued expenditure of precious resources. In other words, the attitude toward termination is in the end sensitive to the calculation of utility. As the expected costs and benefits of continuing are weighed, it may lead at some point to a policy reassessment and a modification of the minimal outcome one is willing to settle for. This process of reevaluation may actually take place on both sides and, in any case, it continues until the two sides agree that settling for less than they had hoped for is preferable to continuing hostilities.

Various factors may erode willingness to continue expenditure of resources on behalf of existing war objectives. The cost of the war may have severe economic consequences which, together with mounting casualties, weaken public support and generate domestic pressures for termination. World opinion may become increasingly critical toward one or both belligerents and bring strong diplomatic pressure on them to moderate their terms for a settlement. International developments may lead belligerent governments to reorder their foreign policy priorities and downgrade the importance heretofore assigned to the war. New threats may emerge in the international arena that require a shift in allocation of resources to the war effort. As a result, one or both sides may be willing, or even eager, to initiate negotiations for ending the war.

III

Many of the observations regarding the nature and process of negotiation presented in Chapter 12 are relevant here. But to an extent that is not usual in other forms of negotiation, war termination typically involves not one but a number of important issues on which the two sides disagree: for example, the timing and other conditions of a cease-fire; the disposition of territories and the drawing of boundaries; arrangements for exchange of prisoners and withdrawal of forces; provisions for reparations; and the nature and composition of a regime.

Accordingly, the process of negotiation leads to the identification of the resistance points of the two sides on each of these issues. Both actors engage in persuasion and bargaining to narrow the gap between their positions not only on an issue-by-issue basis but across issues in search of an overall agreement acceptable to both sides. Persuasion makes use of carrot-and-stick tactics; bargaining employs concessions, conditional offers, quid pro quos, or stonewalling tactics. Complex negotiations often take considerable time. Attempts to bridge the resistance points may be initially successful on only one or two issues. At a later stage in the negotiations, additional questions may be resolved. At still a later stage, compromise may be achieved by linking two issues so that each side trades its concessions on one for concessions by its opponent on another.

Complex, prolonged negotiations of this kind often characterize war termination. One can trace progress toward a final agreement by identifying a number of different phases and turning points in the negotiations that follow on each other. Figure 7 depicts a hypothetical negotiation of this kind. As shown there, progress toward settlement of the different issues proceeds at an uneven pace. Tentative agreement achieved on any single issue in one phase of the negotiations may be dissolved in a subsequent phase. During the course of the negotiations, new developments may take place on the battlefield or in domestic and international arenas that lead to a reassessment of negotiating objectives and tactics. During the process of persuasion and bargaining at the negotiating table, each side may highlight those issues and aspects of issues that are particularly important to it and on which it is least likely to compromise. Mutual adjustment of concessions may then take place, with one side yielding more on one issue and the other side on another issue. Remaining differences may be compromised or made part of a package deal linking several issues in a quid pro quo.

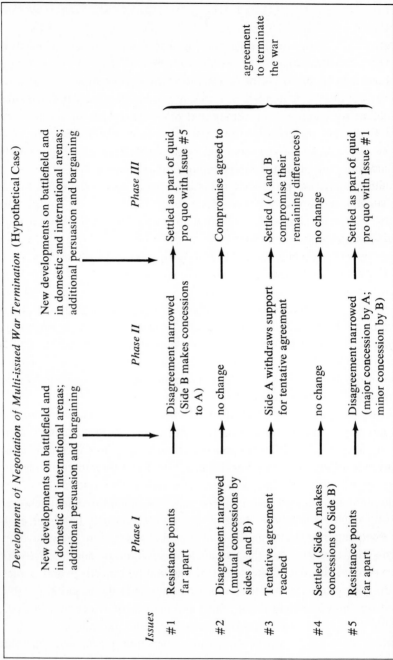

Development of Negotiation of Multi-issued War Termination (Hypothetical Case)

	Phase I	Phase II	Phase III
	New developments on battlefield and in domestic and international arenas; additional persuasion and bargaining	New developments on battlefield and in domestic and international arenas; additional persuasion and bargaining	

Issues

#1	Resistance points far apart	→	Disagreement narrowed (Side B makes concessions to A)	→	Settled as part of quid pro quo with Issue #5
#2	Disagreement narrowed (mutual concessions by sides A and B)	→	no change	→	Compromise agreed to
#3	Tentative agreement reached	→	Side A withdraws support for tentative agreement	→	Settled (A and B compromise their remaining differences)
#4	Settled (Side A makes concessions to Side B)	→	no change	→	no change
#5	Resistance points far apart	→	Disagreement narrowed (major concession by A; minor concession by B)	→	Settled as part of quid pro quo with Issue #1

agreement to terminate the war

Figure 7

Finally, by analyzing the process of negotiations sequentially, we discover that it is often characterized by a series of stopping points at which negotiations are slowed down or temporarily adjourned while the two governments reassess their positions. A sequential analysis of the negotiations should, therefore, take note of new developments on the battlefield, in the domestic situations of the two sides, and in the international context that influence the negotiating goals of both actors.

Negotiations do not necessarily lead to symmetrical agreements. Both sides need not make roughly equal concessions or achieve a settlement which balances their competing interests. The bargaining power (a combination of capabilities and motivation) of the two sides may not be equal. And in any case, one side may negotiate more skillfully than the other. Even when one side is thoroughly defeated, as were Germany and Japan in World War II, it may still possess some residual bargaining power that it can utilize during the course of surrender negotiations in order to achieve somewhat better terms on matters it regards as of vital importance.

We should note, too, that peace negotiations may result in only a partial settlement of the issues at stake. The two sides may agree to terminate military hostilities without having reached an agreement on all of the issues in conflict. They may agree to take them up themselves at a later date, set up ad-hoc international commissions to deal with them, or use the auspices of existing international bodies.

Elements of a peace agreement often lack clarity, suffer from ambiguity, and permit of contradictory interpretations. Sometimes acceptance of such flaws may be necessary if any agreement at all is to be achieved. Some matters dealt with in the peace settlement, therefore, may in fact be in the nature of pseudo-agreements that merely paper over fundamental disagreement and pave the way for future conflict. Or enforcement provisions for key components of the agreement may be so inadequate as to create the likelihood that the settlement will crumble and perhaps entirely collapse at some later point.

Many of the factors that facilitate and impede the process of war termination and the negotiation of multiple issues can be seen in the process that ended the Vietnam War.

Vietnam: A Case Study of War Termination*

The Communist war against foreign domination in Indochina can really be said to have begun in 1930 with the founding of the Indochinese Communist party. From that date until the final collapse of resistance in South Vietnam in 1975, the party of Ho Chi Minh and his heirs never once wavered from its announced goal of a unified, Communist Vietnam. It was less the appeal of Communist ideology per se than Ho's ability to blend it with powerful sentiments of nationalism and anticolonialism that enabled him and his people to fight three wars against, in turn, the Japanese, the French, and the Americans. In contrast to this simple, single-minded aim of the strongly motivated Vietminh, the Americans, like the Japanese and French before them, had other, competing interests that detracted from their efforts in Vietnam. Only this can explain how the Communists could prevail against one of the two world superpowers, the United States of America.

The gradual involvement of the United States in Vietnam originated during World War II when, ironically, the American Office of Strategic Services (OSS) (forerunner of the CIA) actually helped the Communists against the Japanese. Involvement didn't really take on ominous tones until the early 1950s, when the United States aided France against the Communists. This aid must be seen in the context of the Cold War mentality of this period, which created the conditions that ultimately resulted in over five hundred thousand American troops in Vietnam; later on, a change in the Cold War mentality significantly contributed to the final outcome. In 1949, China became a Communist state. In late 1950, Communist Chinese troops entered into prolonged combat with Americans in Korea. Chinese aid to the Vietnamese was increasing substantially after 1949, and there seemed little doubt that the Chinese were part of the Soviet Union's growing collection of puppet states. Beset in both Asia and Europe by Communist expansion, the United States adopted a policy of containment. When the French left Indochina in 1954, the United States stepped in to aid the new nation of South Vietnam maintain its pro-Western independence, much as it had aided Greece after Britain withdrew in 1947.

Hoping for and expecting a political victory, the Communists in South Vietnam conducted a quiet, semilegal struggle to unify North and South.

* This case study was prepared in its original form by Major Clinton Ancker, III, U.S. Army.

But the surprising success of South Vietnamese President Diem in consolidating his position in the South led to renewed warfare beginning in 1959. By 1965, this violence threatened to overthrow South Vietnam, and the United States began sending massive numbers of troops to bolster a faltering ally. To many, including a significant portion of American leaders, it seemed the proper thing to do. The United States had turned back the effort to spread communism by means of a conventional war in Korea, it had stared down the Soviet Union in a nuclear confrontation over missiles in Cuba, and a defeat of a Communist guerrilla army in Southeast Asia would seemingly close off the entire spectrum of violence through which communism could expand. As a world power and as the leader of the free world, the United States had a commitment to prevent Communist aggression wherever it occurred. Several successive administrations had pledged the United States to stand by South Vietnam, and its reputation for resolve and as a world power was seemingly at stake. What is more, under the proddings of President Kennedy, U.S. military forces had been nurturing an unconventional warfare capability, and Vietnam provided an occasion to use it. With a hubris born of repeated successes in the postwar world, with a Cold War mentality that saw communism encroaching everywhere, and with a typical disdain of Third World capabilities, the United States undertook to save South Vietnam. But beyond that vague goal, American leaders never did clearly define how the United States would do it, or what success would look like.

Nevertheless, things seemed to go well. By the end of 1967, American military leaders were confidently predicting victory, domestic opposition to the war was muted by its apparent success, and the rising costs of the war were hidden by President Johnson's decision to rely upon deficit spending. The Communist Tet Offensive in February 1968 once and for all shattered the illusions, and suddenly American leadership had to face a situation that could no longer be ignored. While the Tet Offensive ended in a shattering tactical defeat for the Vietcong and North Vietnamese, it was a strategic victory, for it had a tremendous psychological and political impact on American opinion. Hanoi had never really hoped to defeat the United States in a military confrontation; rather, the North Vietnamese leaders simply wanted to make the war so costly to the United States in manpower, money, and international prestige that it would finally decide that continuing the war was too expensive relative to the possible benefits. The Tet Offensive created a feeling of hopelessness and presented the specter of a long, drawn-out conflict with no end in sight for the American public. Support for the Johnson administration's Vietnam policies plummeted below 50 percent in public opinion polls for the first time since the war had heated up. Widespread vocal protests gained tremendous impetus now that the saving grace of "victory" in the struggle appeared to be a chimera. The media, already hostile to the war, became more and more virulent in opposition to its continuation. Many intellectuals from all walks of life joined the antiwar movement. And just as important, President Johnson's advisers now convinced him that a purely military solution to the insurgency was beyond reach. North Vietnam was more than willing to sustain the level of losses and suffer through the level of deprivation that could be imposed on it by U.S. military forces in South Vietnam and the bombing of the North.

As a result of the foregoing, Lyndon Johnson radically altered the U.S. strategy for the war. He now sought to deescalate American involvement and to seek a negotiated settlement. This, however, proved to be very difficult. Hanoi was under little time pressure, and the North Vietnamese exhibited a willingness to wait as long as necessary to achieve their unaltered goal of a unified Vietnam. Besides, they were past masters at using negotiations to secure victory when armed force had either failed or merely provided a basis for talks. Thus, when the two sides put forward their preconditions for negotiations, they were found to be mutually exclusive. The North Vietnamese did agree to bargain about negotiations in April 1968 after Johnson halted the bombing of the North, but apparently this was only a ploy to gain a respite from massive air attacks, and nothing of substance was really achieved.

But Johnson was a lame-duck president anyway. On 20 January 1969, Richard Nixon was inaugurated as president, bringing a whole new approach to the war. It was Nixon, and his foreign affairs adviser, Henry Kissinger, who would eventually end the war. As often happens, it took a change in leadership to create an effective change in policy.

Nixon's approach was a multifaceted strategy, each part designed to work on one aspect of the problem, and the whole designed to end U.S. involvement in Vietnam on as good terms as possible. First, to help quiet antiwar sentiment at home, he announced that the United States would begin large withdrawals of troops and a process of reequipping and retraining the South Vietnamese army. This Vietnamization process, as it was called, was meant to result in the South Vietnamese assuming the main role in defending their country and significantly reduce American casualties, thereby, it was hoped, taking the war off the front page of newspapers. To put increased pressure on the North Vietnamese, Nixon drastically widened the war by increasing bombing in the North and by spreading the bombing and ground combat to Cambodia and Laos. Additionally, to bring international pressure to bear on Hanoi, Nixon and Kissinger attempted to link progress on improved relations with China and the Soviet Union to those nations' use of their influence to pressure Hanoi to stop the war. Finally, Kissinger opened secret negotiations with North Vietnamese representatives in an attempt to find a way out of the war.

What might have looked like a comprehensive U.S. strategy was in fact riddled with contradictions. While removing U.S. troops initially calmed the antiwar movement, the expansion of the bombing in the North and the moves into Cambodia and Laos had the opposite effect and caused antiwar protests to burst forth with renewed vigor. Not only did all the old arguments against the war resurface, but the moral question was given much greater play, with the United States cast in the role of an aggressor conducting an immoral war. While violations of morality occurred on both sides, America was unilaterally called to task in both the domestic and international press. Congressmen began to oppose the war in even greater numbers, and administration support, already weak in a Democratic-controlled Congress, diminished further. Inflation, the result of deficit spending to finance the war, was added to the list of evils charged to U.S. involvement in Vietnam. And allies were increasingly critical of U.S. involvement, since it made their relations with the USSR more difficult, created problems in their approaches to China, and, by weakening the dollar abroad, posed a growing threat to international monetary stability.

The increased pressure on North Vietnam caused by the bombing and the invasions of Laos and Cambodia did not change Hanoi's mind about the cost-versus-benefit calculations. Indeed, the beginning of U.S. withdrawal sent a clear message to Hanoi that American involvement was drawing down even if the tonnage of bombs was up. This simply reinforced Hanoi's belief that time was on its side.

The negotiations, too, proved initially to be futile. Kissinger wanted first and foremost to decouple the military and political issues, settling the military question first and then negotiating on the political future of

South Vietnam. Hanoi, which had always considered the military aspect subordinate to its overriding political goals, would not even consider such a decoupling. After all, the North Vietnamese asked, what was the point of the war if not to decide the South's political future? In addition, the Communist negotiators put forth a tough demand for a Communist government in South Vietnam as one of their requirements for a settlement. By adhering stubbornly to this unrealistic requirement, they were able to extract concession after concession from the United States before finally conceding at the last minute in order to bring about a peace agreement that was in other respects highly favorable to them.

Finally, in the international arena, the Nixon and Kissinger attempt at linkage produced limited results. Because the Soviet Union and China each reciprocated Nixon's desire for closer ties, the diplomatic strategy of linkage at first allowed Nixon to expand the war without either of the Communist giants reacting violently and either killing the initiative for better relations or, as Johnson had feared, intervening militarily on Hanoi's behalf. It is also possible that the desire for détente with the United States may have led Soviet and Chinese leaders to exert some limited pressure on Hanoi to reach a settlement. But linkage and the desire for improved relations was double-edged. Nixon and Kissinger had always considered Vietnam as merely a sideshow in a much greater global policy. The endless prolongation of negotiations with Hanoi stood in the way of implementing their grand strategy and increased pressure on them to make damaging concessions in order to end the war, regardless of the ultimate consequences to South Vietnam.

The gradual withdrawal of U.S. forces from South Vietnam was originally linked to a demand for reduction in North Vietnamese activities in the South. Once it was implemented, however, Nixon could not respond to such activities without raising even greater opposition at home, and he thus lost the ability to extract reciprocal reductions from the North. Given this and increased congressional restrictions on U.S. air power in Indochina, the Saigon regime's only hope was to gain the ability to defend itself in the face of Northern aggression. The prospects for doing so did improve in some respects after the Tet Offensive, which shocked and galvanized many elements of the South Vietnamese leadership and population. In addition, progress was made in pacification programs in the South and in the restructuring of the South Vietnamese army; and land reform and a new security orientation were making significant inroads into Vietcong strength and the ability of the North

Vietnamese army to operate at will. But a successful program of this type required time, and time was a commodity in very short supply in 1972, the decisive year of the war.

Negotiations up to early 1972 had really accomplished little and had hardly narrowed the bargaining gap at all. In April, the North Vietnamese launched a conventional invasion of South Vietnam, the so-called Easter Offensive. It was eventually stopped by May of that year through a combination of massive U.S. air strikes throughout Indochina and by the surprising toughness of the South Vietnamese army, which fought the Northern regulars to a stalemate at Au Loc, Kontum, and Quang Tri. As a result of the outcome of the offensive and the upcoming U.S. presidential elections, both sides now had an increased incentive to negotiate a settlement. Nixon was under renewed and increased pressure from both the public and Congress to stop the war. The massive U.S. air strikes had raised howls of opposition, and Congress was closer than ever to passing serious restrictive legislation concerning future U.S. actions in Indochina and the president's ability to wage war at all. With the election coming in November, Nixon felt a settlement in Vietnam would be a tremendous boost to his campaign. But this time Hanoi, too, wanted a settlement. North Vietnamese leaders feared that once reelected, Nixon might take a harder line. Moreover, they were surprised by the resilience of the South Vietnamese army. They recognized that given enough time, American supplies and assistance might help it to close the gap with North Vietnam and that eventually the South might be able to defend itself. Thus, it was prudent to get the United States out of Vietnam while the advantages for eventual victory still lay with the North.

Kissinger and the North Vietnamese negotiator, Le Duc Tho, made rapid progress in secret negotiations during the summer and early autumn of 1972. Both sides made concessions, although the American ones were more substantial than those of Hanoi. The United States agreed to withdraw all its forces without a concurrent withdrawal of North Vietnamese troops. In fact, the United States agreed to allow North Vietnamese troops to stay in South Vietnam, a significant and ultimately fatal concession. Additionally, America agreed to combine the military and political agreements into one document. In turn, Le Duc Tho agreed to drop Hanoi's demand for President Thieu's immediate removal as a precondition for a cease-fire. This had been, from the American negotiators' standpoint, the major stumbling block all along. Having achieved their immediate goal of a withdrawal of U.S. troops without having to abandon their own gains in the South, Hanoi felt a concession on Thieu an acceptable price to pay.

But peace was not yet at hand, for President Thieu exploded in opposition to what he considered a sellout by the United States. Not having been privy to the terms being discussed, Thieu was aghast at the U.S. position. His absolute refusal to consider the terms quashed any hope Nixon and Kissinger had of ending U.S. involvement before the November elections. In reaction to the U.S. failure to ratify the accords, Hanoi reverted to an unacceptable, hard-line position on the political future of the South. For a moment, it looked as if the elusive peace had once again slipped out of U.S. hands.

Nixon and Kissinger, both tiring of the interminable problems of Vietnam and its effects on their cherished global policy, now decided to apply pressure on all fronts. For Thieu, the carrot and stick consisted of massive material aid to bolster the South Vietnamese army, a promise of massive U.S. air intervention if Hanoi violated the proposed accords, and, finally, a threat to conclude a unilateral treaty if Thieu balked. That was enough to secure Thieu's reluctant acquiescence. For Hanoi, a new massive bombing and mining campaign coupled with pressure applied through the Soviet Union and China served to break their hard-line attitude. The agreement finally signed in early 1973 was essentially similar to the aborted October 1972 accords; it included amorphous, predictably unworkable, provisions for implementation. But it ended the war for the United States.

As it turned out, the accords were a poor substitute for a genuine peace. None of the real issues in Indochina was resolved, and the enforcement machinery was virtually useless. Having secured a complete U.S. withdrawal, Hanoi waited two years to mount its massive conventional attack which finally achieved the long-held, never-altered goal of a unified, Communist Vietnam. Time, and U.S. support, had run out for the Saigon regime.

Bibliographical Essay

The general analysis of war termination presented in the first part of the chapter draws upon the following sources: William T. R. Fox, ed., "How Wars End," *Annals of the American Academy of Political and Social Science*, 392 (1970); Morton H. Halperin, "War Termination as a Problem in Civil-Military Relations," ibid., 86–95; Michael Handel, "The Study of War

Termination," *Journal of Strategic Studies,* 1 (1978), 51–75; Fred C. Iklé, *Every War Must End* (New York, 1971); Paul Kecskemeti, *Strategic Surrender* (Stanford, Calif., 1958), which is particularly good on the residual bargaining power of defeated nations; Robert Randle, *The Origins of Peace: A Study of Peacemaking and the Structure of Peace Settlements* (New York, 1973); Janice G. Stein, "War Termination and Conflict Reduction, or How Wars Should End," the *Jerusalem Journal of International Relations,* 1 (1975), 1–25; Major Clinton J. Ancker III, U.S. Army, "The Franco-Algerian War: A Study in War Termination," seminar paper, Political Science Department, Stanford University, 1979; and Helen Milner, "Case Studies in the Termination of Modern Limited Wars," senior honors thesis, Stanford University, May 1980.

Books available on the war in Vietnam and especially on war termination suffer from two problems. First, almost nothing of any real substance has come out of Hanoi, the People's Republic of China, or the Soviet Union. What has appeared has been polemical in nature and so full of rhetoric that the serious scholar must dig long and hard to find relevant facts. Most of it consists merely of paeans of praise to the NVA. Second, only a short period has elapsed since the crucial events. The controversy and emotionalism engendered by the war inevitably distort objectivity. In addition, the authors' desire to defend their war policy makes it necessary to deal cautiously with Henry Kissinger's *White House Years* (Boston, 1979) and Richard M. Nixon's *RN: The Memoirs of Richard Nixon* (New York, 1978), both of which, however, are indispensable sources. Kissinger reportedly delayed publication of his book in order to revise it in response to William Shawcross's *Sideshow* (New York, 1979) and had already incorporated in the book defenses against Tad Szulc's *The Illusion of Peace: Foreign Policy in the Nixon Years* (New York, 1978).

In the last few years, the first attempts at a detached, scholarly look at Vietnam have appeared. Among these are Allan E. Goodman, *The Lost Peace* (Stanford, Calif., 1978); Leslie H. Gelb and Richard K. Betts, *The Irony of Vietnam: The System Worked* (Washington, D.C., 1979), which maintains that, far from being a failure of the American system, Vietnam was a good example of how it should work; and Peter Braestrup, *The Big Story* (New York, 1978), a critical look at media coverage of the war. It will be a long time, however, before the government documents are available which can resolve many of the contradictions found in the above sources. And we may never know just what impact various decisions had on the North Vietnamese.

17
Détente

There has been little systematic study by historians and political scientists of the phenomenon of détente in interstate relations. In the modern era, even the meaning of the term has become opaque, and it is often misused by policy makers as well as by specialists in international relations and members of the general public. The reasons for this are instructive in themselves.

In the United States, the term *détente* came suddenly into vogue following the conclusion of the partial test ban treaty in the summer of 1963. After the brush with thermonuclear disaster in the Cuban missile crisis, Kennedy and Khrushchev attempted to place U.S.–Soviet relations on a new basis in order to alleviate the extreme distrust and conflict that had characterized the Cold War. With the signing of the partial test ban treaty, the first arms control agreement between the two nuclear superpowers, the term *détente* began to be employed by policy makers and commentators. The word was used, somewhat inconsistently, for a variety of purposes: to describe the emergence of a new atmosphere in U.S.–Soviet relations; to characterize the passing of the acute phase of the Cold War; to refer to a new but not too well-defined policy toward the Soviet Union; and to identify a more cooperative relationship with the Soviet Union that might be gradually achieved in the future.

The deep concern, often forcefully expressed, of those who continued to distrust the Soviet Union compounded confusion over the meaning of the term and its applicability to U.S.–Soviet relations. Many people felt

238

that the signing of the test ban treaty did not signify any diminution of Russia's hostility toward the West or any modification of its long-range intentions. They argued that Soviet interest in détente was merely a tactical stratagem designed to lull the West into complacency. Disagreements quickly arose as to what détente did and did not mean, what it should and should not be allowed to become.

It is important to recognize that the problem of ascertaining the correct meaning of détente following the missile crisis was not solely semantical. It was not cleared up by consulting the dictionaries and learning that in the era of classical diplomacy, "détente" meant simply "a relaxation of tensions" in relations between two states whose policies had been previously characterized by considerable rivalry that posed the danger of war. The question remained as to what a "relaxation of tensions" meant in the era of the Cold War and what its implications should signify for future U.S.–Soviet relations.

Clarification of these questions will be facilitated if we recognize that détente was a different phenomenon in the context of the Cold War than it was in the nineteenth and early twentieth centuries. As we have seen, the old European system was a relatively well-ordered multipolar system in which the major actors were committed to the maintenance of a balance of power. Competition and rivalry among them was not unlimited; there was a great deal of cultural homogeneity among the ruling classes; ideological differences were not pronounced; and, finally, the conduct of foreign policy was left largely in the hands of professional diplomats. All these characteristics of the classical era of European diplomacy had long since given way; traces of them could scarcely be found in the period of the Cold War.

Given the striking differences between these two international systems, it is not surprising that efforts to transfer diplomatic concepts from one era to the other should generate confusion and malaise. Such concepts and practices had well-defined meanings and uses in the European system. Diplomats and statesmen of that period had developed a rich, differentiated, and relatively precise set of technical phrases that facilitated communication in the conduct of interstate relations. With the breakdown and transformation of the older system, however, the diplomatic vocabulary of the classical era was debased. Its terminology lost much of its precision and, in consequence, attempts to use the old concepts in contemporary foreign relations were apt to lead to confusion.

We can demonstrate this by recalling how precisely the language of the older diplomacy characterized the progressive stages of improvement that were possible in the relations of two states that were experiencing acute conflict in their policies. The process might begin with "détente" and possibly develop into "rapprochement"; this, in turn, could lead to "entente." Two further developments could then take place: one or both sides could engage in "appeasement" of the other and/or the two sides could form an "alliance." But this stage-by-stage improvement in relations could stop at any point. The specific meanings of these concepts and the relationship among them are depicted schematically in Figure 8.

The following example illustrates the utility of such precise terminology in aiding effective communication between diplomats. In the course of his mission to Berlin in February 1912, the British war minister, Lord Haldane, met with Jules Cambon, the French ambassador at Berlin, to explain to him the object and significance of the talks he was then having with the German chancellor, Bethmann Hollweg, about the possibility of an Anglo-German agreement to limit naval expenditures. Aware that such discussions were taking place and concerned lest they portend the loosening of England's relationship with France and Russia, Cambon met with Haldane at the British embassy and anxiously sought to be informed about the talks. Haldane later recorded in his diary that

> without telling him anything, I said emphatically that we were not going to be disloyal to France or Russia, that the Chancellor agreed that it would be dishonorable in us if we even talked of departing from the existing agreements, and that we believed a better state of public opinion between England and Germany would benefit France. With that he [Cambon] agreed. He suggested that my conversation had no other end than to create a *détente,* as distinguished from an *entente.* I said this was so as regards my conversation. I had not come there to draw up an agreement, or to do more than *tâter le terrain.* But that I hoped more than a détente would follow later on—if my very limited mission succeeded.

The concern for precision in the interest of avoiding misperception and distrust is further illustrated by Haldane's belief that it would be "a useful precaution" if he could see Cambon's telegraphed report of their conversation to the French premier, Raymond Poincaré, before it was sent to Paris. Cambon agreed, and upon reading it Haldane concurred with the way in which the French ambassador described the distinction he had made between "détente" and "entente."

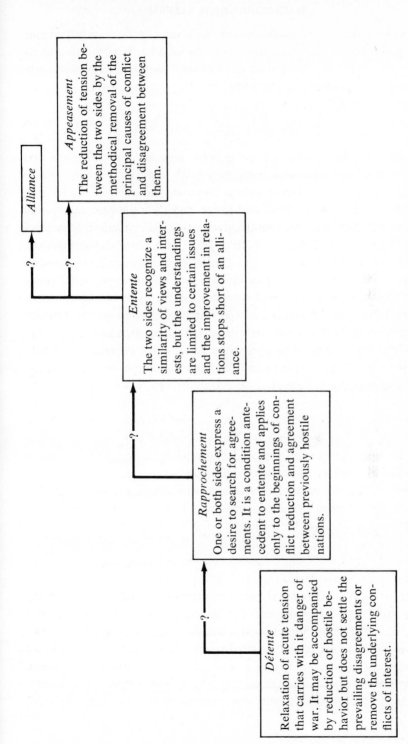

Alliance

Appeasement
The reduction of tension between the two sides by the methodical removal of the principal causes of conflict and disagreement between them.

Entente
The two sides recognize a similarity of views and interests, but the understandings are limited to certain issues and the improvement in relations stops short of an alliance.

Rapprochement
One or both sides express a desire to search for agreements. It is a condition antecedent to entente and applies only to the beginnings of conflict reduction and agreement between previously hostile nations.

Détente
Relaxation of acute tension that carries with it danger of war. It may be accompanied by reduction of hostile behavior but does not settle the prevailing disagreements or remove the underlying conflicts of interest.

The question marks indicate that the process of improvement in relations between the two states need not go beyond détente and could stop at any point.

Figure 8

The relevance of these conceptual distinctions to the conduct of foreign policy in the European system can be further illustrated by tracing their application to the gradual improvement in relations between England and France beginning in 1898.

Anglo-French Entente, 1898–1904

In that year, the protracted antagonism between Great Britain and France in the colonial area came to a head when the French government, seeking to force the British to terminate the occupation of Egypt that they had begun in 1882 and to conclude a settlement that would recognize French interests, sent troops commanded by Colonel Marchand from West Africa to the upper Nile. Here, at a place called Fashoda, the French were met by a stronger British force commanded by General Kitchener, and the danger of an incident that might trigger a European war became obvious. This had a sobering effect upon the French government, distracted by the domestic agitations caused by the Dreyfus affair, with naval forces only half those of Britain, with its only ally too deeply involved in the Far East to be able to give it effective support, and with no expectation of assistance from the Triple Alliance powers, who were not displeased with the possibility of an Anglo-French conflict. The French foreign minister, Théophile Delcassé, a nationalist who believed that the lost provinces of Alsace and Lorraine might be worth a war but that Egypt certainly was not, temporized and, when the British showed no inclination to make concessions, he capitulated in November 1898 by ordering Marchand to withdraw.

Even before the crisis, Delcassé had been telling the British ambassador that he desired a rapprochement with Great Britain, and in a letter to his wife in October he wrote, "I hope it has been realized that the desire for an agreement with England, very freely expressed by me since I became Foreign Minister, came not from a feeling of weakness but from a general conception of policy." The French withdrawal from Fashoda both facilitated and impeded progress toward his goal. It significantly lowered tension and diminished the possibility of war and thus, in a real sense, represented a détente in the relations of the two powers, while at the same time leaving a heritage of bitterness in France and, in some quarters, a desire for revenge. For some time after Fashoda, circumstances were not propitious for an improvement in Anglo-French relations. The British were still giving serious consideration to the possibility and advantages of an alliance with Germany, which Colonial Secretary Joseph Chamberlain believed would provide an effective defense against the expansionist tendencies of France's ally Russia in China.

Détente was nevertheless gradually transformed into rapprochement within the next three years. During the Boer War, the British became aware of the disadvantages of what they had called "splendid isolation," for they were never entirely sure that they might not have to cope with the intervention of one or more of the continental powers. They were particularly suspicious of the German government, for it proved to be an unreliable partner in the Far East, made no attempt to temper the strident pro-Boer sentiment of the press, and, in 1900, pushed through the Reichstag a supplementary naval bill that marked the beginning of Grand Admiral Tirpitz's campaign to build a battle fleet big enough to threaten British security in the North Sea. The British did not react immediately by turning to the French. Their most urgent concern, aside from the war, was Russian policy in China, and to counter this they finally abandoned their isolationist policy, concluding an alliance with Japan in 1902.

But this step had sensible reverberations in Paris. The French government had long been as concerned about Russia's Far Eastern policy as the British (in 1898, Delcassé had said to the British ambassador, "I would rather have England for our ally than that other"), and now the Anglo-Japanese alliance opened up the prospect of a war in the Far East between the new partners and Russia, in which France would be called upon to make good its treaty with the latter. This Delcassé wished to avoid at all costs, and he saw a rapprochement with the British as the best way of doing so. Indeed, as he saw it, an Anglo-French agreement might facilitate a general settlement in the Far East by providing the basis for an accommodation between Japan and Russia. The French foreign minister therefore made soundings in London, which met a cordial response, for British disillusionment with the Germans was now complete. Even Joseph Chamberlain, the most ardent of the advocates of the German connection, was enthusiastic about a settlement with France.

The progress from this initial rapprochement to entente was, if not quick, deliberate. The first approaches were given more weight by an exchange of official visits, King Edward VII making an unprecedented but highly successful trip to Paris in May 1903 and President Loubet returning the compliment by going to London in July. Meanwhile, the diplomats began to deal with the hard issues that had troubled the relationship since 1882. These involved disputes over sovereignty, economic interest, and boundaries in Newfoundland, Siam, and West Africa, which were settled with no great difficulty, and the thornier problem of Egypt. The words *Fashoda* and *Marchand* were still capable of arousing patriotic indignation in France, but on the whole the French had no expectation of regaining their pre-1882 position there and were intent upon receiving an equivalence in the area of their greatest current interest, Morocco.

With a disregard for the interests of the native populations that would seem outrageous today, the French government recognized the British protectorate at Cairo and declared that it would not obstruct British work in Egypt by calling for a time limit to the British occupation. On their part, the British recognized Morocco as a French sphere of influence, adding that it was for France alone to provide order in that enormously rich area and to suggest reforms to its sultan. In secret articles, they agreed further that they would not object to action that the French might consider appropriate in the case of a collapse of the sultan's authority, provided that whatever became of Morocco, the Atlantic coastline should, for obvious reasons, go not to France but to Spain.

The broader significance of the Entente Cordiale that resulted from these agreements was that it marked the beginning of Anglo-French collaboration in other quarters and the first step toward the alliance between the two Western powers in World War I. It was not transformed into a formal alliance earlier largely because of the traditional British reluctance to make commitments for contingencies that had not yet arisen. Even so, in the decade before the war it more and more acquired the normal characteristics of an alliance. After the Moroccan crisis of 1905, in which the Germans sought to drive the new friends apart by menaces, the two governments instituted military staff talks which, in a professedly theoretical and nonbinding manner, discussed joint operations in time of war. In the wake of the second Moroccan crisis of 1911 and in response to Germany's rapid naval buildup, the British government not only authorized a continuation of the staff talks but also assured the French that "if either Government had grave reason to expect an unprovoked attack by a third Power, it should immediately discuss with the other whether both Governments should act together." This action was taken in order to persuade the French to move their Atlantic fleet to the Mediterranean so as to protect British interests while the Royal Navy was being concentrated in home waters.

As this account indicates, the process of moving successively from détente to rapprochement to entente and then either to appeasement and/or alliance was in this case very deliberate. Moreover, entering into a détente did not carry with it any commitment or assurance that the two sides would move on to a further improvement of their relations. What is more, statesmen in the classical European era proceeded cautiously at every stage, assessing carefully the hoped-for benefits and possible risks of moving to the next phase. Whereas diplomats in the European state system understood well the prudential need for taking careful soundings and preparing the diplomatic ground as well as public opinion before engaging in appeasement or entering into an alliance with a former adversary, this practice was not always followed when the impact of the diplomatic revolution had altered statecraft and had introduced new imperatives and constraints into the conduct of foreign policy.

British Appeasement Policy

The policy of appeasement followed by the National government in Great Britain during the prime ministership of Neville Chamberlain, for example, was based upon an earnest desire to create the conditions for European peace and stability, but it was vitiated by Chamberlain's impatience and his contempt for the cautionary expedients of traditional diplomacy. While between 1933 and 1937, the British Foreign Office had sought, however imperfectly, to establish the bona fides of the dictators and to determine whether there were common interests and values that would serve as a basis for cooperation with them before undertaking a systematic removal of specific causes of conflict, Chamberlain saw no point in these preliminaries and soon got rid of those people, like Eden and Vansittart, who insisted on them. With the general support of a Parliament and a public opinion that wanted no repetition of the 1914 war, he heedlessly plunged ahead to what should have been the final stage of a laborious process, on the mistaken assumption that Hitler and Mussolini shared his objectives and that a demonstration of his readiness to satisfy their demands would bring him the peace that he desired. All that it brought him, of course, was new and more outrageous demands, which in the end had to be resisted by force. As an example of how not to conduct a policy of détente, the appeasement policy of 1937–1939 is not likely to be easily surpassed.

The Soviet-American Détente

These comments on the diplomatic practices of the past provide a basis for a comparison with developments in the Cold War in the period after the Cuban missile crisis. It has already been noted that the ensuing relaxation of tension in U.S.–Soviet relations, which some referred to as a détente, was a significantly different phenomenon than its counterpart during the era of the European balance-of-power system. In that earlier context, substantial improvements were possible in the relations between the major powers. Adversaries could become allies; reversal of alliances was not uncommon. What is more, such pronounced shifts could take place and were expected to take place as part of the practices required to regulate and maintain the multipolar European system. This stands in sharp contrast with the bipolar Cold War system, which was characterized by acute hostility bordering on a zero-sum conflict. While détente——→rapprochement——→entente——→appeasement——→alliance were *system-maintaining* processes in the European system, this degree of improvement in U.S.–Soviet relations could take place only as part of a gradual replacement of the Cold War system by one based on a much more cooperative relation between the two superpowers.

Therefore, when a relaxation of tension took place in U.S.–Soviet relations, the question was whether this signaled the beginnings of the gradual displacement of the Cold War system with some other kind of international system (and, if so, what), or whether détente was either only a quite limited modification of the Cold War system or a temporary respite from the acute hostility of the Cold War. Accordingly, it is not surprising that following the partial test ban treaty in the summer of 1963, skeptics questioned both the desirability and feasibility of the apparent relaxation of tensions. Was détente a purely tactical maneuver, an instrument of Soviet Cold War strategy into which the Russians entered to gain time to improve their position and to disarm the West psychologically? Could Soviet leaders be trusted? Would not a relaxation of tensions and the apparent reduction of Soviet hostility create a widespread and dangerous euphoria in the West and lead to a lowering of its guard and a weakening of its defenses? Would not détente between the United States and the Soviet Union have adverse effects on our allies in Europe and elsewhere, weakening the free world alliance system and reducing its alertness to the further spread of communism?

Thus, within the framework of the Cold War system, it was much more critical and difficult to judge the opponent's *motivation* for wanting a relaxation of tensions. Similarly, the possibly adverse *consequences* of permitting a relaxation of tensions were a more pressing concern than in the older European system.

Interestingly enough, uneasy questions of this kind arose not only in the United States but to some extent within the Soviet Union as well. Soviet leaders were obliged to assure those skeptical of détente in their own country that they were not lowering their guard, would not neglect Soviet military defenses, were not naively trusting American leaders, were not betraying Marxist ideology and Socialist aspirations. Both American and, to a lesser extent, Soviet leaders faced the difficult task of obtaining domestic political legitimacy for their efforts to move away from the acute Cold War era to a less dangerous form of competition. The role of ideology, public opinion, domestic constraints and other features of the diplomatic revolution particularly complicated the efforts of American leaders to move beyond a mere relaxation of tensions toward a more significant restructuring and improvement in relations with the Soviet Union.

With the passage of time, particularly in the Nixon administration, the search for an improvement in U.S.–Soviet relations went well beyond a relaxation of tensions. As noted in Chapter 10, Nixon and Kissinger announced that it was their goal to develop a new "constructive" relationship with the Soviet Union that would constitute the foundation for a new international system to replace the Cold War. Nonetheless, it is significant that they continued to use the term *détente* to characterize this more ambitious long-range policy objective. Nixon and Kissinger spoke of maintaining and furthering the "détente process," while in fact the state of Soviet-American relations moved from "détente" to "rapprochement" to partial "appeasement." The term *détente* was stretched to encompass most of the discrete stages in the gradual improvement of relations between previously hostile states. One can, of course, understand Kissinger's reluctance to employ the term *appeasement* to describe his policies and activities, since it had acquired a highly negative and emotional connotation for the American public as a result of the disastrous effort to appease Hitler in the 1930s. But he was unable to dispel the unhappy association, and it haunted the Ford administration when the American public, as we have seen above, turned against the détente policy and forced its abandonment.

The effort to replace the Cold War with détente was by no means monopolized by American and Soviet leaders. During the early sixties, President Charles de Gaulle had unilaterally taken steps to bring France into closer relations with the Soviet Union; and, before the end of that decade, the West German government was moving cautiously to normalize and develop its relations with the USSR, the Eastern European states, and the German Democratic Republic. The lead was taken by Willy Brandt, first as foreign minister in the government of the Great Coalition headed by Kurt Georg Kiesinger, and later as chancellor of the SPD-FDP coalition that emerged after the elections of 1969.

The motivation and general course of Brandt's *Ostpolitik* have been touched on already in Chapter 10, but it is worthwhile dwelling here upon the diplomatic technique of what was a remarkably skillful performance, undertaken in a complex international environment and under difficult domestic political conditions. It was all the more difficult because the procedures that Brandt followed were closer to nineteenth-century practice than more recent experiments in détente diplomacy.

Brandt's Ostpolitik

It should be noted at the outset that Brandt had a clear notion not only of the changes that he wished to effect, but also of the difficulties that lay in his path. His initiative was based on a shrewd assessment of potential risks and gains and of how to utilize leverage to maneuver around obstacles. Since his *Ostpolitik* willingly embraced the possibility of major concessions to the Soviet Union and the East German regime, it certainly contained elements of what we would regard as appeasement; but Brandt orchestrated the complex process of détente to ensure that he gained important benefits in return, not only for West Germany but for Europe as a whole. He established diplomatic relations with Rumania and Yugoslavia and increased economic and cultural ties with other states in Eastern Europe. In 1970, he worked out a major deal with the Soviet Union, exchanging German-made pipe for Soviet natural gas. He dangled the possibility of favorable credit and commercial arrangements before the economically depressed Eastern European governments.

Unlike Chamberlain in his dealings with Hitler, Brandt did not rush the détente process in order to move as quickly as possible into appeasement. The British prime minister had been so certain of the ultimate success of appeasement that he engaged in a gigantic gamble, without assessing what would happen if his calculations proved to be in error and without having a prepared fallback position. In contrast, Brandt made a realistic calculation of the complexity and dangers of the course upon which he was embarking and devised a strategy and tactics that took them into account. Failure of *Ostpolitik* at any point might, to be sure, have led to the chancellor's political demise, but it would not have constituted a catastrophic setback for either West Germany or for NATO. Brandt minimized the risks by moving one step at a time and then waiting until the situation ripened before moving ahead again. He never forgot that he could negotiate successfully with the Soviet Union and its allies only if he operated from a position of strength based upon his NATO connection. At the same time, he did not allow the initiatives that he wished to take to be paralyzed by the sometimes lukewarm support of the United States.

At the same time, Brandt's freedom of maneuver was always severely constrained by divided opinion at home. *Ostpolitik,* therefore, inevitably required a strategy in which diplomatic moves were carefully controlled and timed to solidify domestic support or to neutralize political opposition. Indeed, some of the chancellor's initiatives toward the East were shrewdly calculated to weaken opposition at home.

A good illustration of this is the way in which he dramatized his policy at the outset, by means of his unprecedented trip to Erfurt in East Germany in March 1970, an action that was strongly reminiscent of the visit that King Edward VII made to Paris as part of the preparation for the Anglo-French entente of 1904. In his first policy statement after becoming chancellor, Brandt had announced in October 1969 that he intended to seek conversations with both the Soviet and Polish governments, and almost immediately he sent Egon Bahr to Moscow to sound out Andrei Gromyko on the possibility of a normalization of relations. Simultaneously, Georg Duckwitz, state secretary in the Foreign Office in Bonn, began similar talks with the Poles. The approach to the German Democratic Republic Brandt reserved for himself, doubtless because of the intensity of his feelings concerning the necessity of restoring contact between Germans who had been brutally separated by the results of the Cold War. On 22 January 1970, he wrote to the chairman of the Council of Ministers in the German Democratic Republic, Willi Stoph, and suggested a personal meeting to discuss "practical questions . . . that could alleviate the life of people in divided Germany." After some diplomatic sparring, in which Stoph sought to make the talks conditional upon preliminary concessions by the Federal Republic, he received a favorable reply, possibly because of Soviet pressure on East Berlin. On 19 March, a day that seemed to many European observers to mark a decisive change in the direction of Central European politics, Brandt arrived in Erfurt.

The chancellor did not expect to register a great success at this meeting or at its sequel in Kassel in West Germany. The Erfurt trip was planned for its impact upon public opinion on both sides of the common frontier. Aside from that, Brandt's goal had been to take the initiative in a way that if it accomplished nothing else, would neutralize negative East German influence in Moscow while the Bahr-Gromyko talks were proceeding, while at the same time letting Eastern European governments see that there were areas of policy in which the Federal Republic was able and willing to conclude bilateral agreements. Without in any way loosening his ties with the West, Brandt was making it known that the *Bundesrepublik* was prepared to follow an independent line in the interest of general appeasement.

This had positive results. In August 1970, the Moscow talks ended successfully with the signature of a Soviet–West German treaty that provided for the pacific resolution of all disputes between the signatories and recognized the existing frontiers between the two Germanies and between Germany and Poland, while not excluding the possibility of German reunification "in free self-determination." (This treaty was a way station in the progress of the Soviet Union toward the more comprehensive border clauses negotiated at the Conference on Security and Economic Cooperation and embodied in the Helsinki Agreement of 1975.) Four months later, a similar treaty normalized relations between the Federal Republic and Poland, stipulating the recognition by the former of the inviolability of Poland's frontiers, including the Oder-Neisse line, which Western governments had long insisted was a merely provisional border.

What were the benefits derived by West Germany and the West in general? Brandt wanted to extract from the Soviets and the East Germans an agreement that would guarantee the independent status of West Berlin and access to it by the Western powers. He assured this by indicating to the Soviets that he would not submit the Moscow Treaty to the German parliament for ratification until a satisfactory agreement on Berlin was negotiated by the four occupying powers. This was accomplished in due course, and the Berlin Agreement was signed by the powers in September 1971. Under pressure from the Soviets, the East German government, which had been reluctant to respond positively to Brandt's earlier overtures, now worked out agreements with the Federal Republic governing access to West Berlin and transit between the two parts of the city. The Moscow Treaty was then ratified by the Bundestag in May 1972. Six months later, after numerous meetings between officials of the Federal and Democratic republics, relations between the two Germanies were finally normalized by the so-called Basic Treaty, in which each agreed to respect the other's territorial integrity and to renounce the use of force in settling disputes, while also promising collaboration on practical and humane questions. In 1973, both governments applied, and were accepted for, membership in the United Nations.

With Brandt's fight to win parliamentary ratification of his work, in which he succeeded by defeating a vote of no confidence in April 1972 and, five months later, by forcing new parliamentary elections, we need not concern ourselves here. But it is worth emphasizing that the manner in which he pursued his diplomatic goals illustrates some of the prerequisites for effective use of the détente strategy. Among them, of course, is the importance of skillful political leadership that understands the multiple risks of embarking on such a course. The contrast between Brandt and Chamberlain was in this respect, as we have noted, striking. *Ostpolitik* is also a useful reminder that, while the sequence détente—→rapprochement—→entente—→appeasement cannot be pursued in today's world in precisely the same manner as it was in the European balance-of-power system, the older historical experience with this process retains relevance and value. Although the Cold War provided an entirely different context for the pursuit of détente/appeasement, this strategy remained potentially viable if employed with due caution and with sensitivity to the greater complexity of the situation and the nature of the risks involved. Indeed, the careful step-by-step way in which Brandt pursued *Ostpolitik* bears important similarities with the measured management of the détente process by English and French statesmen at the turn of the century.

Bibliographical Essay

There has been relatively little systematic comparative analysis of the phenomenon of détente by historians and political scientists. Research of this kind is currently being undertaken by Professor Klaus Knorr of Princeton University. Two useful discussions are Evan Luard, "Conciliation and Deterrence," *World Politics*, 19 (1967), 167–89, and John Herz, "The Relevancy and Irrelevancy of Appeasement," *Social Research*, 31 (1964), 296–320. See also Kal Holsti, *International Politics* (Englewood Cliffs, N.J., 1972).

On the Anglo-French entente of 1904, see especially Christopher Andrew, *Théophile Delcassé and the Making of the Entente Cordiale* (New York, 1968); G. P. Gooch, *Before the War: Studies in Diplomacy*, I (London, 1936); Zara S. Steiner, *The Foreign Office and Foreign Policy, 1898–1914* (Cambridge, Eng., 1965); and Paul Kennedy, *The Rise of Anglo-German Antagonism, 1860–1914* (London, 1980). The Haldane quotation is from his diary of his Berlin visit. See G. P. Gooch and H. W. Temperley, eds., *British Documents on the Origins of the War* (London, 1930ff.), VI, No. 506, p. 681. We are indebted to David Jex for calling this to our attention.

For Brandt's views on the development of *Ostpolitik,* see Willy Brandt, *Begegnungen und Einsichten: Die Jahre 1960–1975* (Hamburg, 1976). Other useful sources include Karl Birnbaum, *East and West Germany* (Lexington, Mass., 1973); Michael Freund, *From Cold War to Ostpolitik* (London, 1972); William E. Griffith, *The Ostpolitik of the Federal Republic of Germany* (Cambridge, Mass., 1978); Peter Merkl, *German Foreign Policies, West and East* (Santa Barbara, Calif., 1974); Roger Tilford, *The Ostpolitik and Political Change in Germany* (Lexington, Mass., 1975); Lawrence Whetten, *Germany's Ostpolitik* (London, 1971); and Philip Windsor, *Germany and the Management of Detente* (New York, 1971).

III
Ethical Imperatives
and Foreign Policy

18
The Christian Statesman: Bismarck and Gladstone

It is fair to say that most Americans like their leaders to mention God now and then and to attend church services occasionally. It is generally felt that such actions mark them as good men with moral values and that this is what we want in men in high office.

It would probably be harder, however, to win any general agreement on what relationship there should be between a leader's religious convictions and moral values and his policy. Should his beliefs and values influence his diplomatic style and goals? President Eisenhower's secretary of state, John Foster Dulles, was a practicing Christian. He was a long-time elder of the Presbyterian church who had also been active in the Federal Council of Churches, under whose auspices he had in 1939 founded the Commission for a Just and Durable Peace, an organization established to ensure that the great moral issues of the age were not disregarded when peace was made after World War II. Dulles's Christianity obviously was not, in his eyes, irrelevant to his statecraft, and his moral sense certainly informed his diplomatic style. This did not sit well with all of his fellows, and there were those who believe that it was self-defeating. Richard Rovere scoffed at Dulles's jet diplomacy, saying, "Mr. Dulles flies in for a few days, delivers a couple of dour Calvinist forecasts of doom and retribution, and then heads out to Bangkok or Rio or wherever," having accomplished nothing, he implied, except perhaps to alienate his hosts by his elevated moral tone. Walter Lippmann felt the same way and objected strenuously to Dulles's sermons about American moral excellences. Mr. Dulles was, Lippmann wrote once, "too noble about our ideals and never humble at all about our human, our very human, failures and faults. This alienates, indeed enrages, those who are by national interest our friends and allies. . . . For with great power, which is always suspect, there should go a decent humility." In the same way, the projection of President Carter's Christian convictions into the human rights program which he pushed so strenuously during his first year of office was, although widely praised, considered regrettable by some competent judges. The former ambassador to the Soviet Union, George F. Kennan, regarded the program as gratuitously insulting to the Soviet Union and said, "I think the new Administration has made just about every mistake it could . . . and has defied all the lessons we have learned with the Soviets since the last world war."

More difficult is the question whether religious and moral convictions should impose limitations upon a statesman's actions, so that he will feel compelled to oppose certain kinds of policy as being incompatible with his private beliefs. What should the devout statesman do when he is confronted with a situation that seems to require action in the service of his government that is deeply repugnant to him as an individual? Many who have reflected on this problem have argued that he should resign, but by no means everybody would agree. In a famous essay on Martin Luther, the theologian Karl Holl pointed out that that is too easy an answer. As the Great Reformer had held, the individual Christian undoubtedly had the duty to make his personal behavior conform to God's commands. But God had also given him a vocation, and it was his duty to be faithful to it and its requirements. It was inevitable that there would be conflicts between what Holl called the *Personalethik* and the *Berufsethik,* his personal ethical imperatives and the ethical imperatives of his vocation; and it did not necessarily follow that the latter must always be subordinated to the former.

We do not intend here to resolve these difficult problems but merely to illustrate the way in which they affected the policies of the two most famous European statesmen of the second half of the nineteenth century, Otto von Bismarck and William Ewart Gladstone.

It may come as a surprise to find Otto von Bismarck regarded as a Christian statesman, for one tends to think of him as the pure political animal, the *Realpolitiker.* Yet no one who has studied his life or his career will feel inclined to dismiss the importance of their religious component. When he was a young man, a dissolute, heavy-drinking

Landjunker in Pomerania, he met a young woman named Marie von Thadden, a devout Christian of Pietist persuasion. He was so deeply impressed by her character that he underwent a kind of religious conversion and became a member of a circle of like-minded friends, where he eventually met his wife, Johanna von Puttkamer. This early experience left a permanent mark upon him. Not that he was ostensibly devout, which was far from being the case. When he became famous, he gave up going to church because he said that people gaped at him as if he was some kind of animal and, when he took communion, he did so in the privacy of his own home. Moreover, he seems to have had to struggle to maintain the faith that he had painfully acquired in his youth. His favorite text was "Lord, I believe. Help thou my unbelief" (Mark 12:24); and he seems at times to have believed that his struggle was in vain, comparing himself late in life with Peter sinking beneath the waves because his faith would not sustain him. But however persistent his internal doubts, he clung to his faith in God's providence and found personal comfort in the doctrine of justification. And these things helped determine not only his diplomatic style (Otto Vossler once analyzed a famous passage in one of Bismarck's letters and, noting the emphatic use in it of terms like "justify," "duty," "service," "disloyalty," "caprice," and "right," said that no one could be unimpressed by its moral and ethical earnestness) but also his conception of his office, while at the same time supplying him with the strength to accept its burdens and, ultimately, giving him the confidence to make the decisions his office required of him.

When Bismarck learned that he had been appointed Prussia's ambassador to the Germanic Diet in Frankfurt in 1850 (his first post and the one that set him on his way to his later eminence), he wrote to his wife, "I am God's soldier, and where he sends me there I must go, and I believe that he does send me and that he shapes my life as he needs it." This has sometimes been taken merely as an ingratiating plea to a devout wife who was fretful about being uprooted and forced to move to another city; and it might be accepted as such if it stood alone. But it is one of many statements that show that Bismarck did not regard diplomacy as a mere job, but as a *vocatio,* an office to which he had been called by God. "I didn't ask for the royal service," he wrote to his friend Leopold von Gerlach in May 1860, "or search for personal honor in it, at least in a premeditated way. . . . God set me unexpectedly in it." And if it was God's will that he do this job, then doing it as well as he could was both an expression of obedience and an act of service. "I believe that I am obeying God when I serve my King," he said on one occasion; and, again, "It is precisely my living evangelical and Christian faith that lays upon me the duty—in behalf of the land where I was born and for whose service God created me and where high office has been entrusted to me—to guard that office against all sides." Here certainly we have an expression of Luther's concept of *Beruf* or vocation as work specifically assigned by God to the individual so that in performing it he might at one and the same time do his duty to God and his fellow men.

Bismarck's belief in this helped him bear the burdens that went with his office and the authority that was invested in him after he became the prime minister of Prussia in September 1862 and from 1870 to 1890 when he combined that office with the chancellorship of the new German Reich. This authority included the heavy weight of decisions that could bring war and even defeat to his country. Despite the undeniable personal satisfaction that he derived from wielding power, he never took its responsibilities lightly or callously, and he was always sensitive to the charge that he was ruthless, without scruple or conscience. His job was a lonely one, in the sense that the great powers of decision in foreign policy were concentrated in his hands; he could not delegate them to others or leave the ultimate choice up to the king whose chief adviser he was. He had to decide, and this meant often that he had to do things or choose courses of action which by the ethical standards of any religion in the world were wrong. In 1865, an evangelical pastor named Andrae-Roman wrote him a letter in which he asked him how he could condone the kinds of things he did and square them with his conscience as a Christian. Bismarck responded, "Would to God that I didn't have other sins upon my soul besides those the world knows of." But, he went on, he did not believe that anyone could accuse him of being a ruthless man or one without Christian conscience. As a matter of fact, he wrote,

> As a statesman I am not ruthless *enough* but rather cowardly in my feelings; and this is because it isn't always easy in the questions that come to me to win that clarity in whose soil grows confidence in God. Anyone who reproaches me for being a politician without conscience does me injustice and should sometime try his own conscience on *this* battlefield.

The fact of the matter, he continued, was that the dirty jobs had to be done, and the man whose duty it was to see that they were done had to continue to hope that God's grace would be extended to him. On another occasion, after 1870, dealing with the same question that Andrae-Roman had posed, the chancellor said, "If it hadn't been for me, there wouldn't have been three great wars, 80,000 men would not have died, and parents, brothers, sisters and widows would not be in mourning. But that I have had to settle with God."

The faith that sustained Bismarck in the big questions of peace and war quite clearly supported him in the lesser, but nonetheless important, tasks of his office. At the outset of his career as a diplomat, he wrote to his wife, "I will do my job. Whether God gives me the brains for that purpose is *His* business." A decade later, he put this idea in more elegant language when he said that the God who had made him unexpectedly a diplomat would watch over his actions "as long as I search for what is for His service in my office, and if I go wrong He will hear my daily prayer and change my heart or send me friends who will do so."

It is clear from all this that the decisiveness and sureness of touch so much admired by Bismarck's followers were not merely the products of a dynamic personality or of professional virtuosity but had other roots; and the religious component of his thinking makes it easier to understand not only the passion and dedication that he brought to his vocation but also the confidence with which he performed his duties. It was characteristic of him that, once he had made a decision, he did not worry about it but went forward confidently as if the decision was a shared one—indeed, as if the saying of one of his admirers, Maximilian Harden, that "God gave him the word while he slept" was really true and his decision was preordained and therefore right. This assurance, which so impressed other statesmen, was certainly rooted in his religious convictions.

And yet, as the liberal deputy Ludwig Bamberger once suggested, it is possible that Bismarck made it easy for himself. Bamberger's way of putting this was to say: "Prince Bismarck believes firmly and deeply in a God who has the remarkable faculty of always agreeing with him." That is cynical but not entirely wide of the mark. It would perhaps be more accurate to say that Bismarck's insistence that serving the state was a divine service made it easy for him to believe that anything that could be regarded as a requirement of the state became a divine requirement. In this sense, although he had only a fleeting acquaintance with Hegel, he often sounds Hegelian when he talks about the Prussian state, and he seemed to regard it as a thought of God, a historical force with its own dynamics. He believed that it was the duty of the statesman not to question those dynamics but to understand them, not to question the state's requirements of power and growth but to find ways of satisfying them. He put this idea in religious rather than philosophical terms, but nevertheless in terms that Hegel would not have rejected, by saying that the statesman must listen for the footstep of God in events and then leap forward and seize Him by the hem of His garment. What might have been an agonizing dilemma for another Christian— a continued conflict between his personal conscience and his responsibility to his job—was reduced in Bismarck's case to a somewhat simpler problem of persuading himself, on any given occasion, that he was performing his duties *as a statesman* well. Once he had convinced himself that that was true, he could, and did, assure himself that he had done his duty by God as well. There might be some personal delinquencies that had to be taken care of, but in protecting and maintaining state interest he had performed the big duties required of him.

It is instructive for anyone interested in Bismarck to visit his estate at Friedrichsruh near Hamburg. Here one can wander in the Sachsenwald among trees planted by the chancellor himself and see in the museum memorabilia of a long and fruitful career. And here one can visit the Forest Chapel and see the family sarcophagi—Bismarck's and Johanna's before the altar, his son Herbert's and his wife's below in the vault. On Johanna's sarcophagus are engraved the words "God is Love and who abides by Love, he abides in God and God in him." On Bismarck's, the inscription is shorter. It reads simply "A loyal German servant of Emperor William I." The words, in this particular setting, are a lapidary summary of the principles that guided Bismarck's career: the belief that service to the state and its ruler was the supreme duty and that this, according to his reading of Luther, was also a service to God. In Bismarck's career, if there was a conflict between *Berufsethik* and *Personalethik,* he had no great difficulty in resolving it by giving priority to the demands of his vocation.

In the case of William Ewart Gladstone, the conflict between these principles was more acute, and the willingness to accept the requirements of state policy without question was not present. Gladstone was the son of a hard-headed Lowland Scots businessman with extensive interests in India and the West Indies and a romantic and spiritual mother who was fervently religious and who brought her son up in the bosom of the Evangelical wing of the Church of England. An idealistic, emotional, and highly argumentative youth, he went to Eton in 1821 where he had a successful career, being elected to all the best societies and becoming coeditor of the *Eton Miscellany,* which printed his first writings. He went up to Oxford in 1828, as a member of Christ Church College, where he became one of the most powerful debaters in the history of the Oxford Union, and where he won a double first—that is, first-class honors in both classics and in mathematics, a remarkable achievement. The first stirrings of the Oxford Movement—that force of reform in the Church of England that was led by people like Newman and Manning—occurred during his time in Oxford and strengthened his already profoundly religious temperament. If he had had his way, he would have taken religious orders. His father, a blunt and forceful man, would have none of that and insisted that his son turn to politics. Gladstone did so, entering the House of Commons at the age of twenty-three in 1832 and beginning a parliamentary career that lasted until his death in 1898 and brought him four times—in 1868–1874, 1880–1885, 1886, and 1892–1894—to the position of prime minister of England.

His religious passion did not abate when he went to the House. Peter Stansky has written,

> He conceived of his life as dedicated to God; politics was a second-best way of trying to achieve a more Christian community. He would sooner hear a sermon than see a sight, and he did not allow his career to interfere with his church-going. In his youth, he had a tendency to be narrow-minded in an Evangelical fashion, but he was not unbending—he played cards (though not without qualms), he never opposed drink, and he would, if he must, travel on the Sabbath.

As he grew older, his religious views broadened and became more tolerant, and his early suspicion of Catholicism was tempered by a growing respect for that church (which Newman, the leader of the Oxford Movement, whom Gladstone admired, had in the end joined). His views became steadily more ecumenical as he grew older, and he was always opposed to the narrow sectarianism of the kind that denied seats in Parliament to those who did not subscribe to the thirty-nine articles of the Church of England and sought to maintain that church as the established church in Ireland. Indeed, he came to the conclusion that religion would be best served by freeing the church from the state.

His personal faith was intense and untroubled by the kind of doubts that affected Bismarck. He genuinely tried to live his life according to the Sermon on the Mount, and succeeded to an extraordinary extent for one who was leader of a powerful people. He was admired in the Victorian age, which yearned for both power and morality, for suggesting, as Stansky has said, how one could both be moral and get along in the world. He was never hesitant to do what he considered to be his Christian duty even when it shocked the pious or seemed injudicious to the calculating. For years he made it a personal mission to attempt to alleviate the lot of London's prostitutes and, even when he was prime minister, spent a remarkable amount of time walking the streets, talking with these women, sometimes going to their rooms with them, wholly oblivious to the criticism that this attracted.

What effect did these religious convictions have upon his politics? They determined his goals and the way in which he pursued them. Gladstone was one of the great reformers in the history of British politics, a man who would have earned his place in history even if he had never become prime minister, for even in his middle years, as chancellor of the Exchequer in Aberdeen's cabinet in 1852–1855 and that of Palmerston and Russell in 1859–1866, he distinguished himself by promoting the free trade policy, by abolishing the excise tax on paper (which reduced the price of books and newspapers), by devising an effective postal savings and insurance system that was much used by the poor, and by systematically reducing direct and indirect taxation. But it was only after he became prime minister for the first time in 1868 that the true spirit of his reforming activity became manifest, and it became clear that, while not a democrat, he believed that the vulnerable members of society, particularly the working class and the Irish, should not be treated differently from the middle class and should be given opportunities that would enable them to win complete political and social equality. His had been the key voice in the passage of the Reform Bill of 1867, for he had been the first to say that "every man who is not presumably incapacitated by some consideration of personal unfitness or of political danger is morally entitled to come within the pale of the constitution." The Liberal victory that made him prime minister in 1868 was an expression of the electorate's acknowledgment of authorship of the reform; and he in turn responded to that vote of confidence by pushing forward new measures—the civil service reform of 1870, which opened the bureaucracy to talent, the reform of the army that accomplished the same for that body by doing away with the purchase of commissions, and the Education Act of 1870, which gave a tremendous impetus to popular education.

In Gladstone's mind, the most important of his reforms had to do with Ireland which had chafed, since Elizabeth's time, under British rule. When Gladstone came to office in 1868, he said, "My mission is to pacify Ireland!" and his first step in this direction was to call for the disestablishment of the Anglican church in that country. He followed this up with measures to improve the lot of Irish tenant farmers, by protecting them from arbitrary eviction and providing them with compensation for improvements to the land. Once that basis was laid, the logic of events and his own conscience led Gladstone, in his three remaining terms as prime minister, to work for an extension of autonomy to Ireland, for the establishment, in short, of an Irish free state. He fought for this goal implacably, never hesitating to place the political tenure of his cabinets in jeopardy, never stayed by the vitriolic attacks of the Conservatives and defectors from his own party, who called his plan "a monstrous mixture of imbecility, extravagance and political hysterics," preaching his cause on the hustings to the detriment of his own health, and in the end he failed. But as he said during one of these intermittent campaigns in old age, "I went in bitterness, in the heat of my spirit, but the hand of the Lord was upon me." He was fighting for a principle that his conscience told him was a right principle, and he was willing, in the last resort, to incur defeat for a great cause. Some of his colleagues, who wished he would forget Ireland, whispered that he wanted martyrdom, a remark prompted by the fact that Ireland engrossed all of the old man's attention during his third and fourth prime ministerships and led in both cases to his government's fall.

How did Gladstone's religious views affect his positions on foreign policy? For one thing, unlike Bismarck's, his thinking was not influenced by Hegelian or Lutheran ideas about the state and its demands. The state was a term that did not fit easily into an Englishman's mouth in any case, and Gladstone, knowing that British policy was made in the House of Commons, did not objectify the state or attribute to it thoughts of its own. His view of what the government did in foreign policy was always critical, in both a negative and positive sense. He believed that it was beneath the dignity of his country, which he regarded as the most progressive nation in the world, to indulge in the sin of pride, by vaunting itself above others, or of greed, by lusting after the possessions of others, or of murder, by indulging in war for base ends or for any but defensive reasons.

His first speech on foreign policy was in June 1850, at a time when he was still the Tory member for Oxford and a member of the opposition. The occasion was a debate on an action taken by Lord Palmerston, foreign secretary in the government of Lord John Russell. Palmerston had sent ships to blockade Greece because the Greek government had refused to pay compensation to a Portuguese moneylender named Don Pacifico, whose house had been looted. Don Pacifico, who had been born in Gibraltar, claimed British citizenship, and it was on that basis that Palmerston had authorized the naval action, which culminated in a bombardment. A vote of censure was brought against him in the House of Commons, and Palmerston defended himself in a brilliant five-hour speech that ended with the words: "As the Roman in days of old held himself free from indignity when he could say . . . 'Civis Romanus sum!' so also a British subject, in whatever land he may be, shall feel confident that the watchful eye and the strong arm of England will protect him against injustice and wrong."

The narrow patriotism and false pathos of this speech outraged Gladstone, who rejected the Roman comparison by saying that it implied that the British, like the Romans, should enjoy the privileges of a special kind of law that set them above others. "The English people are indeed a great and noble people; but it adds nothing to their greatness or their nobleness that when we assemble in this place, we should trumpet forth our virtues in elaborate panegyrics and designate those who may not be wholly of our mind as a knot of foreign conspirators. . . . The only knot of foreign conspirators against the noble Lord is the combined opinion of civilised Europe." In words that show the intimate relationship between his religious fervor and his foreign political views, Gladstone declared: "It would be a contravention of the law of nature and of God, if it were possible for any single nation of Christendom to emancipate itself from the obligations which bind all other nations and to arrogate, in the face of mankind, a position of peculiar privilege." Gladstone always opposed this tendency of the British to assume that they were a superior nation, untouched by the rule that they insisted should bind all other nations, as he opposed the policy of imperialism which was justified by it.

Gladstone's most complete and eloquent statement of his positive views about what Britain's policy should be was delivered during his great electoral campaign—the so-called Midlothian campaign of 1879–1880—and the deep Christian coloration of this speech is evident even in its headings.

1. "To foster the strength of the Empire . . . and to reserve it for great and worthy occasions."

2. "To preserve to the nations . . . the blessings of peace—especially were it but for shame, when we recollect the sacred name we bear as Christians, for the Christian nations."

3. "To cultivate to the utmost the Concert of Europe" [because one can thus] "neutralise and fetter the selfish aims of each."

4. "To avoid needless and entangling engagements."

5. "To acknowledge the rights of all nations. . . . In point of fact all [nations] are equal, and you have no right to set up a system under which one is to be placed under moral suspicion or espionage, or made the subject of constant invective. If you do that, and especially if you claim for yourself a pharisaical superiority . . . you may talk about your patriotism as you please, but you are a misjudging friend of your country and are undermining the basis of esteem and respect of others for it."

6. Finally, foreign policy "should always be inspired by love of freedom [and] a desire to give it scope, founded not on visionary ideas but upon the long experience of many generations within the shores of this happy isle." (It was this principle that Gladstone felt had been violated at the Congress of Berlin by the Disraeli-Salisbury government when it signed a treaty that left the Balkan Christians under Turkish control, thus actually appearing to make a deal with the Turks in return for the cession of the island of Cyprus.)

It is easy, when one reflects upon this statement of principle, to understand why Woodrow Wilson, another statesman whose politics reflected his religious convictions, was a great admirer of Gladstone. But principles are not always easy to cling to when one is charged with the conduct of the policy of a great nation, and Gladstone was to discover that only two years after he made these ringing declarations.

In June 1882, Egyptian nationalists led by a colonel named Arabi (an early Nasser or Sadat) rose against the corrupt administration of the khedive. Egypt was a country in which both Britain and France had economic interests, and Britain, since Disraeli's time, had financial control of the Suez Canal. The British government had a sizeable stake to protect, but the French were disinclined to cooperate in restoring order in Egypt, and Gladstone, always opposed to imperialistic adventure, did not want to act alone. True to his principles, he appealed to the European concert to act, but was rebuffed. Bismarck, not displeased by Gladstone's difficulties and seeing the possibility of using Egypt to drive a wedge between England and France, ended any hope of action by the concert by saying, "Let the Powers interested settle it as they please, but don't ask me how, for I neither know nor care." Against his will, Gladstone found himself impelled to action, saying rather lamely to the House, "We should not fully discharge our duty if we did not endeavor to convert the present interior state of Egypt from anarchy and conflict to peace and order. We shall look . . . to the cooperation of the powers of civilized Europe. . . . But if every chance of obtaining cooperation is exhausted, the work will be undertaken by the single power of England."

In July, the admiral of the British fleet lying off the Egyptian coast sent an ultimatum to Arabi, ordering him to stop fortifying Alexandria. When no answer was received, he opened fire and destroyed the fort. After rioting and anarchy ensued, Gladstone asked Commons for funds to send an expeditionary force under General Wolsey, which landed at Port Said in August, defeated Arabi's forces in a pitched battle, and restored order. All of this led John Bright, one of Gladstone's oldest colleagues, to resign from the cabinet, saying that the action was "simply damnable—worse than anything ever perpetrated by Dizzy."

There is no doubt that Gladstone wanted to withdraw the British garrison from Egypt as quickly as possible, but he had in reality taken the step that turned Egypt into a British protectorate. Unforeseen events promoted this result. In 1883, a revolt took place in the Sudan led by a religious zealot named the Mahdi and, late in the year, his forces met and cut to pieces an ill-disciplined Egyptian army led by Hicks Pasha. It seemed necessary for Britain to use troops to save the hapless Egyptian forces and liquidate the Sudan situation; and for this purpose the government sent General George Gordon to Khartoum. But no sooner had this strange compound of adventurer and religious enthusiast got to Khartoum than he proclaimed that, if Egypt were to be kept quiet, the Mahdi must be smashed. This fantastic enterprise came to no good end and, by March 1884, Gordon was surrounded and besieged in Khartoum by the Mahdi's forces. The question of sending a force to relieve him now became the order of the day, but its resolution was delayed by Gladstone's fury at Gordon for launching what he called "a war of conquest against people struggling to be free" (which seemed to many to be a strange inconsistency, for if the Mahdi represented a people struggling to be free, why hadn't Colonel Arabi?). He refused to believe that Gordon was in danger. One of his colleagues said that Gladstone could "persuade most people of most things, and above all he can persuade himself of almost anything"; but his attitude was not merely obtuse; it was instead rooted in his determination that Britain must get out of Egypt rather than become more involved in it. The result, however, of his mental tergiversations was that the debate about a relief expedition dragged on much too long. It was not until July that Wolsey was authorized to move; he was not ready to do so until October; and when his advance guard reached Khartoum on 28 January 1885, Gordon and his men had been killed two days earlier.

The Gordon affair (while assuring that Britain stayed in Egypt) did much to kindle the bitterness that split the Liberal party and led to its loss of office in June 1885, and it led to fierce attacks upon Gladstone. The Queen herself said emphatically, "Mr. Gladstone and the Government *have* Gordon's innocent, noble heroic blood on their consciences"; and, in his biography of Gladstone, Philip Magnus has cited a music hall song that reversed the initials G.O.M. (Grand Old Man), often used with reference to Gladstone, to make them signify Murderer of Gordon.

> The M.O.G., when his life ebbs out,
> Will ride in a fiery chariot,
>   And sit in state
>   On a red-hot plate
> Between Pilate and Judas Iscariot.

Quite respectable people called Gladstone a traitor, and, in view of his other reforming goals, a Communist. During the election campaign of 1886, Lord Randolph Churchill jeered: "Mr. Gladstone, in his speech at Edinburgh on Friday, recommended himself to the country in the name of Almighty God. Others cannot and will not emulate such audacious profanity."

What these people were raving against, of course, was an attempt, however clumsy, by the country's leading statesman to remain true to the principles of foreign policy which he had enunciated during the Midlothian campaign in 1880 and which they had applauded to the echo. In their rage, they were now using Gladstone's Christianity against him. The story of the Egyptian affair of 1882–1885 is a striking example of the way in which the man of principle can become involved in a mass of contradictions that make clear decisions impossible. There is no doubt what Bismarck would have done in this long crisis. He would have made a careful calculation of Germany's interests in the area and acted on that basis, telling himself, perhaps subconsciously, that he was doing God's work. Gladstone could not permit himself that kind of indulgence. His principles of foreign policy were not guided by a narrow conception of national interest but rather by his view of what his country *should* be like and how it could contribute to a more perfect community of nations; and his religious convictions imposed those broader goals upon his mind as a duty. But in the myriad of problems posed by the Egyptian-Sudanese question, Gladstone discovered that there was no easy way to apply those principles unambiguously. His stubborn refusal to abandon them completely led to his rejection, not only by a public opinion that was inflamed by the jingoistic press, but also by colleagues who felt that, in this instance, morality was nothing but weakness. It is easier to govern one's private behavior according to the Sermon on the Mount than it is to run one's foreign policy in accordance with it.

Bibliographical Essay

The role of religion in Bismarck's statecraft is the theme of A. O. Meyer, *Bismarcks Glaube,* 4th ed. (Munich, 1933); Friedrich Meinecke, "Bismarcks Eintritt in den christlich-germanischen Kreis," *Historische Zeitschrift,* 90 (1902), 56–92; Otto Vossler, "Bismarcks Ethos," ibid., 171 (1951), 263–92; and Leonhard von Muralt, *Bismarcks Verantwortlichkeit* (Gottingen, 1955). In the latest major biography, decided weight is placed on it: Lothar Gall, *Bismarck, der weisse Revolutionär* (Frankfurt am Main, 1980).

On Gladstone's faith, see the classical biography of John Morley, 3 vols. (London, 1904) and the modern one by Philip Magnus (London, 1954). Concise and provocative is Peter Stansky, *Gladstone: A Progress in Politics* (Boston, 1979), and there are interesting *aperçus* in Asa Briggs, *Victorian People: A Reassessment of Persons and Themes* (London, 1954) and a forgotten but valuable work, A. A. W. Ramsay, *Idealism and Foreign Policy* (London, 1925). The role of religion in the Gordon affair becomes very clear in Lord Elton, *Gordon of Khartoum* (New York, 1954).

19

The Problem of Ethical and Moral
Constraints on the Use of Force
in Foreign Policy

How to find ways of restraining the use of force has been a perennial problem in the theory and practice of international relations. Since the ideal of abolishing war completely is evidently unattainable, statesmen, political philosophers, and specialists in international law have turned to other methods of limiting resort to force as an instrument of foreign policy. The development of international law and institutions like the League of Nations, the World Court, and the United Nations has not been without some relevance and influence in this respect. But despite repeated attempts to define aggression and to limit the conditions in which resort to arms is justified, agreement on these matters has proved to be elusive, and nations have been unwilling to surrender the sovereign right to decide for themselves when to use military force to protect or advance their interests.

Nevertheless, in all of the international systems of the modern period, some basis has existed for the restraint of force, if only through the operation of deterrence. As we have seen, the consensus of the great powers comprising the concert of Europe in the nineteenth century discouraged individual states from embracing hegemonial aspirations in their foreign policies. This restriction of objective, in turn, often encouraged a limitation of the means employed in the pursuit of legitimate policy objectives.

Another type of restraint is that derived from the moral and religious principles of national leaders. Some statesmen experience, as Gladstone did, a psychological conflict between their conception of moral behavior

269

(and the moral standards of the community to which they belong) and the requirements of foreign policy that impel them on occasion to intervene by force in the affairs of other countries. On the other hand, as the comparison of Bismarck and Gladstone in this respect has revealed, there are important differences in the extent to which private scruple and conscience constrain a statesman's actions in foreign policy, and some statesmen experience little or no conflict between their moral beliefs and the requirements of their position.

I

Although the question of the role that moral and ethical principles can, or should, play in the conduct of international affairs has engaged the attention of moral and political philosophers for centuries, it has not been resolved even on the theoretical level. The problem is often put in the form of a question: Does the end justify the means? This is the way in which many people address such policy questions as: Was President Truman morally justified in using the atomic bomb against Japan? Was President Kennedy morally justified in approving the Bay of Pigs invasion of Cuba and, later, in risking a thermonuclear war by attempting to coerce Khrushchev into removing the missiles from Cuba? Was Nixon justified in using covert methods to try to prevent the election of a Socialist, Allende, in Chile and, afterward, to bring about the downfall of Allende's Socialist government? Similarly, was the Soviet Union justified in using its army to put down the Hungarian revolution in 1956 and to intervene in Czechoslovakia in 1968 and Afghanistan in 1979? There are, unfortunately, many other American and Soviet foreign policy actions about which the same question can be raised. But this question can also be raised about the foreign policies of other governments. For example, during the early part of World War II, the Swedish government, having adopted a policy of neutrality, felt it prudent to deny Norwegians being hunted by the Nazis who had occupied their country from escaping into Sweden. While recognizing the policy dilemma created for Sweden, many observers questioned the morality of its decision. As this example suggests, the morality of foreign policy can be questioned not only when a state takes actions that conflict with ethical principles but also when it fails to take actions to further a moral objective. Thus, many persons thought that President Eisenhower was morally delinquent when he refused in October 1956 to give strong support and military assistance to the Hungarians who had overthrown their Communist regime, thereby allowing their revolution to be crushed by the Soviet army. And, to cite a more recent example, many persons believe that the U.S. government is morally delinquent because it will not intervene more energetically against the apartheid policy of the South African government.

II

As noted earlier, there is a long history of controversy over the question whether and how moral principles should apply in foreign policy. Three schools of thought may be identified, each of which takes a different position on the issue "Does the end justify the means?" There is, first, the *amoral* point of view, a designation that can be given to all those who believe that the question of morality applies only to the ends or goals of foreign policy, not to the selection of means to achieve those ends. This position is taken by adherents of an extreme *Realpolitik* approach to world politics as well as by a variety of political activists— whether ideological fanatics like Hitler and the old Bolsheviks or extreme nationalists and terrorists. They argue in effect that since the objectives they pursue are morally justified, that's all that matters. *Any* means to an end is then justified, with one caveat, to be sure, and that is that the means chosen should be effective. For the amoralists, then, the criterion to be applied in choosing methods is not their morality but rather their efficiency. They are interested only in whether the means chosen will be effective in promoting the moral objective.

It should be noted, however, that those who subscribe to the amoral position do not always feel free to choose morally questionable means. Sometimes they feel obliged to respect the moral standards of others, for they realize that to be completely ruthless can create strong opposition and set back their cause. Amoralists, therefore, may restrain themselves from taking certain actions, but they do so out of prudence and coldly calculated self-interest, not because they have moral scruples of their own.

The *perfectionist* approach to the question "Does the end justify the means?" is another familiar position. The perfectionist argues that no matter how noble and virtuous the end, it *never* justifies the use of means that violate moral/ethical standards. The moral perfectionists and the amoralists, therefore, stand at opposite ends of the spectrum.

271

Perhaps the best example of a thoroughgoing moral perfectionist is the pacifist—one who excludes the use of military force and violence in all circumstances, even in self-defense. For the genuine, full-blown pacifist not even circumstances in which the physical survival of the nation is at stake can justify a resort to violence in self-defense. However, we must not assume that pacifists are cowards. Faced with aggression against his own country, a pacifist may rely on *nonviolent* techniques of passive resistance to frustrate the aggressor. A courageous pacifist may be willing to risk his own life in passive-resistance efforts.

Similar to the pacifists in some respects are those persons in the United States and elsewhere who some years ago used to criticize Cold War policies on the grounds that they plunged the world into crises, such as the Berlin crisis of 1948 and the Cuban missile crisis, which raised the danger of a thermonuclear war. These critics were not pro-Communist or pro-Soviet; they did not favor the spread of communism throughout the world. Rather, they felt that reliance on deterrence and military threats to defend against the spread of communism was immoral and unacceptable because such policies increased the risk of a thermonuclear holocaust. Many of them, like the pacifists, were willing to pay a stiff price in order to avoid the danger of World War III. They recognized that if American leaders followed their advice and did not use force and threats of force to deter communism, then communism would inevitably spread. But they took the position that such an outcome, however distasteful, was preferable to a thermonuclear holocaust, and this position they expressed in the colorful phrase "Better Red than dead." This slogan was quite popular twenty years ago among some members of the peace movement and those who favored unilateral disarmament by the United States.

Even if one disagrees with pacifists and those who argued "Better Red than dead," one can respect them for their willingness to face up to the logical and political consequences of their beliefs. Of quite a different stripe, on the other hand, are other perfectionists, often referred to as *moralizers,* who avoid dealing with the question of the costs (to others as well as to themselves) if their moralistic views on foreign policy are actually adopted. Moralists of this kind are often accused by their critics of wanting to retain the comforts of a good conscience for themselves in matters of foreign policy without being prepared to pay the price. Moralists often are more concerned with the symbolic aspects of foreign policy than its actual substance. They frequently appear to be less concerned with influencing foreign policy than with registering virtuous attitudes.

There are other interesting aspects of the perfectionist position which deserve some attention. Some perfectionists have argued that states should behave in accord with the same high standards of morality that apply to individual persons in a well-ordered community. They recognize that states and their rulers do not behave according to these standards; but they believe that they *ought* to do so and that it is the task of enlightened leaders to create an international system in which they will. A well-known exponent of this view was Woodrow Wilson. As Wilson phrased it in his message to Congress in 1917 declaring war on Germany: "We are at the beginning of an age in which it will be insisted that the same standards of conduct and responsibility for wrong done shall be observed among nations and their governments that are observed among the individual citizens of civilized states."

Various objections have been raised against this kind of perfectionist view, not all of which can be taken up here. One of the criticisms is that states are different from individuals and that therefore moral standards that can be appropriately held up to guide and judge the behavior of individual persons in a well-ordered community cannot apply to states that are trying to provide for their security in an anarchic international system. Elaborating on this, some writers (for example, E. H. Carr, in *The Twenty Years' Crisis*) say that moral standards can take precedence only in a well-developed, well-ordered international community, one in which people agree that the good of the whole community must take precedence over the good of the parts. Viewed from this standpoint, it is obvious that loyalty and adherence to a world community are not yet powerful enough to override what individual states consider to be their "vital national interest."

Another familiar criticism of the perfectionists is that their emphasis on morality easily leads to a self-righteous moralism in foreign policy. Such a criticism was leveled against John Foster Dulles, Eisenhower's secretary of state. Dulles and moralists of his kind, it was charged, are dangerous people to have in charge of foreign policy because they tend to convert conflicts of interest among states into conflicts between "good" and "evil." This kind of moralization of foreign policy can have catastrophic consequences. The more passionately a moralist leader believes he is right in a dispute with another state, the more likely he is to reject compromise and accommodation and strive instead to secure a complete

273

victory over the opponent on behalf of his moral principles. Thus, it is possible that a moralistic approach in foreign policy, if carried to an extreme, can end up in fanaticism, which in turn can lead to catastrophic results. This type of concern was registered by Hans Morgenthau, a leading proponent of the "realist" approach to international affairs, when he wrote: "We cannot conclude [merely] from the good intentions of a statesman that his foreign policies will be either morally praiseworthy or politically successful. . . . How often have statesmen been motivated by a desire to improve the world, and ended by making it worse?"

So much for the perfectionist answer to the question "Does the end justify the means?" This formulation of the problem is rejected by a third school of thought, the *nonperfectionists,* for whom Arnold Wolfers was a leading spokesman. For the nonperfectionists, there is no simple, unequivocal answer to the question as there is for the amoralists and the perfectionists. Nonperfectionists insist that this question has to be reformulated in a significantly different way, as follows: "Under *what* conditions do *which* ends justify *what* means?" And as their reformulation of the question implies, the nonperfectionists believe that whether morally questionable means are justified cannot be answered abstractly but depends on the specific circumstances of the situation as well as on the character of the objectives the policy maker pursues in that situation.

Because nonperfectionists stress the critical importance of the circumstances of each case, they are often said to take a *contextualist* approach to the problem. That is to say, the nonperfectionists employ *situational ethics,* not absolutist ethical standards.

Who, then, subscribes to the nonperfectionist view, a view that takes issue with both the amoralists and the moral absolutists? It may come as a surprise to learn that the original *Realpolitik* and "realist" approach to international politics subscribed not to the amoral position but to this contextualist view of the role of moral principles in the conduct of foreign policy. The realist approach, identified in modern times with the writings of Hans Morgenthau, goes back at least as far as Machiavelli. It is important to recall that the Florentine thinker, although he often sounded as if he adhered to the amoral position, was in fact a contextualist of the nonperfectionist stripe. It is true that many realists have misread Machiavelli's *The Prince* as saying that "the end justifies the means" and that international politics being what it is—a kind of "dog-eat-dog" contest—one has to take a cynical, amoral stance toward the problem of selecting means to pursue foreign policy objectives. Those who oversimplify Machiavelli's position in this way may be referred to as the *vulgar realists*—"vulgar" because they have misunderstood and distorted his realist approach to international politics. Actually, as Kenneth Waltz and Michael Walzer have emphasized, Machiavelli attached important qualifications to his advice to the ruler. Thus, Machiavelli says that *not all ends,* but only some ends, justify morally dubious means; they must be constructive, beneficent ends.

An even more important qualification is Machiavelli's additional caveat that whether unsavory, morally questionable means are justified depends upon what he calls "the necessity of the case"—that is, whether in a given situation there are no alternative modes of action that promise success in achieving the constructive end. The realist position on this issue has been developed further by academic theorists such as Morgenthau and Wolfers who defend the original realist position and distinguish it from the oversimplified, distorted views of the vulgar realists.

Whatever the philosophical or political attractiveness of the nonperfectionist approach, it is much more difficult to apply in practice than either of the two other approaches. The amoralist and the perfectionist positions can be implemented much more easily than the situational ethics which are supposed to guide the realists. Thus, the perfectionist operates with a flat prohibition against using morally dubious methods even on behalf of the most virtuous ends. The amoralist's rule of action is exactly the opposite and almost as easy to apply: any means, however immoral, is acceptable so long as it promises success and is efficient. In contrast, it is impossible to convert the nonperfectionist point of view into simple rules of action that give explicit and clear-cut guidance to the decision maker. Since so much depends on the specific circumstances of the case, nonperfectionists can formulate only very general guidelines for decision-making. Four such guidelines have been spelled out by Arnold Wolfers, and in listing them now it will become obvious why they are best regarded as general guidelines rather than specific rules for correct behavior.

The first is that the objective of a foreign policy action must be genuinely constructive and praiseworthy if the decision maker is even to consider choosing morally dubious methods on its behalf. Some would say that, if this guideline is taken seriously by the policy maker, then he would use force only to defend the truly "vital interests" of the nation.

The second is that morally dubious means should not be employed when less dubious means that may achieve the same objective are available.

Third, a statesman should choose that course of action which, in the given circumstances, promises to cause the least destruction of things of value.

Finally, the statesman who attempts to apply situational ethics in making difficult decisions of this kind should be constrained in the choice of means—particularly when military force is employed—by what theologians have referred to as the "principle of proportionality." This is an enjoinder to the effect that the dubious means employed must at least have a rational relationship to the ends pursued. In practice, this requires the statesman to avoid profligate use of force that will inflict more loss of life and more damage than is necessary or congruent with what is at stake. It will be recalled that American war policies in Vietnam were severely criticized, even among those who were not totally opposed to U.S. objectives, on the grounds that they grossly violated the principle of proportionality. The military means employed by U.S. forces and the enormous destruction they wrought were felt to be out of any conceivable proportion to the American interests involved.

III

What is the practical utility of the four guidelines offered by nonperfectionists for dealing with moral dilemmas arising from the use of force as an instrument of foreign policy? They are relevant and better than no guidance at all as to how situational ethics apply in practice, but nonetheless it must be recognized that their vagueness permits considerable subjectivity and elasticity in the way in which they are likely to be employed. The guidelines may have some useful effect, particularly where policy makers are not unduly pressed, but there is no guarantee whatsoever that they will force even those decision makers who subscribe to them to give conscientious attention and adequate weight to moral considerations in determining their foreign policies and actions.

Most policy makers and their advisers in a country like the United States probably regard themselves as practitioners of the nonperfectionist approach. But they generally apply it in very subjective, loose, and highly inconsistent ways, and they do so not only because these guidelines are so vague but because other pressures on policy-making are often so much stronger than the force of moral considerations. The decision maker is under pressure to protect and advance his country's position in world affairs, even when vital national interests are not at stake; he is under pressure to achieve results and to be successful in foreign affairs; and he is usually concerned also to protect his personal political interests and those of his party, and to win elections. Considerations of this kind tend to have greater importance for most policy makers than what may seem to them to be an overly squeamish concern with the morality of the means employed. It is all too easy for decision makers to justify their resort to morally questionable means, to engage in self-deception, and to offer convenient rationalizations as to the necessity to do so.

Certainly it is the case that so long as more stringent guidelines for employing situational ethics are lacking, the policy maker can easily end by believing that results are more important than the moral purity of his actions. When hard-pressed by the exigencies and political controversies that surround his performance, the statesman tends to fall back to a last line of defense, arguing that the ultimate justification for what he has done is whether it turns out to be successful. Leaders of many different persuasions have at least one thing in common: they prefer to be judged by "history" when their compatriots render harsh judgments. Unfortunately, ample precedents—some of them highly respectable—are available to be called upon by leaders caught in such circumstances. It was, after all, Abraham Lincoln who on one occasion responded to criticism by stating that "if the end brings me out all right, what is said against me won't amount to anything. If the end brings me out wrong, ten angels swearing I was right would make no difference." This may be a good political argument—certainly it appealed to President Nixon, who quoted Lincoln to justify his highly controversial invasion of Cambodia, and to Bert Lance, director of the Office of Management and Budget in the Carter administration, who also quoted Lincoln when defending his unusual financial transactions before a Senate committee—but it remains a questionable approach to political morality.

Given the limitations of the nonperfectionist approach and the fact that nonetheless many statesmen will continue to make use of it, it is perhaps appropriate to end with a good word for the moral perfectionists—those persons who have an irrepressible tendency to express moral condemnation of this, that, and almost every aspect of foreign policy. While their preachments are often irritating and naively impractical, we should still appreciate the contribution they make to public debates about foreign policy. For their criticisms are a valuable reminder that foreign policy is often imperfect from a moral standpoint, and they provide a useful safeguard against the tendency of practical men to engage in moral self-deception. It is often forgotten that Machiavelli, even while advising the prince that circumstances would force him to use morally questionable means on behalf of worthwhile goals, also remarked that it was important that the prince should know that he was doing so and that he should suffer a bad conscience so that moral values would at least survive their violation.

Bibliographical Essay

Particularly useful in preparing this chapter were Arnold Wolfer's essay, "Statesmanship and Moral Choice," in his book *Discord and Collaboration* (Baltimore, 1962), and Michael Walzer, "Political Action: The Problem of Dirty Hands," *Philosophy and Public Affairs,* 2 (1973), 160–80. See also Machiavelli, *The Prince;* Kenneth Waltz, *Man, the State and War* (New York, 1954), pp. 210–17; Hans Morgenthau, *Politics Among Nations,* 4th ed. (New York, 1967), chapter 1; Michael Walzer, *Just and Unjust Wars* (New York, 1977); Stanley Hoffmann, *Duties Beyond Borders: On the Limits and Possibilities of Ethical International Politics* (Syracuse, 1981); Sissela Bok, *Lying: Moral Choice in Public and Private Life* (New York, 1979); and Edward H. Carr, *The Twenty Years' Crisis,* 2nd ed. (New York, 1956).

Index

Aberdeen, Earl of (George Hamilton Gordon), 209, 210, 214–15, 262
accommodative strategy, 164
Acheson, Dean, 116–17
Adams, John, 53
Afghanistan, 143, 144, 147–48
agendas, for negotiations, 159–60
agreements
  enforcement and verification of, 164–65
  peace, 229
  types of, 158–59
Aix-la-Chapelle, Congress of (1818), 174–75
Alexander I (czar, Russia), 29, 31, 174–75
Alexander II (czar, Russia), 181
amoral position, 271, 275
Anglo-Russian Agreement (1907), 42
Angola, 137, 139, 141
Anne (queen, England), 8
antiwar movement, 232, 233
appeasement policy, 134, 247
  Brandt's 248–51
  Chamberlain's, 57, 69, 85, 93–95, 98, 181, 183, 245
Arabi Pasha, 265–67
Arab-Israeli Wars, 187
  of 1967, 180–81
  of 1973, 137, 139, 141, 199–200, 212–19
Arab oil embargo (1973–1974), 198–201
armaments
  during Cold War, 121–22, 124–27

Congress of Vienna and, 33
in crisis management, 207–8, 216–18
in current policies, 151–52
détente period agreements on, 136, 137, 141, 143
in Middle East, 180, 181, 184, 185, 187, 212, 213
pre-World War II, 82–84
public opinion on, 63–64
technical changes in (1870's), 37
in Versailles Treaty (1919), 69, 70, 79, 84, 96, 97
of World War II, 101
al Assad, Hafez, 181
Atlantic Charter, 108, 110–11
August III (king, Poland), 23
Augustus II (the Strong; king, Poland), 9
Austria
  Congress of Vienna and, 33
  Crimean War and, 209
  Egyptian crisis of 1838–1841 and, 194
  French Revolution and, 25–26
  Hitler and, 98
  intervention in Naples by, 175
  under Maria Theresia, 19–21, 23
  in mid-nineteenth century, 36
  after Peace of Utrecht, 8
  pre-World War I, 43
  after Thirty Years War, 4, 6
  in World War I, 210–11
Austria-Hungary, 38, 39

Bahr, Egon, 249, 250

279

Eden, Anthony, 94, 95, 97, 245
Edge, Walter E., 80
Edward VII (king, England), 243, 249
Egypt
 Anglo-French conflict over (1898), 242, 244
 crisis of 1838–1841 in, 193–95, 201
 Gladstone's policies in, 265–68
 Israel and, 137, 179–81, 186, 187, 199, 200, 212, 213, 215
Eisenhower, Dwight D., 123, 173
 commitment to Israel by, 179, 180, 184, 185
 Hungarian revolution and, 119, 270–71
enforcement of agreements, 164–65
Engels, Friedrich, 90
England, 8. *See also* Great Britain
Entente Cordiale (1904), 42, 244
ententes, 240–45
Erfurt (East Germany), 249, 250
escalation, 190, 219, 221–22, 224
Esher, Lord, 42
Eshkol, Levi, 179
ethics, 256, 270
 in history of diplomacy, 12–13
 situational, 274–77
Ethiopia, 62, 64, 69, 94
Eugene (prince, Savoy), 8
European Economic Community (Common Market), 167
exploratory discussions, 160
extension agreements, 158

Falkland Islands, 189
Fashoda (Sudan), 242, 244
Ferdinand VII (king, Spain), 175
Ferdinand (prince, Austria), 211
Foch, Ferdinand, 77
Ford, Gerald, 137, 139–41, 169, 247
Four Power Directorate, 57
Fourteen Points, 54, 74
France
 in 1600, 4
 Bismarckian Europe and, 38, 39
 Congress of Vienna and, 30, 187
 in Crimean War, 209, 210
 economy of (1930's), 83–85
 Egyptian crisis of 1838–1841 and, 193–95
 Egyptian revolution of 1882 and, 265–66
 entente between Britain and (1898–1904), 242–45
 Foreign Ministry established in, 12

at Geneva disarmament conference (1932), 64, 69, 79, 80
 in Indochina, 230
 League of Nations and, 54–55
 under Louis XIV, 6–8
 under Louis XV, 23–24
 under Louis Philippe, 34
 in mid-nineteenth century, 36
 post-World War I, 55–57, 75–78
 pre-World War I, 41
 pre-World War II, 66, 71
 Quadruple Alliance and, 174–76, 182–86
 Revolution (1789) in, 25–26
 Richelieu and, 5–6
 Soviet Union and, 92, 248
 in Suez crisis, 121, 179
 in World War I, 211, 212
Francis I (emperor, Austria; II emperor, Holy Roman Empire), 24
Franz Joseph (emperor, Austria), 209
Frederick IV (king, Denmark), 9
Frederick I (king, Prussia), 10
Frederick II (the Great; king, Prussia), 19–23
Frederick William (the Great Elector, elector, Brandenburg), 10
Frederick William I (king, Prussia), 10–11
Frederick William III (king, Prussia), 29

Geneva (Switzerland)
 Conference on Security and Cooperation in Europe in (1973–1975), 166–70, 250
 Disarmament Conference (1932) in, 64, 68–69, 79–81, 90
Geneva Protocol (1924), 55, 56
Genoa (Italy), 76, 90
Germany. *See also* East Germany; West Germany
 Anglo-French Entente and, 243, 247
 under Bismarck, 37–39, 258–60
 at Brest-Litovsk Conference, 88
 Congress of Vienna and, 31
 French Revolution and, 26
 under Hitler, 56–58, 62, 64, 71, 81–84, 93–99, 245
 League of Nations and, 54
 Poland invaded by, 176–78, 182–86
 post-World War I, 52, 55–56, 74–79
 post-World War II, 111, 114
 pre-World War I, 40–43, 215
 in seventeenth century, 3, 4, 6, 7